Beyond States and Markets

Seeking to extend our understanding of the contemporary global political economy, this book provides an important and original introduction to the current theoretical debates about social reproduction and argues for the necessity of linking social reproduction to specific contexts of power and production.

It illustrates the analytic value of the concept of social reproduction through a series of case studies that examine the implications of how labor power is reproduced and how lives outside of work are lived. The issues examined in countries including the Ukraine, Chile, Spain, Nepal, India, and Indonesia, consist of:

- human trafficking and sex work;
- women and work;
- migration, labor and gender inequality;
- microcredit programs and investing in women;
- health, biological reproduction and assisted reproductive technologies.

The book lends a unique perspective to the understandings of transformation in the global political economy precisely because of its simultaneous focus on the caring and provisioning of the everyday and its relationships to policies and decisions made at the national and international levels of both formal and informal institutions.

With its multi-disciplinary approach, this book will be indispensable to students and scholars of international political economy, development studies, gender or women's studies, international studies, globalization, and international relations.

Isabella Bakker is Professor of Political Science and Women's Studies at York University in Toronto, Canada.

Rachel Silvey is Associate Professor in the Department of Geography and Programme in Planning at the University of Toronto, Canada.

RIPE Series in Global Political Economy

This series, published in association with the *Review of International Political Economy*, provides a forum for current debates in international political economy. The series aims to cover all the central topics in IPE and to present innovative analyses of emerging topics. The titles in the series seek to transcend a state-centred discourse and focus on three broad themes:

* the nature of the forces driving globalisation forward
* resistance to globalisation
* the transformation of the world order.

The series comprises two strands:

The *RIPE Series in Global Political Economy* aims to address the needs of students and teachers, and the titles will be published in hardback and paperback. Titles include

Routledge/RIPE Studies in Global Political Economy is a forum for innovative
new research intended for a high-level specialist readership, and the titles
will be available in hardback only. Titles include:

Beyond States and Markets

The challenges of social reproduction

Edited by
Isabella Bakker and Rachel Silvey

Routledge
Taylor & Francis Group

LONDON AND NEW YORK

HC
79
.I52
B49
2008

First published 2008
by Routledge
2 Park Square Milton Park, Abingdon, Oxon OX14 4RN

Simultaneously published in the USA and Canada
by Routledge
270 Madison Avenue, New York, NY 10016

Routledge is an imprint of the Taylor & Francis Group, an informa business.

Typeset in Times New Roman by
Taylor & Francis Books
Printed and bound in Great Britain by
TJ International Ltd, Padstow, Cornwall

British Library Cataloguing in Publication Data
A catalogue record for this book is available from the British Library

Library of Congress Cataloging-in-Publication Data
Beyond states and markets : the challenges of social reproduction /
edited by Isabella Bakker and Rachel Silvey.
    p. cm. – (RIPE series in global political economy)
    Includes bibliographical references and index.
    1. Industrial productivity–Social aspects. 2. Economic development–
Social aspects. 3. Sexual division of labor. 4. Globalization–Social aspects.
5. Equality. 6. Feminist economics. I. Bakker, Isabella, 1956- II. Silvey,
Rachel.
    HC79.I52B49 2008
    306.3–dc22
                        2007045358

ISBN 13: 978-0-415-77585-4 (hbk)
ISBN 13: 978-0-415-77586-1 (pbk)
ISBN 13: 978-0-203-92849-3 (ebk)

Contents

Part III
Social reproduction and transnational migrations

Part IV
Social reproduction, health, and biological reproduction

Illustrations

Figures

Tables

Contributors

Meena Acharya is currently General Secretary of a research/advocacy NGO, Tanka Prasad Acharya Memorial Foundation, a voluntary position. She is also a senior advisor and trustee of another action-oriented NGO, SAHAVAGI, which she helped to establish and from where she does her consulting work. Dr Acharya has degrees from the Universities of Wisconsin, Moscow State and Delhi. From 1990 to 1994 she was executive director of the Institute for Integrated Development Studies. From 1966 to 1990 she worked for Nepal's central bank, Nepal Rastra Bank. From 1980 to 1982 she worked as an economist in the Development Economics Department of the World Bank in Washington DC.

Isabella Bakker is Professor and Former Chair of Political Science at York University in Toronto. Her published works include *The Strategic Silence; Gender and Economic Policy; Rethinking Restructuring: Gender and Change in Canada*; and *Power, Production and Social Reproduction: Human In/ Security in the Global Political Economy.* She is involved with several NGOs working on engendering economic policy and alternative women's budgets.

Wendy Chavkin is an MD and Professor of Public Health at Columbia University. She has written extensively about women's reproductive health issues, including the consequences of welfare reform for the health of women and children, reproductive health in medical education, HIV and illegal drug use in pregnancy. She has served as the Editor-in-Chief of the Journal of the American Medical Women's Association and Director of the Bureau for Maternity Services and Family Planning in New York City.

Christina Ewig is Assistant Profesor of Women's Studies at the University of Wisconsin-Madison. A political scientist, her research interests center on gender and social policy in Latin America, both historically and under neoliberalism. Her current research is a cross-national study of health sector reforms in Peru, Chile, Mexico and Columbia. She is the author of "Piecemeal but Innovative: Health Sector Reform in Peru" and "The Strengths and Limits of the NGO Women's Movement Model: Shaping Nicaraguan Democratic Institutions."

Maria Floro is an Associate Professor in the Economics Department at American University, teaching in the fields of gender, development finance, and development economics. Her publications include books and several articles on topics including time allocation, informal sector, credit, savings and asset ownership along gender lines. Her recent research focuses on gender dimensions of financing strategies for development, and the intersection of gender, finance, and informal sector work among urban poor households in Latin America and Asia.

Stephen Gill is Distinguished Research Professor of Political Science, Communications and Culture at York University, Toronto, Canada and Fellow of the Royal Society of Canada. His publications include "The Global Political Economy" (with David Law, John Hopkins University Press, 1998); "American Hegemony and the Trilateral Commission" (Cambridge University Press, 1991) and "Gramsci, Historical Materialism and International Relations" (Cambridge University Press, 1993). His "Power and Resistance in the New World Order" (Palgrave 2003) won the Choice, Outstanding Academic Title Award. It will be published in a second enlarged edition in 2008.

Pregs Govender was a Parliamentarian in South Africa from 1994 to 2004 and served as Chair of the Joint Monitoring Committee on Women to consider questions of power, utilizing her expertise on effecting gender budgeting, legislation and institutional change.

Gioconda Herrera is Founder and Director of Gender Studies in FLACSO (Faculty of Latin American Social Sciences) in Ecuador. Her research interests center on gender and public policy and gender and migration. She has published on these issues in Spanish in "Women's Issues in Ecuador" for *The Greenwood Encyclopedia of Women's Issues.*

Hella Hoppe is a political economist now working at Friedrich Ebert Stiftung. Her main research interests are globalization, labor markets, and feminist economics. She has held a research position with the secretariat of the German Parliament for which she contributed to the reports on the labor market, social standards, and gender justice. One key piece of her writing is titled, "The Doha Development Round, Gender and Social Reproduction."

Lakshmi Lingam is Professor in the Women's Studies Unit at the Tata Institute of Social Sciences in Mumbai, India. She has conducted research on women-headed household, sex-selective abortion, reproductive rights, women's health, migration, and structural adjustment policies and gender. She has contributed to gender and equity mainstreaming activities in the governments of Indian states and to gender and equity issues in participatory action in Afghanistan. Among her publications are "Taking Stock: Women's Movement and the State" and "Migrant Women, Work Particpation and Urban Experience."

Olga Pyschulina is Senior Research Fellow, National Institute for Strategic Studies under the President of Ukraine, Department of Economic and Social Strategy. She has extensive experience in developing policy briefs and research summaries for government officials in the domain of social issues in general, and human trafficking and women's migration in particular.

Rachel Silvey is Associate Professor of Geography at the University of Toronto. Her research interests include gender and feminist geography, migration studies and transnational Islam. Her work has appeared in a number of gender and geography journals, edited volumes, and the Blackwell Companion to Feminist Geography. She has worked with migrant rights NGOs, development organizations, and the ILO to cultivate better understanding of the issues facing transnational migrant women.

Preface and acknowledgments

This book is the result of the authors' collaborative efforts over the course of the last few years. The Fulbright New Century Scholars (NCS) program first brought us together in 2004 as members of the international group of scholars focused on the program's theme that year: "Toward Equality: The Global Empowerment of Women." Our collective work has challenged each of us to move beyond our individual research agendas in order to engage in collective, interdisciplinary debate and dialogue. We are grateful to the New Century Scholars (NCS) program for providing the platform and the funding that has made it possible for us to develop the cross-cutting themes that are reflected in this volume. We thank the leadership and staff of NCS for all the work that went into making our meetings run smoothly and successfully, and we thank Carolyn Elliott for serving as the Distinguished Scholar Leader during the program year.

At the first NCS goal-setting meeting, we organized a sub-group of scholars concentrating on the themes of gender, globalization and neoliberal governance. In our group's original statement of aims, we wrote that we would explore "national and transnational processes, structures, and institutions of production and social reproduction, [in order to. ...] develop alternative conceptual and methodological tools that will enhance the empowerment of women." We exchanged our individual research proposals and discussed conceptual connections among our projects. In particular, we found that each of us aimed to move beyond the foundational conceptions of economic governance that posit limited conceptions of states and markets. We also decided that as a group we would extend these classical concepts to attend more effectively to gendered inequalities of power, production and distribution. We thank each of the group members for contributing to these efforts. In our individual chapters, each of us also thanks numerous people and institutions who both directly and indirectly supported our research.

At the conclusion of the NCS program, we proposed a follow-up workshop to permit us to see our collaborative work through to publication. We thank the Rockefeller Foundation's Bellagio Conference Center for providing the venue and funding for this phase of the project. Over the course of a week in the summer of 2006, we concentrated on critiquing and refining our individual chapter contributions, and we drafted the introduction to the present volume. We provided constructive feedback to one another, and this allowed us to forge deeper connections among our diverse interests. We are grateful to have had the time at Bellagio, where the inspiringly beautiful conference space overlooking Lake Cuomo made our work a distinct pleasure. We also acknowledge the hard work of the staff at Bellagio, and thank them for carrying out the reproductive labour that made this book possible.

We have also benefited tremendously from the editorial input of Nancy Mann and the expert research assistance of David Roberts, Adrienne Roberts, and Tim DiMuzio. Their work has led to substantial improvements in the book, and we offer sincere thanks to them for their commitment to the project.

We also thank the University of Toronto Faculty Association and the Canadian Social Science and Humanities Research Council for their funding.

Abbreviations

ANC	African National Congress
AP	Andhra Pradesh
ARTs	Assisted Reproductive Technologies
CEDAW	UN Convention on the Elimination of All Forms of Discrimination against Women
DWCRA	Development of Women and Children in Rural Areas
FDI	Foreign Direct Investment
FONASA	*Fondo Nacional de Salud* (National Health Fund, Chile)
GATS	General Agreement on Trade in Services
GATT	General Agreement on Trade and Tariffs
GEAR	Growth, Employment and Redistribution
ILO	International Labor Organization
IMF	International Monetary Fund
ISAPREs	*Instituciones de Salud Previsional* (Health Provider Institutions, Chile)
MDGs	Millennium Development Goals
NAFTA	North American Free Trade Agreement
OBC	Other Backward Caste
OECD	Organization for Economic Cooperation and Development
PAHO	Pan American Health Organization
Plan AUGE	*Plan de Acceso Universal con Garantías Explícitas* (Plan for Universal Access with Explicit Guarantees, Chile)
PMG	*Programa de Mejoramiento de Gestión* (Program to Improve Management, Chile)
RDP	Reconstruction and Development Program
SAPs	Structural Adjustment Policies
SC	Scheduled Castes
SERMENA	*Servicio Médico Nacional para Empleados* (Employee Medical Service, Chile)
SERNAM	*Servicio Nacional de la Mujer* (Chilean State's Executive Women's Agency)
SNS	*Servicio Nacional de Salud* (National Health Service, Chile)
ST	Scheduled Tribes

TRIMs	The Agreement on Trade-Related Measures
TRIPs	Agreement on Trade-Related Aspects of Intellectual Property
UN	United Nations
UNCTAD	United Nations Conference on Trade and Development
UNRISD	United Nations Research Institute for Social Development
WTO	World Trade Organization

Introduction

Social reproduction and global transformations – from the everyday to the global

Isabella Bakker and Rachel Silvey

Feminist scholarship in international political economy has worked to correct for the exclusions of mainstream development models (Andrew *et al.* 2003; Scott 1995; Jackson and Pearson 1998). Much of this work has responded to the increasingly hegemonic neoliberal models of development that have been characterized by reduced expenditures on state services, the privatization of formerly public services, and the expansion and creation of new markets (Peck and Tickell 2002). In response to classical political economy, which has focused primarily on formal state policies and monetized production processes, feminist scholarship highlights the centrality of gender and social reproduction in (re)constituting production and exchange relations.

The theorization of social reproduction can be traced to the period of the Enlightenment and was tied to the idea that modern capitalist societies have a biological metabolism and reproductive cycle (Caffentzis 2002). An initial theorization of social reproduction was mapped out in Quesnay's *Tableau Economique* in the mid-eighteenth century. Adam Smith advanced these earlier insights in *The Wealth of Nations*, broadening the analysis of social reproduction to include industrial labour as value producing. Marx furthered these ideas on the commodification of labour power and also linked the value of labour power to notions of subsistence and the family.[1] However, Marx's emphasis is on the process of production and accumulation of capital rather than the process of social reproduction. Marx's key discussions of social reproduction relative to capitalist social relations are found in volume 1, chapter 23 of *Capital*, entitled "Simple Reproduction," and volume 2, part 3 of *Capital*, entitled "The Reproduction and Circulation of the Total Social Capital":

> A society can no more cease to produce than it can cease to consume. When viewed, therefore, as a connected whole, and in the constant flux of its incessant renewal, every social process of production is at the same time a process of reproduction. The conditions of production are at the same time the conditions of reproduction.
>
> (Marx 1976: 711)

There is a significant history that precedes the neoclassical economics of classical economists who understood the cost of social reproduction to be at the centre of the system of capital accumulation. This insight is an important one to hold onto in thinking through current theoretical and empirical discussions of social reproduction, since it suggests that the work of social reproduction does not stand outside of the mode of production or the determination of surplus, but rather is at its centre (Bezanson 2006).

This volume builds on this central insight of classical political economy and speaks to the re-emergent interest in feminist conceptualizations of social reproduction (Katz 2001a; 2001b; Federici 2004). Foundational feminist notions of social reproduction focused on integrating women's domestic labour power into analyses of production and power relations (Safa 1996; Hartmann 1981; Molyneux 1979; Benería and Sen 1981). In this early work, social reproduction was located within a framework of state-led development and collective responsibility for realizing the current and future reproduction of the labour force, social values and social care (Benería and Feldman 1992; Mies 1986). Inspired by feminist political economy, it sought to understand the historical, materialist, and dialectical processes that are productive of gender and class oppressions. One central concern was to understand the gender politics of domestic labour and their relationship to capitalism (Laslett and Brenner 1989). Seccombe (1974), for example, argued that domestic labour is necessary for the reproduction of the labour force, and that capitalist production should therefore be understood as dependent upon the work carried out within the home. The central insight was that housework is unpaid, usually women's labour, which enables the usually male labourer to work longer hours, and thus the gender division of labour lies at the base of surplus value creation (James and Dalla Costa 1973).

Furthermore, feminist political economists such as Antonella Picchio (1992) theorized the relation between social reproduction and the capitalist process of accumulation, arguing its centrality at five levels: (1) production, since labour is a produced input but one that is constituted outside of the sphere of production (see also Armstrong and Armstrong 1983 on this point); (2) distribution, since any saving on social reproduction to the capitalist or the state means higher profits (Katz 2001a also underscores this point); (3) circulation, since the consumption of wage goods is the largest part of aggregate demand (Keynes' observation); (4) institutions, since insecurity of access to the means of reproduction is a fundamental source of "command" over the work process; and, (5) politics, since there is a fundamental conflict between profits and living standards manifested in the process of social reproduction.[2]

Social reproduction refers to both biological reproduction of the species (including its ecological framework) and ongoing reproduction of the commodity labour power. In addition social reproduction involves institutions, processes and social relations associated with the creation and maintenance of communities – and upon which, ultimately, all production and exchange rests (Bakker 1999; Edholm *et al.* 1977). As Bakker and Gill note:

> "In today's world social reproduction involves institutions that provide for socialization of risk, health care, education and other services – indeed many of the key elements of what the early Marx called 'species-being,' social institutions that distinguish the life of human beings from that of animals (Marx 1964)"
>
> (Bakker and Gill 2003 b:18).

From this perspective of ontology, which is the study of existence or being, we employ Bakker and Gill's *social* ontology, which is an historical and human process. This process involves human agency in the creation of the institutions and structures of social life. A social ontology is therefore a "process associated with the reproduction and transformation of dominant and subordinate structures of thought and practice in a given historical period" (Bakker and Gill 2003 b:19). The authors in this volume illustrate, through various applied considerations, that "social reproduction is both a productive potential and a condition of existence for the expanded reproduction of capital in capitalist social formations" (Bakker and Gill 2003 b:22); different forms of social reproduction can be associated with various social formations such as feudalism or state socialism. Hence, what interests us here is the degree to which particular patterns of social reproduction are shaped by and also shape socio-economic and political orders. Therefore, our conception of social reproduction not only encompasses what feminist economists refer to as "the care economy" (Elson 1991; Folbre 1994) but also transcends this notion to include wider questions of power and production (Bakker and Gill 2003). From this vantage point, the family and the state become important sites where the needs of reproduction are linked to the need for accumulation and where the state intervenes to offset or offload the high costs of social reproduction onto or away from the family at different moments in different locales.

A central goal of this volume is to build on previous conceptualizations and to grapple with questions of how social reproduction is constructed in particular geo-historical contexts (Mitchell *et al.* 2003). In so doing, our aim is to theorize social reproduction not only in terms of the ways in which it functions for capital, but also to understand the ways in which its organization shapes markets, their meanings and gender orders (Connell 1987). Moreover, we aim to explore the ways in which women from diverse social and geographic locations understand and navigate their roles in social reproduction both in relation to states and markets and also in terms of their own value systems and human agency.

By extending the Marxist understanding of social reproduction beyond the perpetuation of modes of production and the structures of class inequality, feminists broaden the definition to include "the work of maintaining existing life and reproducing the next generation" (Laslett and Brenner 1989: 383). Katz refers to it simply as "the fleshy, messy, and indeterminate stuff of everyday life" (2001b: 711). We are interested in both the ways that responsibilities for such fleshy, messy work are assigned to particular groups of people (women versus men, immigrants, low-income people, women of colour) and institutions (state or non-state) and how these assignments and workloads are shifting in the contemporary period. In addition, we examine the effects of recent reorganizations of governance at the transnational, national and local levels on the dynamics of daily social reproduction practices and possibilities.

In the context of global neoliberal restructuring, feminists have high-lighted the increasing tensions, contradictions and crises emerging within the domain of social reproduction (Andrew *et al.* 2003; Bakker and Gill 2003c; Mitchell *et al.* 2003; Federici 2004; Brodie 2005; Bezanson and Luxton 2006). Our work further elaborates on this current literature to examine social reproduction in diverse yet increasingly *interrelated* contexts within the North and South, and across various scales of social relations. Through our case studies, we argue for the necessity of linking social reproduction to specific contexts of power and production. We build on previous literature to continue to broaden conventional notions of states and markets through attention to the relations of power and production that operate outside of the boundaries of formalized government and monetized exchange.

Attention to social reproduction requires an analytic approach to governance that extends beyond a focus on the formal regulatory mechanisms of the state. For while the state is a key actor in shaping many features of the political economy, the consequences of formal state policies and their gender dimensions are shaped in conjunction with other less formal and more "private" dynamics (Brodie 2005). Thus, we situate our exploration of social reproduction within a conceptualization of governance that involves both the public and the private processes and mechanisms that shape social and economic outcomes (Bakker and Gill 2003a). Governance, as under-stood by the authors in this volume, involves the struggles over regulation and legality within both state institutions and civil society, as these operate within particular sites or across national boundaries in regional and global frameworks. Furthermore, "governance involves *ideas* that justify or legit-imate political power and influence, *institutions* through which influence is stabilized and reproduced and *material practices* which sanction or act as incentives to compliance with rules, regulations, norms and standards" (Bakker and Gill 2003a: 5). One aspect of global restructuring which is echoed throughout the contributions to this volume, is a shift towards *the increasing privatization of social reproduction*. In recent decades a variety of states in the wealthier countries and the former Soviet bloc have shifted away from providing some social services (e.g. public transportation, public health services, public sector employment) and towards the expectation that private individuals, organizations, and corporations will fulfil these needs.

Governments have increasingly opted out of service provision and "contracted-out" multiple services to private businesses, non-governmental organizations, and individuals. As Bakker and Gill's contribution (Chapter 1) to this volume points out, global transitions towards privatization and informalization are part of the international shift towards a new social contract, a "new constitutionalism" (Gill 1998). In the global South, developmental states with infrastructure to meet social reproduction needs (e.g. Latin America) experienced a pronounced squeeze on finances due to: (1) the distributional effects of tax reform; (2) the net effect of fiscal spending cuts on social safety nets and welfare; (3) the effect of fiscal retrenchment on employment; and (4) the privatization of public utilities, enterprises, services and common property resources (UNRISD 2005: 44). Despite improvements in per capita social spending (on health, education, social security and welfare) in the late 1990s, these expenditures as a share of gross domestic product (GDP) have declined in a number of developing countries, most significantly in sub-Saharan Africa and Eastern and Central Europe (UNRISD 2005: 45). In some countries, such as Nepal discussed by Acharya in Chapter 3, market infiltration more so than state retrenchment is reshaping social reproduction and gender roles. Hence, we also document a process of *marketization and informalization of social reproduction*.

Social reproduction lends a unique perspective to understandings of transformation in the global political economy precisely because of its simultaneous focus on the caring and provisioning of the everyday and its relationships to policies and decisions made at the national and international levels of both formal (governments, courts, the World Trade Organization (WTO), World Bank, the International Monetary Fund (IMF), United Nations (UN) conferences) and informal (World Economic Forum) institutions. Each of the contributions to this volume reveals these linkages as they play out in different substantive and geographic arenas. Through our different case studies, we find that the dynamics of shifting global–local relations are more complex than would be expected from a straightforward understanding of state withdrawal from social provisioning or a clear-cut decline of the welfare state. Rather, we find new, surprising, and often contradictory outcomes of global restructuring for international regulatory institutions, national public health, reproductive technologies, local agricultural economies, recipients of micro-lending, international migrants, and "trafficked" persons.

In addition to contributing to feminist political economy, this volume, which builds bridges between geographically diverse case studies drawn from multiple analytical scales, moves our work beyond identity politics. Rather than focusing on the debates about identity that have been central to much recent feminist research (see Benhabib 1994 for a discussion), we are interested in using the lens of social reproduction to examine the ways in which multiple inequalities between and among various groups of women are relationally reproduced, challenged, and transformed in the current moment of global political-economic development. In so doing, we align our work with recent feminist scholarship that underscores the importance of understanding the potential for political alliances that link different social groups and the analytical interconnections between processes occurring across places, scales, and groups (Grewal and Kaplan 1994; Rai 2002; Moghadam 2005). Although there have been a number of contributions to the literature on social reproduction in recent years (Mitchell *et al.* 2003; Federici 2004; Bezanson and Luxton 2006), we would suggest that this volume goes farther than others in developing an analysis of the concept that spans a diverse geographic and analytic expanse.

Theorizing social reproduction and the global political economy

The contributors to this volume come from various branches of the social sciences and have a diversity of regional and institutional specializations. One of the goals of our common project is to foster a dialogue amongst these various disciplinary traditions; and second, to contextualize the transformations in social reproduction in the specific locales and institutions on which our research focuses. For instance, we emphasize the spatiality of social reproduction. Locating social life in a spatial context means not only analyzing economic globalization in the context of intensified internationalization of social and economic relations. In addition, attention to spatiality involves locating individuals and local communities in an international context that takes account of the multiple scales within and across which political economic processes are reworked. The contributors to this volume illustrate the centrality of space with some regions of the global political economy integrated into the process of economic globalization to a considerable degree, others much less so. Hence, we illustrate that current transformations in the global political economy are by no means part of a homogeneous process but must be understood in specific spatial contexts and in terms of the relationship between places.

Our approach aligns with recent multi-disciplinary views of transnationalism as a key analytic (e.g. Ong 1999; Mitchell 2004). The rise of transnational mechanisms of governance – as discussed in Part I of this volume – illustrates the challenges posed by a transnational optic to conventional conceptions of space and territoriality, specifically the limitations of long-standing conceptions of the boundaries around national economies and the sovereign state. As these geographies shift, so too do the spaces within which people carry out social reproduction. More women than ever before are migrating worldwide for domestic work, childcare, elder work, nursing and sex work. Much of their transnational socially reproductive labour remains place-bound at the point of destination. That is, while migrant women are crossing national boundaries in increasing numbers, housework, nursing, childcare or sex work must be carried out in the site where the social reproduction is needed.

As Helleiner points out, "[t]he contemporary conjunctural and short term economic globalization phenomenon also appear to be intensifying certain forms of geographical inequality" (1997: 100). Income inequalities have increased both within and between nations in recent decades, as have the inequalities between different groups of women. Furthermore, hierarchical structures within countries also appear to be intensifying. As the United Nations Research Institute for Social Development (2005) notes in a recent study, the question of whether neoliberal policies of global liberalization have led to an improvement in well-being is a debate fuelled by different conceptions of well-being. There is however, according to the study, "substantial evidence of persistent and even widening income and resource gaps within countries." The study cites evidence of these patterns in China, the United States, a number of Latin American countries and several Eastern European countries (UNRISD 2005: 31–32). Thus, a variety of standpoints yield different interpretations of current global transformations: those near the top of the world's social hierarchy see a positive expansion of material well-being and freedoms, while those at the lower end of the hierarchy experience greater threats to human security and those aspects of social reproduction provisioning that enhance overall well-being and life chances.

Overall, we note a conjunctural separation of production and social reproduction. In the post-World War II era golden age, many countries of the global North experienced this separation through the provisioning of a family wage premised on a male breadwinner model (McDowell 1991; Bakker 2003). This system was based on a wage packet to the male worker and different degrees of state provisioning which supported in a collective sense, the social reproduction work of the wife.[3] In the more recent period of neoliberalism, we see the abandonment of the family wage, declining state supports – less socialized aspects of social reproduction – and an increase in the labour force participation rate of women and other family members. We are also seeing the encroachment of monetary relations into more and more aspects of social reproduction, including, as Chavkin points out (Chapter 9), fundamental components of biological reproduction.

In the global South, the intensification of the boundaries between production and social reproduction has been less distinct and shorter term. Assets such as land, water or agricultural seeds are increasingly appropriated by the state or private interests, reflecting new forms of "primitive" accumulation that challenge the previously fluid boundaries between expanded household relations of social reproduction and care, food provisioning and sustainability. Increased urbanization and marketization are also contributing to a greater distinction between production and social reproduction. At the same time, the spaces of informalization often "bring home" paid work, as is the case for domestic workers and industrial home-based workers. Here, the contradictions between maintaining the boundaries between work and what Mitchell *et al.* (2003) call "life's work" become more pronounced and difficult to regulate.

In the examples from both the North and South explored in this book, there appears to be a common trend towards increasing emphasis on individual responsibility for, and informalization of, social reproduction. Yet here too states play a role in policing this boundary: states can offload to the local and the individual due to fiscal constraints; states can turn a blind eye to labour regulation or actively regulate standards downwards for the sake of competitiveness; and states can actively monitor (or selectively ignore) the activities of non-citizens such as domestic servants and nannies who are fulfilling a need to care for children of women who work outside the home.

The example of transnational care work is a compelling one because it clearly illustrates the spatial and hierarchical aspects of global transformations, illustrating the ways in which social reproduction takes place transnationally. From the view of the *longue durée*,[4] contemporary transnational motherhood, Sedef Arat-Koc notes, really continues a long "legacy of people of colour being admitted to some countries only through coercive systems of labour that do not recognize family rights" (2006: 76). What is new in terms of the conjunctural moment is the size and nature of the migrant labour force – currently 175 million people live outside their country of birth and there is an increased feminization of this labour migration with women now constituting half of this migration flow (Arat-Koc 2006: 77).

From a short-term perspective, as Arat-Koc points out, migrant domestic workers are ideal subjects of a neoliberal state "since they are workers whose social reproduction is not just privatized in the home but can be totally hidden with the economic, social and psychic costs transferred to a different location and state" (2006: 88). They also conceal not just their own reproduction but their employer's – middle-class women whose citizenship rights are mediated on the condition they participate as if they were men in the labour market. As Arat-Koc concludes, having flexible domestic help enables some women to participate equally in the labour market. In addition, it diffuses pressure that might otherwise be directed towards changes in gender relations in the home or in broader state policy (2006: 89). Finally, transnational work in the area of social reproduction challenges the neoliberal myth of self-sufficiency and independence, laying bare the relations of dependence that link workers and employers in different parts of the globe (Arat-Koc 2006: 91).

Outline of the volume

Part I: Social reproduction and economic governance

This part explores the social consequences of neoliberal economic policies, new forms of flexible accumulation, and the constitution of informal and formal labour regimes. The nature and direction of economic policies – especially trade, investment and finance – are often incongruent with international and national commitments to enhance development for all social reproduction needs. In tandem with these processes, women's roles in fulfilling social reproduction needs are neglected by states and the private sector, prompting us to argue for an expanded understanding of labour that includes unpaid care work, informal women's work and other unpaid labour responses to the deepening of markets into everyday life.

Key questions that we address in this section include: How have recent national, regional and transnational economic agreements impacted on systems of social provisioning and gender equality goals? What would greater policy coherence for realizing gender equality goals entail?

The first two chapters flesh out the key definitions and contextual processes providing the background to our collective work. First, Bakker and Gill analyze shifts in the economic and juridical frameworks at both the international and intra-national scales that have promoted and required the adoption of increasingly market-based frameworks. Floro and Hoppe's chapter extends the framework of the book to grapple with the neglect of social reproduction by international trade and financial institutions. They reveal the disjunctures between the espoused principles and the grounded outcomes of neoliberal policy implementation. While the neoliberal paradigm promotes increased market efficiency, the strategies for assessing efficiency do not attend to the "costs" embedded in, for example, unpaid work, informalized work, or decreased food security. In failing to attend to these costs, the model excludes the contributions that women and the poor, often at great cost to themselves and their communities, make to social reproduction and thus to economic development.

Bakker and Gill's chapter traces the implications of the new regulatory mechanisms that require governments and international financial institutions to abide by neoliberal policy priorities, and then discusses the significance of such shifts in governance for social reproduction. They describe the global neoliberal shift away from social interests towards private ones, and points to the particularly detrimental consequences of this shift for poor people and women in their everyday efforts to survive. They proceed with a discussion of some alternative approaches to understanding and reworking globalization, and illustrate the value of these new paradigms for understanding the relationships between the state and social reproduction. Their discussion demonstrates that scholars and policy-makers need not subscribe to reductionistic views of the state's linkages with markets and the public. Rather, social reproduction can be integrated into macroeconomic policy and national development frameworks, so that social needs are incorporated into conceptualizations of economic priorities and evaluations.

Floro and Hoppe provide additional background for understanding how international financial institutions, including the IMF, the World Bank, and the WTO, are pressuring developing countries to liberalize, deregulate, and privatize their economies. As these global institutions increasingly adopt and coercively implement neoliberal sets of policies and development priorities, they limit the power of developing nations to implement their own development agendas. In addition, the market-oriented priorities of the international financial institutions put them in conflict with other international platforms that focus more on social development, such as the Beijing Platform for Action and the United Nations Millennium Development Goals (MDGs). This chapter indicates that trade liberalization, the primary goal of the international financial institutions, in fact threatens both food security and livelihoods, which are at the heart of the social development platforms.

The authors argue that a policy focus on social reproduction would reflect better vertical (i.e. linking local to national to global) policy coherence, and this orientation could lead to global policies that would better meet the basic livelihood and survival needs of poor people and women worldwide.

Part II: Social reproduction and marketization

The broad economic policies analyzed in the first part of this volume rely on, and shape, the often invisible world of social reproduction. These economic processes also affect the state's capacity to support social reproduction. The shift towards individualization, marketization and privatization of the state's traditional social responsibilities has increased the state's reliance on women's social reproductive activities and has dramatically altered women's lives, gender relations, and the everyday social fabric of communities across the globe. Some of the questions the authors explore here include: What are the positive and negative consequences of increased market expansion and greater reliance on market incomes on systems of livelihood and social reproduction? Have poverty reduction strategies such as microcredit enhanced women's economic and social status?

Acharya provides the volume's first country case study, illustrating the dynamics laid out in the first two chapters. She examines the gendered impacts of globalization in Nepal from the 1970s into the present period. She traces the effects of market incursion on women workers, pointing in particular to rising rates of rural–urban migration, a movement from free to waged labour, the narrowing of the agricultural market, and the erosion of the local and national food security system. Social and gendered discrimination has not been alleviated in this context. Rather, old forms of discrimination are simply increasingly enacted in modern spaces, such as factories. As the IMF and the World Bank pressure Nepal to open up its markets to global investment, the Nepali state has played a largely facilitative role. State services were never widely provided in Nepal, so the increasing marketization has not involved a withdrawal of the state. Yet women have faced persistent devaluation and intensified workloads, as they have continued to be held primarily responsible for domestic and caretaking work, and as their livelihood options have continued to depend on the assets, income, and status of their husbands. Interestingly, Acharya notes that dowry has acquired new dimensions, as prospective husbands have started to view it as seed capital for new businesses or for their own overseas trips, motorbikes, cars, TVs, and other consumer durables. Although this is more of a middle- and educated-class phenomenon, it is putting much social pressure on the lower middle class as well. Moreover, her survey suggests that dowry is spreading even among communities that did not have it before. Thus, globalization and its consumer culture have not done away with the onerous system of dowry, but converted it into a vehicle for promotion of consumerism and capital for new business, making it more onerous for families to have girls.

Lingam's chapter examines social reproduction through the lens of microcredit programmes in two regions of India: Andhra Pradesh and Mehbubnagar District. She finds, along with other feminist critics of neoliberal reform, that structural adjustment programmes in India are reducing livelihood options, increasing impoverishment, amounting to a falling support for social reproduction. Microcredit programmes are development initiatives that emphasize investing in women as micro-entrepreneurs by providing formal credit to them. She views the programmes as an extension of privatization and liberalization agendas into local lives, and a strategy that turns women's social reproductive work into an instrument of the market. Yet through her detailed fieldwork, she finds that overall, this form of women's incorporation into market exchange is providing some hope. In particular, she finds that despite the general exacerbation of poverty in the region, microcredit seems to be offering limited ways to mitigate their poverty and mobilize solidarity with one another. Her chapter highlights women's agency and sees women mobilizing social reproduction as a resource for creating solidarity and for their own well-being.

Part III: Social reproduction and transnational migrations

This section demonstrates that shifting social reproduction dynamics are at work in both the global North and the South, and that attention to changing social reproduction regimes is a particularly valuable way of tracing the relationships that link people, processes, and regions across such imagined divides. We hope to contribute to rethinking the foundational geographic understandings of nations and politics as polarized in terms of "North" and "South" or as delimited by the territorial boundaries of sovereign nation-states. The contributing authors further problematize the dualism of the North/South analytic in distinct ways in each chapter. First, Chapters 5 and 6 focus on transnational migration; both examine the migration politics and social reproduction patterns of a lower-income country (Ecuador [Chapter 5] and Indonesia [Chapter 6]) *in relation to* reproductive labour needs and migration into more economically developed countries (Spain [Chapter 5] and East Asia and the Gulf States [Chapter 6]). Women migrants are also involved in the social reproduction processes associated with human trafficking of women and children, a process explored by Pyshchulina (Chapter 7). Pyshchulina's focus on trafficking in the Ukraine further highlights the gendered problems with policies aimed at rapid marketization and privatization.

We examine the ways that gender roles and relations have changed in response to the macroeconomic forces fuelling the shift from public to private support of social reproduction. We find tensions and contradictions in the types of gendered change different women are experiencing in their specific work/reproductive lives. For example, women in OECD countries are trying to reconcile employment and childcare pressures by relying on migrant social reproductive labour and, by having fewer children. The growing global migration of women relies on women's traditional roles as domestic workers and childcare givers, yet it also involves dramatic changes in terms of women's mobility and wage-earning status. Migrant women's children refract the shifting formations of particular family roles induced by their mothers' migration. As women have increasingly travelled transnationally, the actors and institutions seeking to regulate their migration have also proliferated. This part of the book asks how gendered migration, and changes in patterns of biological reproduction are affected by, and reflective of, broader transnational shifts in social reproduction.

Herrera's chapter examines global shifts in social reproduction through the lens of Ecuadorian immigrant domestic workers in Madrid, Spain and their children left behind in Ecuador. She develops analytical connections between the informalization and privatization of social reproduction in Spain and Ecuador with the increasing transnational mobility of Ecuadorian women. She examines the transnational networks of care and work that link working mothers in Spain with those of immigrant domestic workers and their children from Ecuador. She examines these themes through immigrants' interpretations of the meanings of work and the emotional vocabularies of children of emigrants. She illustrates the importance of states and individual migrants in shaping liberalization trajectories across transnational space.

Silvey echoes Herrera's interest in female transnational migration. Her chapter centres on the regulation of Indonesian overseas contract labourers, most of whom are women, at the immigration terminal set aside to process migrant labourers as they return from abroad. The terminal was originally founded by the Indonesian state in order to provide protection to returning workers who faced high rates of theft, harassment, and abuse on their journeys home. Despite the state's intentions, the terminal has become a site of concentrated harassment and abuse for women migrants. This chapter argues that social differentiation and gender inequality are reproduced through the terminal's spatial segregation of migrant workers from other travellers. Migrants are monitored and governed in gender-specific ways at the terminal, and their subordinate gender and class status within Indonesia is reinforced as they are processed back into the nation. The space of the terminal is a site of social reproduction in itself, and it is aimed at the management of migrants who have carried out reproductive labour as part of transnational circuits.

Pyshchulina (Chapter 7) looks at informal criminal elements of the deepening processes of commodification and transnational migration by examining the social reproduction processes associated with human trafficking in the Ukraine. Economic globalization has pushed growing numbers of women and children into poverty, which has increased their vulnerability to trafficking. She shows that the growing traffic in persons from the Ukraine reflects the social reproduction of the dominance of Western European nations over Eastern European ones; men over women; wealthy people over poor ones; and corrupt officials over relatively powerless citizens. She argues that the monetization of social and personal relationships has laid the backdrop for the growth of prostitution and trafficking in women. As the Ukraine has moved away from the centrally controlled and planned economy under Russia, women have faced particular hardships. Women's poverty pushes them to seek jobs abroad and increases their risk of being trafficked. Gender inequality is socially reproduced through the objectification and commodification of women who are bought and sold for sex work.

Part IV: Social reproduction, health and biological reproduction

The broad economic policies and social processes analyzed in Parts I–III of this volume rely on and shape the often invisible world of social reproduction. These economic processes also affect the state's capacity to support social reproduction. The shift towards individualization, marketization and privatization of the state's traditional social responsibilities has increased reliance on markets as well as women's unpaid socially reproductive activities, thereby often dramatically altering women's lives, gender relations and the everyday fabric of communities across the globe. In particular, issues of women's health care and the very capacity to have babies are two aspects of social reproduction interrogated here.

Chapter 8 by Ewig explores the effects for women of neoliberal health sector reform in Chile. In the 1990s the Chilean state shifted responsibility for biological reproduction towards individual women and private sector interests. The women's movement responded by pressuring the state to re-centre women's interests and social reproduction in health policy in the new millennium. Ewig argues that this contestation between feminists and entrenched state interests was a struggle over whether the costs of social reproduction should be socialized or privatized. Feminists developed their own political machinery and gained some voice within the Chilean state. While Chile's neoliberal technocracy continues to dominate the state, women's movements have also grown more organized and vocal in demanding that the state support their social reproduction roles and work.

In the wealthy countries, as discussed by Chavkin in Chapter 9, growing numbers of women are relying on assisted reproductive technologies (ARTs) after having postponed childbearing. Chavkin provides an analysis of changing demographic patterns and their linkages to the growth in ARTs. In highly developed economies, women have increasingly postponed child-bearing, had fewer children, and participated at higher rates in full-time paid employment. In the context of global fertility decline, as growing numbers of women face shortened windows for childbearing, more are turning to assisted reproductive technologies to address their infertility, which, according to Chavkin, is problematic for both women and children. While ARTs may help as a technical solution to some people's desires to have children at later ages, they do not resolve the more basic gender inequity associated with the unequal division of social reproductive responsibilities. She argues that in order for states to support gender equity and child-bearing, they must take into account women's reproductive life cycles when determining both employment policies and the provision of social services.

In her Afterword to the volume, Pregs Govender draws on her insights as a parliamentarian and social activist in the first post-apartheid government in South Africa. She is particularly interested in reflecting on the possibi-lities of global transformations and alternative notions of power and lea-dership that rest on foundations of love and courage. Govender notes that

> the dominant understanding and exercise of power is too often pre-mised on the negation or destruction of self and community. This authoritarian notion of power vests authority elsewhere – in the parent, husband, leader, or political, economic, religious, and other social institutions – away from self and community – away from the potential leader within every one of us.

At the same time, she suggests that

> our most powerful acts of courage have emerged from an understanding and experience of love that enables us to recognize, respect, and express our individual and collective humanity beyond the differences that are used to divide and destroy ourselves or each other. This is the power of life itself.

South Africa is an interesting microcosm of many of the issues we reflect upon in this volume. It conforms to new constitutionalist imperatives that have been internally and externally imposed. This has led to a shift in macroeconomic policy that reflects a move away from earlier African National Congress (ANC) commitments to growth through redistribution. Yet, as she reveals through examples of political choices on issues such as macroeconomic policy, military spending, HIV/AIDS, rural women's right to land, and privatization of water, there are choices in using power and leadership in the interests of that countries' citizens as opposed to global neoliberal interests. In particular, she discusses examples of women's work in social reproduction and emphasizes that it cannot be conveniently manipulated or erased – it must shape global transformation.

Govender echoes the hope behind this collection: that the spirit of collaboration and learning from each other will help to inform greater cross-disciplinary dialogue and debate. She also notes the significance of identifying policy changes that would weaken the pressure of inequality which results in people holding contradictory aspirations between care and self-fulfilment, need and material possessions, survival and creative engagement with the world. In large part, the struggle for progressive social reproduction is a struggle for both resources and for control over time. Institutions like public education and childcare are crucial to the realization of such possibilities, as several of the authors point out.

We also suggest that historical shifts in philosophies of governance reorder the social and the political. They suggest a particular configuration of the public and private sector (the state versus the economy) and the public and private sphere (the state and economy versus the family and the individual) (Brodie 2005: 246). Feminist interventions in discussions of governance have evaluated the construction of historically specific gender orders and how they integrate processes of production and social reproduction. We have also detailed this process in the context of the chapters in this volume, being careful to link neoliberal restructuring to cultural and space-bound shifts in gender orders. What is implicit in all of the restructurings explored throughout are policy choices about the gender division of labour and the ways in which social reproduction needs are met (or not). These are key entry points for making explicit the nature of the architecture of social reproduction and for envisioning different futures.

Notes

1 In later writings, after Senior, the wage is purely determined by forces of supply and demand replacing the natural price of labour and thereby externalizing the process of social reproduction in economic analysis (Picchio 1992; Bezanson 2006).

2 See Bezanson, K. (2002) "Gender, the State and Social Reproduction: household insecurity in Ontario in the late 1990s," unpublished thesis, York University.

3 Some women's roles in social reproduction were better supported than others in this period; low-income women and women of colour have historically been involved in both productive and reproductive activities.

4 Fernand Braudel's notion of the *longue durée* refers to a historical period or wave of great length, focusing on those aspects of what he called material life that might remain relatively unchanged for centuries, such as what people ate, wore, what they produced and what shaped the "structures" that define the limits of potential social change for hundreds of years at a time (Braudel 1995).

Part I

Social reproduction and economic governance

1 New constitutionalism and social reproduction

Isabella Bakker and Stephen Gill[1]

The principal argument that underlies this chapter and is reinforced by most of the contributions to this volume is that mainstream neoliberal development thinking and practice have failed to deliver progressive supports for social reproduction, or human security, for the majority of people in the world. Neoliberalism is linked to social and political forces that tend to increase the human insecurity of the vast majority of the world's population, while redistributing income in an increasingly unequal world from the poor to the rich, in ways that tend to intensify a worldwide crisis of social and caring institutions (UNRISD 2005).

The backdrop to the current crisis of development and social reproduction in our societies is the "worldwide market revolution" that has taken place over the last 20–25 years – a revolution associated with economic, political, legal, and social processes that fall under the general rubric of "neoliberal globalization." This chapter focuses on the economic and juridical frameworks designed to regulate bilateral, regional, and international trade, investment, and financial agreements. We are also interested in the shift in the internal economic policies and governance arrangements within countries away from state-led development towards "market enabling" approaches. We examine the implications of these internal and external development trajectories in the context of what Gill (1998) calls neoliberal "new constitutionalism," a governance process that effectively locks in national and international commitments to market-based frameworks of accumulation and distribution.

New constitutionalism refers to how international legal measures and national constitutional measures have increasingly institutionalized neoliberal reforms and disciplines as fundamental economic policy over the last 20–30 years. These disciplinary measures constrain types of government economic intervention, limit capacities for social redistribution and welfare, and tend to promote more privatized systems. They thus govern not only the political economy but also social reproduction.

International mechanisms that have had the most significant effects on poorer countries include the transnationalization of liberal laws, regulatory frameworks, and conditions on trade and investment agreements. These new frameworks guarantee greater legal rights and freedom of movement for capital, as well as guarantees against expropriation of investments (e.g. nationalization). They are designed and implemented by organizations such as the World Trade Organization (WTO) that exercise juridical or quasi-juridical (law-making) functions. An example of national measures is the growing trend for governments to create independent central banks with legally defined low inflation targets, rather than, for example, mandates to maximize employment. What is important about these new constitutional frameworks is that they are intended (in the phraseology of the World Bank, a key sponsor of the Millennium Development Goals) to "lock in" liberal economic commitments – to guarantee individual rights and freedoms, to protect private property rights, and to lock in neoliberal social and economic regulation.

Such measures are seen by proponents as delivering economic efficiency and growth. Critics, however, contend that new governance frameworks contribute to democratic deficits (democratic controls over the economy are restricted) and undermine progressive forms of social reproduction by allowing market forces to largely determine social priorities. They undermine human rights, human security, and human development for the majority of the world's people.

While at first glance these governance frameworks appear to be narrowly focused on economic questions, in reality they are serving to reshape the conditions under which a central activity – the care and reproduction of human beings – is taking place. A good example of this (also discussed by Floro and Hoppe in Chapter 2) is the General Agreement on Trade in Services (GATS). GATS seeks to progressively liberalize the provision of services, including public services in health care and education (as well as in agriculture, finance, tourism, and other fields). The goal of GATS is to open services to market forces and facilitate greater competition on the assumption that enhanced market competition leads to increased efficiency and growth.[2] GATS is one of a range of mechanisms that is aimed at promoting greater privatization of public assets and mandating the equal treatment of both foreign and domestic buyers of these assets. Whether this leads to equal treatment of all citizens is, however, much more open to doubt, not least because private provision is based on fees for service and thus demands that consumers are able to pay.

New governance frameworks raise particular challenges for the many governments that are already facing difficulties in funding their prior obligations to social reproduction. Many governments are confronting shortfalls in revenue, and many poorer countries must tackle such shortfalls in the face of a legacy of accumulated foreign debts, the servicing of which takes up a large proportion of government expenditures. In these contexts of shortage, governments in both the global South and OECD countries are pressured to sell off public assets in order to fund current expenditures. For example, the city of Dresden in Germany in March 2006 sold its entire stock of 48,000 city-owned apartments to an American private-equity firm for US$1.2 billion, thus wiping out its entire public debt. Ten other German cities are undertaking similar initiatives.[3]

As observers have noted, and as both Ewig's chapter on Latin America and Lingam's on India illustrate, the results of privatization, liberalization, and deregulation are varied. Outcomes depend on the institutional arrangements through which these measures are executed, and negative outcomes under neoliberal regimes may be exacerbated by other conditions such as rigid social stratifications, communal tensions, demographic challenges, epidemics, pre-existent macroeconomic conditions, and natural disasters (Scholte 2005).

While proponents of the mainstream neoliberal development paradigm argue that market liberalization makes for higher growth rates, prosperity, and peace, others argue that the mainstream approach has served to intensify a global development crisis. Indeed, a recent United Nations (UN) study notes that neoliberal policies have coincided with slower rates of growth in most regions except East and South Asia (UNRISD 2005: 29). Slow growth has in turn resulted in limited employment options and the growth of forms of work with no protection or security, such as casual work and self-employment. Policies directed at liberalizing financial flows have contributed to delete recessions and depressions with increasing regularity and severity, and these crises "have extensive costs in terms of lost growth, and contribute to a more unequal income distribution at the country level" (UNRISD 2005: 30). As Scholte (2005) notes, "we have the twenty-first century with some 7.7 million superrich, each holding more than $1 million in financial assets, while 2.8 billion others are living on less than $2 a day" (4). Similar impacts of marketization and trade liberalization on the exacerbation of poverty are discussed in further detail by Floro and Hoppe (Chapter 2, this volume).

This chapter explores the links between social reproduction and three sets of new constitutional mechanisms designed to regulate economic policy and extend private property rights: (1) the reconfiguration of governments and constitutional forms in order to make them operate in the context of greater market discipline; (2) the construction and extension of liberal capitalist markets and the associated extension of the scale and scope of the commodification of land, labour, and money; and (3) the attempts that state and international institutions are making to manage the dislocations and contradictions associated with the liberalization of economies. The conclusion calls for developing macroeconomic policies that attend to social reproduction needs, and ensuring that governance institutions and policies work towards shared social and economic purposes. It also presents a series of global feminist responses to the contradictions that neoliberal forces have generated in conditions of social reproduction. Finally, it provides a set of alternative scenarios for meeting social reproduction needs as a way to visualize some paths towards the emergence of different, more equitable gender orders.

Social reproduction and new constitutionalism

This section discusses the two key concepts of this chapter – social reproduction and new constitutionalism – and illustrates how they are intertwined.

New constitutionalism refers to the specific types of internal and external mechanisms of governance that have emerged in the past 20 years, and that have been heavily promoted by adherents to the mainstream development paradigm. Such mechanisms are designed to provide the legal foundations for an extended market order, to regulate economic policy, and to fully protect private property rights, including intellectual property rights (e.g. proprietary rights to knowledge relating to health care systems, medicines, and plants and other life-forms) (Gill 1998; 2002).

What feminist theory calls *social reproduction* involves fundamental social processes and institutions associated with the intergenerational mechanisms and activities through which communities are reproduced and develop over time – and upon which all production and exchange ultimately rest, as for example on the general health of the population. Social reproduction largely depends on some form of income, which may be in the form of wages and transfers by governments or access to arable land and informal sector activities (Picchio 1992). As Kate Bezanson points out, social reproduction, then, shifts the concept of the economy away from merely market measures to a more ample and dynamic understanding of the economy. Many of the insecurities that are inherent in the labour market, and to some extent in other forms of access to money, are absorbed and mediated at the household level. The degree to which households are able to bear the effects of a market downturn in turn affects the ways in which economic growth occurs (2006: 15).

The significance of new constitutionalism for social reproduction becomes highlighted when one considers the relationship between, on the one hand, mobile capital (e.g. the investment and disinvestment power of multinational corporations) and, on the other, the nature of production and reproduction of territorially based communities. Capital relies on the state and the legal order to ensure its conditions of existence and potential for accumulation. But when it is fully mobile between jurisdictions, capital may exercise social power relatively independently of particular communities. While dependent on state power, a firm can potentially emancipate itself from control by a particular state by deploying/locating its assets elsewhere.

New constitutional measures

New constitutionalism involves three sets of interrelated measures that combine not only to minimize investor uncertainty across different jurisdictions, but also and more fundamentally to expand the scope of operation of corporations and investors to new markets (new avenues of activity/new territories) both now and in the future (Gill 1998). These measures are:

Measures to reconfigure governments and constitutional forms in order to make them operate in the context of greater market discipline, and to allow entry and exit options for mobile capital. Here the clearest cases are the new and more liberal constitutions produced in the former Eastern Bloc after the collapse of communist rule. However, constitutional change needs to be understood as something that occurs not simply within a particular national jurisdiction but in a transnational context. International treaties have constitutional weight, as the case of Mexico and the North American Free Trade Agreement (NAFTA) illustrates. In anticipation of entry into NAFTA, the Mexican government made many amendments to its revolutionary nationalist constitution of 1917. Entry into NAFTA required removing many existing social rights, for example the right of peasants to collective lands as a means of livelihood. In addition, NAFTA required the removal of various corporatist restrictions that protected both state and capital within Mexico from competition from overseas corporations. The advent of free trade therefore meant not only the creation of new rights, and equality of rights between foreign and domestic capital, but also the removal of other rights, such as the Mexican state's right to expropriate foreign investors. Other new constitutional trade and investment agreements, such as the GATS, contain similar provisions, with specific stipulations that include rights of capital to both enter and exit new markets and territories. In this way constitutional forms that were forged in a nationalist or revolutionary historical moment are being reformed by transnational interests in trade liberalization.

In countries as diverse as Russia, China, Mexico, South Africa, and Iraq there have been constitutional and legal changes designed to create more liberal market systems and frameworks of accumulation, as well as to protect the value of capital by preventing inflation (Gill 2002). Thus during the 1990s many nations have moved to fully independent central banks or currency boards that cannot be made to fund government deficits. These institutions are now committed to publicly specified inflation targeting as the centrepiece of monetary policy (as opposed to the promotion of full employment, which was a key goal of central banks during the post-1945 welfare era), in many cases locking in the anti-inflation bias by statute. This explains why one of the most important purposes of these institutional changes is to insulate the making of economic policy from legislative or popular accountability and control. Bank and currency boards' independence from governments is seen as a means to help enforce "budgetary discipline" and restraint on expenditures, particularly social expenditures, which might grow if economic policy were made more accountable to popular demands. Changes of this type – to cordon off monetary and fiscal policy from democratic accountability – can also occur indirectly through international agreements. For example, the International Monetary Fund (IMF) makes agreements, often secretly, with governments to create macroeconomic stabilization and deal with national financial and balance of payments crises. Similarly, the World Bank imposes structural adjustment programmes on governments, and does so without reference to democratic process (Gill and Bakker 2006).

Significance for social reproduction: One result of liberalization has been to reduce the contributions of corporations (and to an extent highly mobile, professional, elite labour) to public goods and thus to the collective costs of social reproduction (Katz 2001b). In low-income countries, from 1970 to 1998, trade taxes as a share of total taxes decreased on average from 40 per cent to 35 per cent. The further emphasis on private domestic investment and foreign direct investment (FDI) decreased tax rates on capital and, to compensate, increased taxes on labour. In many developing countries, this shift in the tax burden has had to be offset further by regressive sales and value-added taxes, because formal sector employment in those countries is small relative to informal sector employment (UNRISD 2005: 30–31). This fiscal squeeze means that governments in both the global North and South have less revenue and are forced to cut capital expenditures on infrastructure and/or social expenditures related to health, education, welfare, and social safety nets. As well, governments have less manoeuvrability in their public finances and are often obligated to prioritize international debt repayment or deficit reduction over the social spending that supports some of the work of social reproduction. As a result, social reproduction is absorbed into the unpaid sphere of (largely) women's work or, in the case of more affluent women, marketized and mediated through monetary relations.

As the critical literature on structural adjustment policies (SAPs) documents, the poorest people – often women, children, and the aged – tend to be hardest hit when provisions for social reproduction are removed or reduced (Benería and Feldman 1992; Bakker 1994; Brown 1995; Çağatay *et al.* 1995; Gutierrez 2003). Cutbacks tend to undermine the broader socialization of risk for the vulnerable (e.g. pensions, health, unemployment insurance, social security, transfers for small farmers and other producers) that is key to social reproduction. This in turn affects the sexual division of labour and more broadly, the gender discourse that supports this division of labour and the existing gender order (Connell 1990).[4] Yet as Meena Acharya's chapter on Nepal illustrates (Chapter 3, this volume), in societies where deeper market penetration, rather than state cutbacks, is the key force, a similar pressure on gender orders is nonetheless taking place.

A more progressive scheme of public finance, which we call the Integrationist Model of Social Reproduction, would maximize the proportion of the budget going to social sector ministries such as health, education, and welfare, as well as environmental protection and housing. In contrast, neoliberal fiscal policy has focused heavily on reducing budget deficits, reducing inflation, and reforming tax laws to favour the business and capital sectors. Balanced budget legislation, a ubiquitous aspect of new constitutionalism, limits the debt-to-GDP (gross domestic product) ratio and thus the ability of governments to undertake counter-cyclical (redistributive) tax and spending measures during depressions; this inhibits policies aimed at increasing employment. From the vantage point of social reproduction, public spending on basic social services is squeezed and universal access to these services is undermined in many countries in both North and South. Cuts have adversely affected the education and health budgets of virtually all countries (Sen 1997; Vanders *et al.* 2000).[5]

Monetary policies also have an impact on social reproduction. For instance, policies aimed at reducing inflation in order to maintain "sound money" and thus investor confidence operate in tandem with financial reform. Such policies usually liberalize the financial sectors in an effort to draw in foreign capital. Indeed deflationary or anti-inflation measures should be seen as part of a general macroeconomic package involving both fiscal and monetary policies. Such measures are designed to reduce social expenditures and the redistribution of income, and they do so as a result of their emphasis on fiscal restraint and high interest rates. The soundness of public finances is interpreted strictly from the perspective of large private investors, both foreign and domestic.

The framework of macroeconomic policy embedded within international agreements reflects the needs of capital markets – the "three Cs" of credibility, consistency, and confidence (Gill 1998). Similarly, the low inflation bias emerging through liberalized financial markets, which at least for most countries (the USA and Japan are exceptions to the general rule of higher interest rates) prioritizes high interest rates, tight monetary polices, and fiscal restraint, reflects the ability of financial institutions and investors to exercise *direct voice* over macroeconomic policies. Governments develop their macroeconomic policies in line with the interests of financial institutions because they fear that investors might postpone or cancel investments or even withdraw existing capital, perhaps causing a balance of payments crisis and worsening external indebtedness. By contrast the poor, at best, have only *voice*, since they tend to be place-bound and hemmed in by unresponsive domestic political structures without meaningful influence on the decisions made by governmental, multilateral institutions, or capital interests. In this sense, macroeconomic decisions can constrain the room for manoeuvre in changing budgets in a more pro-poor and gender-equitable direction (Elson 2001).

The emphasis on the three Cs may also reinforce three gender biases identified by Elson and Çağatay (2000). *Male breadwinner bias* results "from assuming that the nonmarket sphere of social reproduction is articulated with the market economy of commodity production through a wage which is paid a male breadwinner and which largely provides for the cash needs of a set of dependents" (1355). *Deflationary bias* refers to the ways in which financial markets induce most governments to adopt "credible" policies such as high interest rates, tight monetary policies, and fiscal restraint. This has led to a drop in investment rates and growth rates over the period of financial liberalization. Deflationary bias in macroeconomic policy has a disproportionately negative effect on women and ties governments' hands in dealing with recession. *Commodification bias* occurs when macroeconomic policy decreases taxation and, via fiscal squeeze, lower public expenditure. This leads to greater reliance on wages and market provisioning for meeting the needs of social reproduction (1354–56).

A second set of new constitutional measures is intimately related with the first. Since capitalist systems rest on a combination of public and private power, efforts are required both by state and capital to *construct and extend liberal capitalist markets* and thus to extend the potential scale and scope of the commodification of land, labour, and money. There are two broad dimensions involved here: (a) "original" or "primitive" accumulation (see below), when capitalist forms of accumulation and law replace other systems of livelihood and property relations; and (b) creation of new markets through the extension of the frontiers of private property rights and commodification.

Primitive accumulation replaces collective rights with systems of control based on the primacy of private property. Such privatization of collective goods is often facilitated by constitutional and legal changes initiated by the state. Thus the early modern European enclosure movements, justified as "improvement" of lands, are being repeated in the early twenty-first century, as state and capital combine to dispossess peasants and indigenous communities of their rights to land and livelihood throughout the world, not just in Mexico (e.g. Chiapas) and Amazonia. Capitalist markets are being consistently extended through various mechanisms. For example, intellectual property rights have been redefined since the mid-1990s to encompass private rights claims over life forms and the output of life science corporations as commodities. Similarly, it is now possible to purchase and own patents over seeds or even parts of the human genetic structure, parts of the natural world that were historically viewed as uncommodifiable elements of the commons (Gill and Bakker 2006).

Significance for social reproduction: The privatization of basic aspects of livelihood such as water has a disproportionately negative impact on poor households, imposing time costs on poor women in particular. How does privatization increase these burdens? The introduction of user fees for water in South Africa is a good example of the problem of water privatization. Water was available free of charge in the Mpendle area in KwaZulu-Natal from the early 1980s, after tap water supplies were laid on by the apartheid government following a severe drought. The free water supply was, however, terminated by the post-apartheid government as a result of cost recovery systems implemented in accordance with the government's neoliberal Growth, Employment and Redistribution (GEAR) strategy, introduced in 1996. Poor people who could not afford to pay for water had to resort to polluted river water, and this, according to the Ministry of Water Affairs and Forestry, contributed to a cholera outbreak, with thousands stricken and some deaths (Cheru 2001: 510).

Once state assets are privatized in this way, new constitutional mechanisms, i.e. legally binding commitments, lock in the rights of the new owners, who gain rights to control a basic resource necessary for public health as well as the capacity to irrigate and therefore farm dry areas. The issues that this entails are very complex, but they are partly illuminated by the case of externally driven water privatization in Bolivia, where water was privatized under pressure from the World Bank and the IMF. The Bolivian government agreed to privatize water supplies in Cochambamba, selling the contract to a subsidiary of Bechtel Corporation. The effects were similar to those in South Africa, though in the Bolivian case they provoked a general strike and forced the Bolivian president to resign. The Bolivian government then sought to reverse the privatization. When it did, it was challenged by the water company, which had reincorporated in Holland so as to take advantage of the Bolivia-Holland bilateral investment agreement. Like NAFTA, this agreement allowed a private firm to sue the government for damages – in this case for the amount of five times its original investment (Schneiderman 2000). In the Bolivian water case the new constitutional locking-in mechanisms were of two kinds – those of international organizations, in particular international financial institutions that had the power to withhold loans and thus force policy changes, and those of bilateral investment treaties.

The commercialization of life forms, including patenting of indigenous seeds and herbal potions and the market for human body parts, are extreme examples of the extension of private property rights by transnational firms and illegal forces into the biological bases of social reproduction. The law fails to protect specialized local communal practices and local biological resources as forms of both knowledge and communal property, while the WTO's agreement on Trade Related Aspects of Intellectual Property Rights (TRIPS) privileges capitalized inputs and consequently the interests of large transnational corporations.

A third set of measures   connects to the emergence of the World Economic Forum and other organizations that are concerned to protect neoliberal globalization by mitigating its own consequences: the growing frequency and depth of financial and economic crises, widespread impoverishment of populations, irreversible ecological damage, and the generalized social crisis. One reason for these mitigation measures is that neoliberal accumulation requires dismantling certain types of protection for industry, agriculture, and workers; therefore it is resisted, as people seek to protect the basic means of their livelihood and the conditions of their existence. Advocates of neoliberal reform seek to constrain any political repercussions of such resistance through various compensatory measures and efforts to co-opt political opposition. A range of state and international institutions engages in crisis management to deal with the wide range of dislocations noted above. The World Bank supports the idea of "social safety nets" and "poverty alleviation," for example. A wide variety of measures are designed to try to make neoliberalism politically sustainable while it restructures state forms and enlarges the world market for capital (Gill and Bakker 2006).

Significance for social reproduction: The UN Millennium Development Goals (MDGs) have recognized some of the problems for social reproduction that have resulted from the neoliberal policy mix. However, the thinking behind the goals does not appear to acknowledge the link between new constitutionalism and problems of human and social development. Left out of most analyses linked to the MDGs, such as the 2003 *Human Development Report*, are two key obstacles to broad-based social and human development:

1   The extension and strengthening of private property rights of large capital, achieved partly through new constitutionalist means and measures, which tends to reinforce unequal power relations between states; between particular states and market forces; and between different institutions and groups within states, reflecting inequalities within civil society.
2   The lack of expertise and capacity on the part of many parliamentarians and governments, not only in the developing countries, but also in the OECD, with respect to the new constitutionalism and its interrelationship with social policies.

It may well be that the combination of inequalities of power and inequalities in expertise (and therefore informed engagement) concerning links between economic and social policies is central to the emergence of "democratic deficits" at both the national and international levels. The phrase "democratic deficits" refers to the widely documented and apparently growing lack of legitimacy of both national governments and international/multilateral organizations and initiatives in the eyes of citizens and civil society groups. The deficit is intimately connected to the new government and international/multilateral organizations' policies for social and economic development.

In this sense the MDGs reflect a regression in development thinking, as well as a type of fatalism or defeatism about the problems they address. We need a change in mindset. Otherwise, initiatives such as the MDGs will tend to reinforce a system that is not only increasingly unequal but also patently failing to deliver progressive development to those most in need. Similarly, as Bergeron (2003) argues, although the World Bank's "post-Washington consensus" approaches attempt to better integrate social and economic dimensions of development and have placed greater emphasis on gender concerns, the new approaches continue to filter the more socially attuned agenda through a relatively narrow analytical lens that perpetuates many aspects of the old neoliberal model.

In sum, new constitutional governance has reinforced a shift in states and markets, and in power and production relations, in a manner that prioritizes private interests over social ones. The increased global mobility of capital has weakened the fiscal health of many governments and created a "fiscal squeeze" that limits their social expenditure capacity. Hence, capital is less and less responsible for subsidizing any of the costs of social reproduction; states are squeezed to trade off debt reduction/repayments for social expenditures; and households and communities increasingly absorb the costs of social reproduction either locally or transnationally, as is the case with foreign domestic workers (Gill and Bakker 2006; 2003).

Transnational mothering – as discussed by Herrera (Chapter 5, this volume) – is a compelling example of the transnational inequalities shaping social reproduction: it is both under-compensated in monetary terms in the West and in pockets of urban wealth in the South, and simultaneously productive of much needed income for the sending states and the families of women workers who can send remittances home. On the one hand, domestic labour and childcare is poorly paid and often carried out by women with little access to citizenship rights, who find themselves subject to extreme forms of surveillance and control. On the other hand, it is highly valued as a source of remittances sent by these workers to their country of origin and an important source of foreign currency. Host states also benefit from this work, as it privatizes, individualizes, and transnationalizes the cost of social reproduction (Bezanson and Luxton 2006: 8).

Conclusion

The redefinition of property rights under new constitutionalism partly determines the very nature of public systems, and of the institutions and relations of social reproduction as well as the conditions under which they operate. This is because new constitutionalism extends and deepens the domestic and world markets, subjecting public functions to competition or supplanting them with both national and foreign private firms seeking profit. In other instances, where state provisioning of social reproduction functions were previously minimal or non-existent, individual households and communities are struggling to meet their social reproduction needs in the face of the new demands created by increased links to the money economy. This may involve their increased labour in survival or informal activities (see Acharya, Chapter 3, this volume) or their migration to other parts of the world (see Herrera, Chapter 5, and Silvey, Chapter 6, this volume) as domestic servants and nannies to women who are facing their own tensions around social reproduction.

After the ascendancy of capital through much of the 1990s, perhaps one of the most important, and in some senses optimistic developments in global politics has been the emergence of globalized forms of resistance. The organizations involved in such oppositional activism have been variously called the "anti-globalization," "anti-capitalist," or "social justice" movements. The variety of terms used to describe them simply reflects the diversity of objectives and institutions that fall within these contemporary progressive ranks.

Among these, the debt relief movement has attempted to raise the issue of debt cancellation among G8 leaders, multilateral and bilateral donors, and creditors. The Jubilee 2000 Campaign, Jubilee Debt Campaign 10, and Jubilee South 11 focus on partial debt "relief" or total debt cancellation, or even reparations for the damage caused by debt in developing countries (see www.jubileedebtcampaign.org.uk; www.jubileesouth.org). These campaigns are important to conditions of social reproduction because economic policy – especially in the global South – is frequently driven by external considerations such as debt repayment and macroeconomic measures that enhance the shift towards disciplinary neoliberalism. Many developing countries use over 50 per cent of their government revenues (equivalent to 20–25 per cent of their total export earnings) for debt service. In the case of Ethiopia, which has one of the highest mortality rates in the world, the US $197 million spent annually servicing the external debt in 2001 would have provided a basic health care package for all mothers and children in the nation. In Tanzania, the $4 per capita per year spent on debt servicing could have otherwise been used to increase per capita health expenditures by 50 per cent. Not only does this illustrate the opportunity costs for governments associated with unrepayable external debts, but also it demonstrates "the shocking failure of the Heavily Indebted Poor Countries Initiative [of the World Bank] to convert debt liabilities into human-development investments" (Fraser *et al.* 2004: 22).

Despite statements by major governments regarding their support of socially progressive agendas (e.g. pledges made under the MDGs), governance mechanisms for regulating international debts continue to be linked to policy rules and mechanisms that guarantee first and foremost the rights and security of capital (in this case, creditors). In the view of international financial institutions, these rules are political counterparts to the need to discipline market forces and to implement what they call "sound economic policies." The question is, sound for whom? Missing from this policy framework are measures to guarantee and secure the rights of workers, and for the collective provisioning of care and social reproduction needs (Bakker and Gill 2003).

The movement to change international trade rules and barriers has drawn attention to the repeated creation of trade obstructions in Northern countries for Southern products, and the simultaneous undermining of Southern industrial and agricultural capacity through export dumping by rich countries (Ghimire 2005). An interesting network of feminist activists and policy advocates is the International Gender and Trade Network (IGTN; see www.igtn.org), which draws specific links between trade agreements and social reproduction (see Williams 2003a). The international umbrella group links seven regional networks in Africa, Asia, the Caribbean, Latin America, North America, Europe, and the Pacific. The group organizes grassroots responses to trade and investment agreements, and attempts to directly influence decision-makers in and around the WTO to change institutional and regulatory practices.

An example of women's responses to the non-regulation of informal sector work is Women in Informal Employment: Globalizing and Organizing (WIEGO; www.wiego.org). WIEGO is a global research-policy network that seeks to improve the status of the working poor, especially women, in the informal economy. It does so by highlighting the size, composition, characteristics, and contributions of the informal economy through improved statistics and research; by helping to strengthen member-based organizations of informal workers; and by promoting policy dialogues and processes that include representatives of informal worker organizations. WIEGO organizes international meetings that bring together representatives of female informal sector workers in efforts to target legislative change around working conditions, regulation, and pay.

Another increasingly influential form of engagement with officials responsible for economic policy is Gender Audits and Budgets (see www.gender-budgets.org). This movement's goal is to support government and civil society in analyzing national and/or local budgets from a gender perspective and applying this analysis to the formulation of gender-responsive budgets. As the discussion above on fiscal and monetary policy revealed, government budgets reflect the social and economic priorities of governments, yet they often contradict the commitments governments have made at the international and national levels to human rights and gender equality (see www.policyalternatives.ca/Reports/2005/09 for "Why Gender Budgets Matter" by I. Bakker). At this moment there are some 70 examples of gender budget initiatives taking place in regions throughout the world. They are one instrument to hold governments accountable for providing more progressive conditions of social reproduction.

All these examples show a shift away from simply protesting what is wrong and towards advancing proposals that seek to influence regulatory institutions and practices (Ghimire 2005).

Finally, as a counter-strategy, it is important to begin to identify new approaches that bridge economic development and social reproduction. This will involve identifying the components of such an alternative,[6] generating new mechanisms for incorporating social reproduction into macroeconomic frameworks (scenario planning, for example), and determining what a gender progressive model would look like. For instance, one can identify three models of social reproduction.

Model 1: the minimalist informal model of Social Reproduction

Very basic public revenues for SR; little tracking of links between public expenditures and revenues, on the one hand, and gender equity and poverty alleviation goals, on the other; informalization or market-ization (depending on income status) of significant portions of SR (commodification bias and fiscal squeeze); minimal if any public policy/political recognition of work/family balance; SR as an externality (something that is assumed to take place outside economic relations).

Model 2: the regulationist model of Social Reproduction

High or significant degrees of state support for work/family balance (recognition of duality of childbearing and labour market attachment); use of state-based entitlements to fund SR, but perhaps through a male breadwinner bias (separate spheres of production and reproduction); counter-cyclical investment in social and public infrastructure and programmes; gender-sensitive tracking of fiscal policy impacts; women's participation in setting regulation model.

Model 3: the integrationist model of Social Reproduction

Social sector given credibility as part of macroeconomic policy frame; counter-cyclical policies; effective women's mobilization and rigorous analysis demanding that states deliver on policy promises to do with gender equality; exposure of contradiction between the processes of capital accumulation and the SR of the working population (commo-dification/informalization of SR versus socialization of collective costs of SR); privileging of the rights of SR over capital rights; consideration of SR as integral to economic relations and economic workings of society (no separation but rather SR acknowledged as constituting a productive set of social relations); adequately paid parental leave including a time period for fathers; time policies that include fewer hours in paid work; negation of deflationary bias, male breadwinner bias, commodification bias; bolster global governance in the area of capital income taxation.

Thinking about social reproduction in terms of differing models allows us to rethink what would constitute a progressive approach in the context of neoliberal governance models. It also allows us to think about different types of gender orders that relate to the local context and its historically constituted structures.

Notes

1 Thank you to the Fulbright New Century Scholars' Program for the opportunities created through this unique programme. Particular thanks to the scholars who are part of this book for their enthusiasm and willingness to engage with a process that really was unmapped and exploratory. Thanks to the former director of the NCS Program, Patti McGill Peterson, for her impeccable leadership and vision. Also Micaela Iovine and Stacy Bustillos were our unwavering guides through the Fulbright process and lots of fun to be with. Carolyn Elliott provided exceptional intellectual leadership to the overall group of scholars and was always supportive of our ideas. The late Alice Ilchman at the Rockefeller Foundation also deserves our great thanks for supporting the team at Bellagio. A special thanks to Rachel Silvey for her editing of this chapter and her collaboration on this project.

2 Services dominate the economic activity of OECD economies, accounting for 60–70 per cent of production and employment, somewhat less in developing countries. Many of the fastest growing sectors of world production are in services (e.g. telecommunications, health, finance). The share of services in world trade and investment has been increasing to about 20 per cent of total trade by the end of the twentieth century (about $1.3 trillion in 1999), and giant services firms are pressing for further liberalization, e.g. through GATS.

3 See "German Public Housing Attracts Foreign Buyers," *International Herald Tribune,* 4 May 2006.

4 A gender order refers to a historically specific and constituted configuration of state–labour and market–household relations that underpin the work of maintaining and reproducing people on a daily and generational basis (Walby 2000; Connell 2005).

5 As the United Nations Research Institute for Social Development (UNRISD) (2005: 45) notes in its report *Gender Equality: striving for justice in an unequal world,* there have been improvements in per capita social expenditures (education, health, social security, and welfare) in the late 1990s, but these expenditures as a share of GDP have declined in a number of countries and have been most pronounced in sub-Saharan Africa and in Eastern and Central Europe. Moreover, as the authors of the study note, given the need for expanded social expenditure, even some of the increases in expenditure in some countries are insufficient at their current levels (see Table 3.3).

6 The UNRISD report on gender equality in an unequal world (see note 5 above) highlights several changes in policy direction:
- monetary and fiscal policies that are more expansionary;
- taxation policies that provide adequate revenues to fund social expenditures and protect the erosion of state's protective capacity;
- selective strategic liberalization of flows of trade and capital to avoid great ups and downs in employment and exchange rates so that FDI becomes a tool of development, not an end in itself;
- greater policy space for countries so that they can choose from a wider array of policy tools.

2 Towards globalization with a human face

Engendering policy coherence for development

Maria Floro and Hella Hoppe[1]

Introduction

Several governments and civil society organizations have voiced concerns about the current direction of policy coherence being shaped by international trade and financial institutions, namely the World Trade Organization (WTO), the International Monetary Fund (IMF), and the World Bank. The expanded mandate of these institutions has serious consequences for national policy and economic sovereignty and has distributional and gender implications that must not be ignored. Given the world's deep-seated, persistent imbalances in wealth and opportunities, a fair and balanced globalization requires us to coordinate macroeconomic policies to serve social and sustainable development objectives as well as human rights standards. There is need to make international trade and financial agreements fully support United Nations (UN) commitments, especially as regards gender equality, poverty reduction, and women's empowerment. This process will require multi-level efforts and institutional mechanisms.

We argue here that unless critical gender and governance concerns are given priority in the emerging process of policy coherence, it will be difficult for coordinated macroeconomic policies to serve the goal of sustainable human development. We also demonstrate that horizontal policy coherence requires a better understanding of the vertical linkages between the macroeconomic environment created by multilateral trade and investment agreements and micro-level adjustments and changes, particularly those experienced by women. This is particularly crucial in the context of social reproduction and the manner in which it can either be undermined or supported by policy. Social reproduction involves both the market and non-market production of goods and services needed for human maintenance and development.

In this regard, we argue in this paper that policy coherence and social reproduction are dynamically interrelated. First, policy-making itself is inevitably a part of the process of social reproduction. Policy-making is intentional planning and programming of the ways in which states and markets work, and it affects the ways in which social reproduction is maintained, organized and structured. Second, the evolving coherence of trade and financial policies has large implications for social reproduction. Using the definition presented by Bakker and Gill (see Chapter 1, this volume), we explore the effects of policies on three key dimensions of social reproduction, namely biological reproduction, the reproduction of the labour force and the reproduction of provisioning and caring needs.

Institutional setting

The evolving coherence of trade and financial policies is part of the Doha ministerial negotiation process[2] in which WTO member states have emphasized the need for joint measures of the WTO and the Bretton Woods institutions to respond to a rapidly changing international environment (WTO 2001: 2; see also Bretton Woods Project 2003 and Nageer 2004). Efforts to systematize policies and agreements in IMF, World Bank, and WTO negotiations have increased the pressure on developing countries to adopt market liberalization, deregulation, and privatization (Caliari 2004; Nageer 2004). For example, the IMF and the World Bank are increasingly involved in trade and trade-related policies in support of the WTO, providing trade-related technical assistance, research and training activities, and ex ante mechanisms such as country performance assessments before loan approval or grant disbursement (Caliari and Williams 2004: 6). This particular direction of policy coherence can potentially limit the sovereignty of governments in implementing domestic policies and strategies that would put people at the centre of the development process. It is also leading to incongruence between the multilateral trade agreements and other international commitments, particularly the Beijing Platform for Action and the Millennium Development Goals (MDGs). Although the founding principles of the World Bank, IMF, and WTO commit them to work towards the attainment of people-centred objectives, fundamental power asymmetries are being strengthened between the international institutions that deal with trade and finance and those that support human rights and the social content of development policies, leading to growing tensions and contradictions (World Commission on the Social Dimension of Globalization 2004: 113).

International organizations, policy-makers and civil society, as well as academics, have raised grave concerns that the needs of vulnerable groups, and especially those of poor women – decent work, social protection, and empowerment – have become subservient to or are derived from (market-driven) economic growth and financial policy objectives (see, for example, Sheinin 1996; UN 2003a; Williams 2003b; Çağatay and Erturk 2004; Nguyen and Zampetti 2004; World Commission on the Social Dimension of Globalization 2004; Arestis and Sawyer 2005). More generally, this shift towards privatized governance arrangements has strong effects on caring institutions as well as on processes of social reproduction, which encompass biological reproduction of the species and the ongoing reproduction of commodity labour power (see Chapter 1, this volume).

The horizontal approach to policy coherence

The incongruence between increasingly coordinated international macro-economic policies and the objectives and mandates of key international organizations and conferences, is due partly to the typical focus of negotiation on specific sectors or issues such as trade, finances, health, social affairs, and development assistance. This compartmentalization reflects, to a large extent, a parallel situation faced by national governments, where departments with separate spheres of governance often fail to coordinate their actions to achieve development goals (World Commission on the Social Dimension of Globalization 2004: 78). The compartmentalization leads to incoherent policies not only at the national level but at the international level as well. Economic and trade ministers commit themselves to trade liberalization in multilateral, regional, and bilateral negotiations; at the same time, other government officials and representatives are signing legally binding and non-binding conventions, resolutions, and declarations concerning human rights, environmental protection, and the empowerment of women (Walker 2004). Given the dominance of the financial ministries and international financial institutions, their mandate often sets the terms of the other discourses and negotiations. Attention to social goals and human development goals is lacking or inadequate, and distributional concerns are not addressed. Thus market expansion tends to benefit only certain countries and certain groups within societies, intensifying existing economic inequalities.

Several examples illustrate the importance of policy coherence at the horizontal level, as shown in Figure 2.1. In agriculture, lack of coherence is evident between the goals of trade liberalization – as formulated in the WTO Agreement on Agriculture – and food security as a core human right (see article 25 of the Universal Declaration of Human Rights, and article 14 of CEDAW, which stresses the specific role of women in attaining food security). Rural women in Africa are especially affected by imports of subsidized food and price dumping, which have endangered local economies and threatened the livelihood of small-scale farmers, especially women, and the food security of poor households (Young and Hoppe 2003: 19). Substantial reductions in subsidies and improved market access are key elements of a policy coherence that would serve the goals of food security and poverty reduction.[3]

Another area where coherence is lacking is the primary commodities trade. A number of developing countries, and especially Least Developed Countries (LDCs), are caught in a vicious cycle of heavy dependence on primary commodities, unstable and declining world market capacities, and unsustainable external debt (UNCTAD 2003). A key precondition for reducing extreme poverty in these countries is to break this chain and to formulate trade and monetary/financial policies more strategically, that is, in ways more consistent with national priorities and development objectives

Horizontal Dimension of Policy Coherence

Goals of the UN rights framework

Effects of the WTO/trade agreements and BWI loan conditionalities

- fair and inclusive globalization
- achievement of social development for all
- promotion of human rights, gender equality, and women's empowerment

- unequal distribution of wealth, resources, and incomes
- potential undermining of the productive basis of local economies
- subordination of public sector goods and social services to private profit

Figure 2.1 Horizontal dimension of policy coherence

(Singh 1994; Rodrik 2001; UNCTAD 2003). Declining commodity prices, short-term price fluctuations, and the dwindling share of primary producers in the value chain have had, as many studies show, serious negative effects on women, who are strong agents in producing and trading commodities (for a general discussion and review of the literature, see Çağatay 2001 and Ul Haque 2004). Given the role of women in the production process, these trends constitute a threat to food security as well.

International trade and foreign investment in services constitutes a third area where policies are not coherent. Studies show that the current direction of the General Agreement on Trade in Services (GATS),[4] along with private-sector development strategies and the conditioning of loans on fiscal austerity measures and foreign investment incentives, will further weaken essential public and social services in many countries (Çağatay and Erturk 2004; Williams 2004). Studies indicate that liberalization of the services sector has especially negative implications for poor women, both as customers or users of these services and as employees (UN 2003a: 263; Williams 2001; WIDE 2002; Young and Hoppe 2003). As water, utilities, health care, public transport, and other public services become subject to market-determined user fees, poor households are likely to be marginalized and excluded. The resulting increased workload for women as they spend more labour time on survival and reproduction activities has been emphasized in many studies (Bakker 1994; ILO 1999; Elson and Çağatay 2000; Young and Hoppe 2003; Adaba 2004).

A vertical approach: gender analysis of global macro-micro-linkages

In order to effectively address policy coherence at the horizontal level, it is necessary to examine the vertical linkages between the macroeconomic environment created by international trade, investment, and loan agreements and the adjustments and changes involved at the national, sectoral, household, and individual levels (see Figure 2.2).[5] This section explores these critical linkages from a gender perspective. Using case studies, it highlights the important distributional consequences and gendered outcomes of the current international trade and financial policy regimes.

Female poverty and market liberalization

There is a dynamic interaction between policy coherence, policy implementation, and the pattern of gender relations in social and economic life. A growing body of research by feminist economists shows how gender norms and relations are transmitted through a variety of institutions, including markets, governments, and the household (see, for example, Jones 1986; Hart 1992; Floro 1995; Braunstein 2000; Elson and Çağatay 2000; Erturk and Darity 2000; Kabeer 2000; Young and Hoppe 2003; Floro *et al.* 2004). Policy coherence and implementation can alter or reinforce prevailing gender relations and biases. Market expansion and market liberalization have created new patterns of wealth and poverty. They have brought about changes not only in savings and debt but also in patterns of employment and labour allocation between paid and unpaid work.

These changes have spotlighted the heightened vulnerability of poor households. Women experience poverty differently from the way men do because they typically have less control over resources. As Çağatay (2001) puts it, macroeconomic policies are predicated on a set of distributive relations across different social groups, just as they entail distributive choices across different social groups. If this fact is not taken into account, policy

Vertical Dimension of Policy Coherence

Δ in MACROECONOMIC ENVIRONMENT
   Trade Agreements
   Investment Agreements
   Loan Agreements
   ⇑ ⇓
Δ   at   National,
        Sectoral,
        Household, and
        Individual levels

Linkages between the macroeconomic environment created by international trade, investment and loan agreements, and adjustments at the national, sectoral, household, and individual levels

Figure 2.2 Vertical dimension of policy coherence

implementation and coherence may reinforce gender-based inequalities, which in turn hamper policy reform and/or limit potential benefits to poor households.

The situation in several LDCs illustrates the heightened vulnerability of poor households and the varied ways in which the social reproduction work performed by women in these households has grown more onerous. In recent decades, increasing numbers of women in LDCs have taken on the role of income earners and "breadwinners."[6] Women's share of work in farming and in informal-sector small-scale and micro-enterprises has risen in many developing countries (Charmes 1998; Chen *et al.* 1999; Standing 1999; Carr *et al.* 2000; ILO 1999; 2002). Labour flexibility, in particular outsourcing and subcontracting among home-based women workers, has become prevalent. Women have also taken on "nonstandard" forms of work such as part-time employment and temporary work, which tend to offer little or no job security or health benefits (ILO 1999; 2002).

Until recently, multilateral policy negotiations and formulation of domestic policies have paid little attention to the increasing economic insecurity of small farmers, informal workers, and micro-entrepreneurs, particularly women. The issue of economic insecurity and the associated effect on social reproduction have been excluded from multilateral policy negotiations. The financial and economic crises that have affected parts of East Asia, Latin America, and Russia in the late 1990s have exposed the vulnerability of many groups in these countries and the harsh trade-offs that these individuals and their households have to make to deal with risk and shocks. Coping strategies have taken multiple forms – from depletion of assets by pawning or sale in order to pay health expenses to the use of credit that has been earmarked for investment to help meet subsistence needs, withdrawing children from school to help in the farm or family enterprise, replacing market purchases that have become unaffordable with household production substitutes, reducing food consumption or the use of utilities, migrating to urban areas or abroad, and so forth (see World Bank 1998; Sebstad and Cohen 2001; Beckerman and Solimano 2002; Antonopoulos and Floro 2004; Floro and Messier 2005). These coping strategies are key elements of social reproduction, since they directly affect the means of survival and the reproduction of provisioning and caring needs, yet they are not captured in standard macroeconomic indicators.

Women continue to be more vulnerable to poverty than men, owing to persistent gender inequalities in their access to resources, control over property, or earned income (UNIFEM 2000). A study of women farmers in Ghana by Date-Bah (1985), for example, shows how women's limited access to credit and the generally poor system of public transportation have significantly impaired their earnings, and hence their means of survival. In Kenya, women's exclusion from inheriting or owning cattle and land, the main forms of capital accumulation, has effectively denied them access to credit, market opportunities, and technological innovations (Ventura-Dias

1985). Resource allocation is often gendered both within households and in market institutions, additionally constraining women's opportunities to transform their capabilities into incomes and improvement in their well-being. A growing body of ethnographic, feminist, and household economics research demonstrates that resources remain unequally shared within families in many parts of the developing world (see e.g. Roldan 1987; Haddad *et al.* 1995; Kabeer 2000).

The impact of market liberalization policies on structural inequities and inequalities

A key question in this context is whether trade and financial policy reforms enhance or diminish existing gender inequalities. The answer is not always evident or easily measurable. Global trade and investment rules and accompanying national policy reforms affect not only resource allocation and the organization of production, but also legal property rights and rules of behaviour. Changes in incomes and employment patterns greatly influence household members' spheres of control and authority, access to and control over resources, and decision-making roles. Export expansion can increase growth and employment. But it calls also for an understanding of existing structural inequities, which undermine women's welfare rather than enable sustainable human development.

For example, it has been argued that as agricultural markets and exports expand, indigenous land tenure systems evolve from communal ownership to the privatization of property rights that may bypass women farmers (Smith *et al.* 1994). Studies in Cameroon, Nigeria, and Zambia show how market-liberalization-induced commercialization of a particular crop can lead to a situation in which women are forced to cede decisions about crop production to men (Webb 1989; Kumar 1994). When cocoa was promoted as an export crop in Nigeria, it became a men's crop as well. The same is true for irrigated rice in Zambia. Other village-level studies in Nigeria, Nepal, and India show that agricultural commercialization has reduced women's share in household income (Ventura-Dias 1985; Moock 1986; Lipton and Longhurst 1989). In North Cameroon, intrahousehold dynamics and the relative bargaining power of men and women have changed as a result of the introduction of new cash crops (Jones 1986). These study findings suggest that global trade and investment rules lead to changes in incomes and employment patterns between women and men which then have direct consequences on the reproduction of provisioning and caring needs in the household. When states and markets undermine the process of social reproduction, there is excessive demand for women's unpaid labour as households and communities try to cope by stretching household production of non-market goods and services.

Several studies illustrate the transformation in women's and men's roles that accompanies the expansion and deregulation of markets for goods and services. Since the mid-1980s, market prices have either declined or fluctuated severely for several major export commodities of developing countries, including cotton, sugar, cocoa, and rubber. The prices of major export commodities of developing countries, such as cotton, have declined by approximately 54 per cent since the mid-1990s. Subsidies provided by developed countries to their cotton producers have led to an increase in supply and thus to lower cotton prices in the world market. Deterioration in the terms of trade, even if temporary, can seriously reduce employment, wages, incomes, economic security, and well-being. The recent Cotton Initiative proposed by West and Central African countries called for the elimination of subsidies by industrialized countries, primarily the USA, in order to ensure that the cotton market would be open to African and other farmers (Williams 2004). According to Oxfam (2002), US cotton subsidies cost sub-Saharan Africa $300 million in potential revenue in 2001–2. The reduction or elimination of tariff and non-tariff barriers in non-agricultural, manufactured goods has also been associated with declining industrial output in some developing countries.

The expansion of WTO trade negotiations and multilateral trade rules into domestic policy areas can further accentuate the difficulties of countries in diversifying and developing their domestic industries. A recent study of trade in sub-Saharan Africa found that, while partial liberalization yielded insignificant increases in market access (due to erosion of the preferences) it has led to a contraction of industrial output and an increased specialization in agricultural commodities such as grains, sugar, and cotton (Williams 2004). Lack of gender-sensitive data, particularly national, longitudinal data, unfortunately makes it difficult to ascertain the severity and magnitude of these displacement effects.

It has been argued that trade liberalization has substantial benefits for women workers, particularly in Taiwan, Bangladesh, China, India, and Korea, because of a rise in women's labour force participation in the export sector, which has narrowed the gender differences in employment and wages. But even in these economies there are reasons to be cautious, given the terms of employment and working conditions under which the increase in women's paid employment has occurred (Çağatay 2001; Fontana 2002; Çağatay and Erturk 2004). Without accompanying laws to uphold labour standards, women's working conditions – including job security, health and occupational safety, and pay – may not improve, and in fact can deteriorate under the pressure of international competition. Furthermore, the potentially positive gains made by women in the context of the feminization of employment may be temporary and can be reversed (Benería and Lind 1995; Çağatay and Erturk 2004).

Berik's (2000) study of the Taiwanese manufacturing sector, for example, shows the effects of industrial restructuring as Taiwan moves from light manufactured exports to machinery and transportation-related exports. Restructuring has caused a decline in women's employment opportunities relative to men's and a shift from wage to salaried employment. Even in countries where wage inequalities are not increasing, the gender wage gap has not diminished, and in some cases it has even widened (Seguino 2000). Berik *et al.*'s (2004) study of Taiwan and Korea suggests that competition from foreign trade in concentrated industries is positively linked with wage discrimination against women. This suggests that even if trade liberalization enhances women's employment opportunities, their "competitive advantage" as workers remains rooted in lower pay and poorer working conditions. In fact, as Braunstein and Epstein's (2002) study on China's export-processing zones demonstrates, liberalization of trade and investment provides strong incentives to ignore both the poor as well as hazardous workplace conditions. They further find that liberalization provides incentives to keep women's relative wages low in order to ensure that the country remains competitive and attracts foreign investment.

Unregulated import liberalization can also threaten the livelihoods of women working in formerly protected areas of the domestic economy. In many OECD countries, trade expansion with developing countries has resulted in declines in employment that disproportionately affect women (Erturk and Darity 2000; Kucera and Milberg 2000). Increased competition from subsidized food imported from the developed countries has also displaced food producers in developing countries. According to Williams (2003b), this has been the case for Kenyan women farmers. Increased food imports and dumping, coupled with increasing prices for farm inputs, have left many female food producers worse off than they were in the early 1980s before structural adjustment. In most cases, there are few or no assistance programmes, e.g. retraining and compensation schemes, for people who have lost their livelihoods. When priorities are set for allocating limited government revenues, projects aimed at attracting foreign investment often take precedence over such programmes.

Although some rural women farmers who were integrated into village markets have managed to increase their incomes, others have not, particularly those who could not afford to buy modern inputs such as fertilizer or equipment. Thus, even when new markets create opportunities, many groups of women are slow to take advantage of them, as they often lack access to credit, new technologies, and knowledge of marketing. This describes the situation in several Africa and Asian countries where a significant number of women work in strategic productive activities, notably agriculture and the food sub-sector. Services provided by financial markets and institutions, such as credit and insurance, are often skewed in favour of cash crop and export-oriented sectors and of non-agricultural sectors such as real estate. Subsistence producers and women farmers are often left out of the financing circuit, so that they cannot make land improvements and increase their production. The issue of food security entails addressing the present gender and economic inequities that limit rural women's access to land, credit, and farming technology and information. The impact of these changes is likely to be more severe for women-headed households and for poor women.

Donors and non-governmental organizations have addressed these constraints through the provision of microcredit, irrigation, and development of extension and training programmes in villages and communities. These schemes have helped generate earning opportunities for many women and have also increased agricultural production in several parts of the developing world. But are they sustainable in the long term? Irrigation projects, for example, tend to falter after donors leave, for lack of maintenance and repair. In other cases, microcredit schemes and assistance programmes do not reach the poorest and most vulnerable households; some also unwittingly reinforce stereotypical notions of "feminine tasks or roles" (Goetz and Gupta 1996; Ackerly 1997; UNIFEM 2000; Mayoux 2001; Sebstad and Cohen 2001).

Many developing economies need coordination and support of complementary investments to jump-start them out of a "low-level equilibrium trap." Economists have argued that coordinated expansion of several sectors is usually self-sustaining through mutual demand support (Bardhan and Udry 1999). Yet in the face of rapid global market integration, the importance of the tradable sector is often overstated while that of the domestic market is underestimated, and the household and public sectors directly involved in social provisioning and care needs are ignored. One should bear in mind that the growth of tradable sectors requires investment in social services as well as non-tradable, intermediate inputs and services including maintenance, repair, and parts, as well as affordable and nearby transport, distribution, and communications services. The efforts of countries to generate strategic complementarities appropriate to their conditions are likely to be undermined by the emerging coordination of macroeconomic policies. The new macroeconomic policies generally limit the policy space for developing countries to choose between different policy options in designing their development strategies. However, whether or not the remaining policy space can be used by governments and civil society in order to promote women's empowerment and gender equality and to address concerns of social reproduction is a question that needs to be analysed on a case-by-case basis.

Trade liberalization creates winners as well as losers and hence can widen disparities; it tends to advantage large and medium producers as well those with access to productive resources, and to disadvantage smaller producers. As in the agricultural sector, informal sector micro-entrepreneurs, especially women, often lack access to the credit, new technologies, and marketing know-how that are needed to participate in the new and expanding markets. Even when their earnings are the same as men's, women in many parts of the developing world are likely to face discriminatory practices on the part of some financial institutions (Manning and Graham 2000; van Staveren 2002). If nothing else, the notion that men are breadwinners and that women earn supplementary incomes – even though the reality may be just the opposite – tends to permeate market transactions, including credit allocation. Unfortunately, data do not yet exist to allow a systematic study of this issue.

Market liberalization policies can weaken the rights of workers, including casual workers and subcontracted home workers, through labour market deregulation, which has been justified in the name of international competitiveness and economic efficiency. This process is illustrated by the case of Ecuador. Rapid integration of Ecuador's economy into the global market through trade and financial market liberalization has meant that an increasing share of its producers need a more flexible labour force that can be redeployed quickly during expansions, and can be kept "at arm's length" at little or no cost during slumps (Benería and Floro 2006). The reforms initiated by the IMF-World Bank in Ecuador during the 1980s brought about greater labour market flexibility, reducing mandatory employment stability in all activities, introducing wage-setting at market-determined levels, and abolishing the obligation of firms to pay workers on strike. Additional measures aimed at increasing labour flexibility and export competitiveness were incorporated into Ecuador's labour code during the early 1990s, further weakening the bargaining position of workers.

In Ecuador and other parts of the developing world, medium-sized and large firms have directly or indirectly developed increasing links to informal production through outsourcing and subcontracting. This trend has been examined in several studies on the cases of India, Pakistan, and the Philippines, as well as parts of Latin America (Boonmathya *et al.* 1999; Prügl 1999; Pérez-Sainz 2000; Balakrishnan and Huang 2002; Todaro and Yanez 2004). For example, Benería and Floro (2006) demonstrate in their study of urban low-income households the extent of heterogeneity in skill levels and production arrangements within the informal sector. Among those employed in their sample survey data, roughly 95 per cent of workers in Bolivia and 79 per cent of persons employed in Ecuador have moderately or highly precarious jobs. Moreover, women, by virtue of their socially ascribed roles within the household, tend to be over-represented at the lower end of the labour hierarchy, i.e. in more precarious jobs. Social norms and gender-ascribed roles tend to influence their work location, level of schooling, and ownership of assets.

Work arrangements for many workers in poor households also reflect their movement between formal and informal sectors. Given the unsteady and irregular character of many work contracts or micro-enterprises, it is not surprising that the incomes of these workers vary considerably. One outcome of the unsteady nature of this may be to discourage and limit investments in children's education. The growing informalization of employment that has been part of the dramatic transformation of employment patterns is likely to persist under the current policy coordination. The result has been the erosion of workers' rights and bargaining power relative to capital. Informal workers, particularly subcontracted persons and home-workers, earn very low piece-rate wages and work without benefits and protection. One result is the international migration of workers from many low-income countries, primarily towards the Middle East, the USA, Hong Kong, and Europe.

Policy (in)coherence of multilateral trade, financial, and investment agreements

Any assessment of the gendered impact of market liberalization policy regimes on human well-being must look at the regimes' impacts on processes of social reproduction, including women's livelihoods and work conditions and the unpaid care economy. Using time-use data, researchers have observed that increases in women's labour force participation are not accompanied by a commensurate reduction in their unpaid domestic work, as men have been reluctant to pick up the slack (Floro 1995; UNDP 1995; Hirway 2002; Floro and Miles 2003; Pichetpongsa 2004). The findings of feminist studies on household strategies during economic crisis show that intensification of work has been an important coping mechanism and an additional labour burden for many poor working women.[7] In a recent study of home-based workers, Pichetpongsa (2004) examines their time-use patterns using the 2002 urban survey data on households in low-income areas of Bangkok. The results indicate that employment in the informal sector has meant longer working hours for women compared to men, and that women still tend to earn less than men. Pichetpongsa's study also shows that women workers tend to have lower quality of life than men workers, being relatively both money-poor and time-poor. His study relates these gender differences in quality of life both to the gender norms that dictate the household division of labour and to the effect of the market liberalization policies that precipitated the financial crisis.[8] The study emphasizes the important point that because gender inequalities are multidimensional, women who may gain in one dimension, such as employment or access to income, may lose in another, in the form of increased work intensity and reduced leisure and sleep.

Assessment of multilateral trade, financial, and investment agreements therefore requires a more comprehensive horizontal-level evaluation that takes into account not only increased market output or incomes, but also unpaid work burdens and quality of life. The continued invisibility of increased unpaid work, higher stress, and declines in women's capabilities is likely to give a falsely positive impression of the consequences of policies and development strategies. The magnitude of these costs, when properly accounted, is likely to offset the perceived benefits of some of the policies.

In recent years, social and public services (e.g. water and health care), as well as traditional financial and professional services, have become a growing part of international trade.

Services now account for about 50% of GDP in developing countries as a whole (vs. 68% in the developed world), trade in services represents 16% of all their trade and 23% of their share of global services exports, according to an UNCTAD study .... Services now generate about half of all jobs in the formal sector.

(Meltzer 2004: 14)

The GATS and the Agreement on Trade-Related Aspects of Intellectual Property (TRIPS)[9] negotiations have explicitly linked trade with protection of investment and intellectual property rights (Young and Hoppe 2003; Caliari and Williams 2004). The GATS will provide the legal framework for trade in services, and aims to cover a range of areas including investment, financial services, communications, transportation, education, energy, water, and movement of persons. Negotiations regarding the GATS call for pro-gressive removal of regulations that impede trade and investment in services. This move towards liberalization of services is likely to affect access to water, health care, and electricity, which are essential for household main-tenance and human survival (see Chapter 1). Intellectual property rights agreements such as TRIPS are also likely to have impacts on access to affordable medicines, which are critical for human health and morbidity. Owing to their impact on technology transfer, these agreements also have serious implications for traditional knowledge and long-term development.

The current WTO negotiations in services and intellectual property rights will commit member countries to specific policy choices especially in these areas. In economies where self-employment or unpaid family work is prevalent, gender-based differences in resource access and control are likely to entail adverse consequences for many women, especially in vulnerable households. If WTO agreements reduce or eliminate restrictions on imports produced using techniques that harm the environment (such as air-polluting electricity generators or equipment that discharges toxic or hazardous materials into rivers or nearby forests), trade liberalization is likely to lead to environmental degradation and erosion of common property resources as well.

During the 2004 WTO ministerial meeting in Cancún, many civil society organizations, including women's groups, questioned the push under the GATS negotiations to liberalize basic social services such as water, sanita-tion, electricity, health, and education. Liberalization and privatization of these basic services will have tremendous social and equity implications. The findings of case studies such as that of Cochabamba, Bolivia, show that privatization dramatically increases the cost of water and reduces access to it by a majority of the poor in the area (Williams 2003b). The imposition of market-based user fees in cost recovery programmes established in India, the Philippines, and South Africa has deprived the poor of access to essen-tial water services (UNIFEM 2000). In Kwa-Zulu Natal, South Africa, lack of access to safe drinking water, excacerbated by privatization, has been implicated in the outbreak of cholera (Williams 2003b; Caliari and Williams 2004). Several developing countries are therefore seeking the right to regulate these services in order to attain their national development objectives. At the same time, they have challenged the dominant role of financial and commercial interests that underlie many international trade and financial agreements. In addition, some developing countries have called for measures that address the current imbalance between the global movements of capital and labour. Developing countries have also called for emergency safeguards, especially a process for addressing "material injury" to domestic service providers resulting from market liberalization.

International agreements such as TRIPS can seriously affect the use of traditional knowledge, the pace of technology transfer, and access to affordable medicines. It is within this context that the Doha Declaration on TRIPS and public health affirms the right of developing countries to interpret the TRIPS agreement from a public health perspective.[10] But the multilateral trade-related negotiations under the WTO as well as IMF-World Bank loan agreements have explicitly linked trade with the protection of foreign capital and intellectual property rights without regard to likely consequences to social reproduction. The Agreement on Trade-Related Investment Measures (TRIMs), for example, was negotiated during the WTO's Uruguay Round with the goal of eliminating trade-distorting investment measures among WTO members. Of critical importance is the push for the liberalization of financial services, which is likely to have distributional consequences in both developed and developing countries. Likewise, the Bretton Woods institutions have used a variety of mechanisms and instruments to reinforce trade and investment links and promote investment and capital market liberalization (Williams 2004).[11] Given that similar agreements have had negative effects on women and the provision of supports for social reproduction, there is a need for critical scrutiny of the gender dimensions of such negotiations and an extended analysis of their impact on processes of social reproduction (Kucera 2001; Young 2003; Floro *et al.* 2004).

The TRIMs limits the ability of host countries to steer foreign investment in such a way as to contribute to their development processes. In contrast, policies that have enabled countries to harness foreign direct investment (FDI) to their advantage have been the cornerstone of success to a number of countries (Arestis and Demetriades 1997; Arestis and Sawyer 2005). Particularly effective have been policies such as those that require the provision of special credits to domestic firms aimed at enhancing their capacity to develop or absorb new technology, promoting the production of support services and intermediate inputs, or restricting entry to certain segments of the economy in order to incubate domestic firms before they are exposed to international competition. Close management of FDI, for example, was part of the overall industrial policy approach of the East Asian countries during their export-led growth period (Braunstein and Epstein 2002). Japan,

South Korea, and Taiwan developed legislation and mechanisms that enabled them to steer foreign investment into sectors that were considered desirable from the perspective of sustainable human development, to ensure technology transfer at reasonable costs, and to prevent excessive repatriation of profits (Chang and Grabel 2004).

The approach used by the WTO and the Bretton Woods institutions to coordinate trade and financial policies on the basis of the neoliberal paradigm ignores the reality of FDI and other capital flows and their gender implications (Arestis and Sawyer 2005). Although net private capital flows to developing countries grew in 2003 by more than 70 billion dollars (UN 2004: 6), the bulk of these funds remains highly concentrated in the larger emerging market economies. The ten largest recipient countries account for three quarters of total FDI inflows to developing countries, with China alone accounting for nearly one third of the total. In fact, the developing countries as a group experienced negative net financial transfers of close to $250 billion in 2003, as reported in the August 2004 report of the UN secretary-general. This is highly disappointing given that the majority of developing countries have heeded policy advice to create a "stable business environment" and adopt "sound" macroeconomic policies.

Moreover, the policies adopted to attract foreign capital have had adverse effects on the more vulnerable segments of the population (Çağatay 2001; Braunstein and Epstein 2002; Braunstein 2004; Floro *et al.* 2004; Arestis and Caner 2005). For instance, an increasing number of developing countries have improved their physical infrastructure for transportation, energy, and telecommunications in areas and in sectors that are favoured by foreign investors and multinational firms. This, along with tax concessions to foreign investors, has diverted public resources and the attention of policy-makers away from activities and sectors that are crucial for social development and that directly alleviate poverty, such as health care, sanitation, and disposal management. These have documented, serious, gender-asymmetric effects, especially in terms of women's unpaid work and human development (Grunberg 1998; Elson and Çağatay 2000; Barnett and Grown 2004; Elson 2005).

Tacit endorsement of global subcontracting work chains and the relaxation of labour laws are among the policy initiatives undertaken by developing country governments to attract foreign capital. This has important gender implications as well, since the majority of industries and enterprises in subcontracting work chains – as has been pointed out in several studies – generally employ women. Even though there is little empirical evidence in support of the view that concessions on labour standards are conducive to attracting FDI and to sustained productivity growth, governments continue to implement policies that reflect this.

Efforts are being undertaken in some developing countries to expand and improve the access to formal financial-sector services of small and medium-sized enterprises, micro-enterprises, the poor, women, and rural populations.

A key example of such efforts are the global initiatives on microcredit (see Chapter 4, this volume).[12] At the same time, these efforts have yet to recognize other gender dimensions of finance, including savings mobilization (Floro 2001; Seguino and Floro 2003; Nguanbanchong 2004). Furthermore, potential gains for the poor and women from microfinance initiatives are being undermined by macroeconomic policies that encourage the informalization of employment and increased income insecurity for low-income people and women in particular.

A recent study among workers in urban, low-income communities of Ecuador explores the incidence of financial stress and financial fragility. The study demonstrates the interconnection between very high levels of household indebtedness and job precariousness (Floro and Messier 2004). There is growing evidence that the unsteady flow or variability of earnings along with socially ascribed roles of women has caused some micro-entrepreneurs to reallocate credit for consumption-smoothing purposes rather than into businesses. As feminists have pointed out, women workers' position in the labour market is linked to their role in the household as primary caregivers and managers. Homebased micro-enterprises, in particular, enable women to reconcile their productive and reproductive roles (Prügl 1999; ILO 2002). But they also present tensions between workers who require cash to meet subsistence needs when earnings are low and enterprises which require capital.

The negotiations and agreements of the WTO, IMF, and World Bank have failed to induce governments to protect the rights of their worker citizens, especially those of women. In the current economic environment, we must give higher priority to stable employment and social protection. Both governments and international agencies must implement gender-sensitive rules designed to guide employment practices of firms and employers. They must also explicitly integrate gender awareness into the International Labor Organization (ILO) Convention on Homework, which is geared to protect workers' rights and decent working conditions for those who carry out work in homes (ILO 1996).

Concluding remarks on policy (in)coherence and social reproduction

The multilateral trade and financial institutions, namely the WTO, the IMF and the World Bank, currently dominate the coordination of macroeconomic policies, principally trade and financial policies. The evidence summarized here shows that the direction of this form of policy coherence remains incongruent with the internationally agreed commitments on poverty reduction and gender equality, particularly the Beijing Platform for Action and the MDGs. This state of affairs can further limit the sovereignty of countries in formulating and implementing domestic policies and strategies of their own that would put people at the centre of the development process.

Multi-level efforts and institutional mechanisms are required to reorient the mandate for policy coherence towards UN processes and in support of the human development framework. Policy coherence can be achieved only if it is tackled at both national and international levels. Key mechanisms that can help policy-makers respond to this challenge should include gender impact assessment of financial, trade, and investment policies and gender mainstreaming in governmental and international bodies. The current dominant role of the WTO and the Bretton Woods institutions in global economic decision-making can be changed only by strengthening and gender-mainstreaming the UN, by restructuring the Bretton Woods institutions, particularly their decision-making processes and voting rules, and by ensuring that the voices of vulnerable groups, and women's groups in particular, are heard in WTO negotiations and agreements. Finally, in order to develop people-centred policy coherence, all stakeholders, including governments, must strengthen their involvement in and adequate support for to the UN-led processes following up on international commitments. Such an alternative approach that prioritized policy coherence would have to address the crucial interrelations between human development, economic policy and social reproduction, not just in terms of biological reproduction and the reproduction of the labour force but also with respect to provisioning and caring needs. As discussed earlier, critical gender and governance concerns must be given priority in the emerging process of generating policy coherence. Otherwise it will be difficult if not impossible for macroeconomic policies to serve the goal of sustainable human development.

In this regard, the agreement reached during the Millennium+5 summit in September 2005 can serve as a reference and starting point given the commitment of the international community to fulfil the MDGs by 2015 (UN 2005). It is important to note that the summit's outcome document takes a broader perspective on the goal of gender equality than that of Millennium Development Goal 3 and acknowledges the key results of the Beijing Platform for Action. It provides a list of women's key concerns that need to be integrated in policy formulation and coordination: the right of women to own and inherit property; access to health care including reproductive health; equal access to labour markets, generation of decent employment, and implementation of labour standards and adequate labour protection; equal access for women to productive assets and resources, including land, credit, and technology; the elimination of discrimination and violence against women and girls; increased representation of women in governmental decision-making bodies; implementation of Security Council Resolution 1325 in 2000 on women and peace and security; and the elimination of gender inequalities in education. Broadening the perspective of the MDGs is important because the MDGs are a key point of reference in government negotiations with the WTO and the Bretton Woods institutions (Gender Monitoring Group of the World Summit 2005).

The points raised in the summit's outcome document will remain unaddressed, however, unless there is accountability and pressure to implement them at the local, national, and international levels. As in the case of the MDGs, they will require multi-level political mobilization, collective action and social pressure from different sectors of society. Finally, unless there is conscious effort among governments and international institutions to gather gender-sensitive, relevant information and to conduct gender assessments of trade, financial, and investment policy impacts, it will be hard to address the interests of women, particularly those in subsistence agriculture and food sub-sectors, as well as in informal and piece-rate, subcontracted work.

Notes

1 An extended version of this article was published by the Friedrich Ebert Foundation. See Floro, M. and Hoppe, H. (2005) "Engendering Policy Coherence for Development: gender issues for the global policy agenda in the year 2005," New York and Berlin: FES. Online. Available at: http://library.fes.de/pdf-files/iez/global/50085.pdf (accessed 26 June 2006). We thank FES and Frank Schroeder, Sigrid Skarpelis-Sperk, and Jürgen Stetten for their useful comments on an earlier draft of that study.
2 The fourth ministerial meeting of the World Trade Organization (WTO) was launched as the "Doha Development Round" in Doha, Qatar, on 9–13 November 2001.
3 At present, developing countries can provide support to small farmers to ensure food security by invoking Special and Different (S&D) treatment, especially green box exemptions (Zampetti 2004: 307). While there is certainly a need to further strengthen and broaden the WTO's S&D treatment provisions, the key constraint on food security remains subsidies and unbalanced market access.
4 According to Young and Hoppe (2003), the GATS is the first legally enforceable trade agreement that covers trade and investment in services. GATS extends to most services, including transport, investment, education, communications, financial services, energy and water services, and movement of persons (Young and Hoppe 2003: 8).
5 The need to enhance the coherence between national development strategies and global trade and financial processes was particularly stressed at the UNCTAD XI conference in Sao Paulo in July 2004.
6 In fact, the increasing rates of women's economic activity observed in several countries have been shadowed by declining rates for men. Increasingly, women in LDCs remain in the labour force throughout their childbearing years, finding ways to combine family responsibilities with market work (UN 2000).
7 Studies on homeworking and informal sector activities show a high incidence among women workers in Bangladesh, Mexico, the USA, and Spain who combine market work with domestic, reproductive activities such as cleaning, cooking, and childcare (Hossain 1988; Roldan 1988; Benton 1989).
8 With the closing of numerous factories in Thailand following the 1998–99 economic crisis, thousands of laid-off workers entered the informal sector, particularly as home-based workers. Women workers especially found it necessary to combine both paid market work and unpaid domestic work, which led to a higher incidence of time and work intensity.
9 The TRIPS aims to provide minimum standards of protection for all intellectual property (Young and Hoppe 2003).

10 The Doha Declaration also explicitly recognizes the right of countries to grant compulsory licenses and determine the criteria for their issuance. By recognizing that these rights are subservient to public health concerns, it paves the way for interpretations of the TRIPS agreement that are more supportive of public health concerns.

11 These include loan conditionalities; trade-related technical assistance; private-sector development strategies; investment climate assessments, e.g. "doing business" reports; and foreign investor advisory services. These investment-related agreements also argue for the removal of performance requirements with regard to foreign investment, e.g. local content.

12 International cooperation on microcredit initiatives is underway in anticipation of the International Year of Microcredit. The G8 countries announced in June 2004 that they will work together with the Consultative Group to Assist the Poor, the UN Capital Development Fund, and organizations of the UN system in preparing a global market-based finance initiative to stimulate sustainable, pro-poor financial sectors.

Part II
Social reproduction and marketization

3 Global integration of subsistence economies and women's empowerment

An experience from Nepal

Meena Acharya[1]

Since the early 1980s the global processes of market integration have accelerated rapidly all over the world. In South Asia also, these processes accelerated during the 1990s. State intervention in the economy began to decrease, with a minimalist state philosophy and the introduction of policies facilitating market development and integration into the global economy. In Nepal, economic liberalization started in the mid-1980s and accelerated after the 1991 consolidation of democracy under a new democratic constitution. Reforms encompassed both domestic and international trade sectors. Changes were aimed at a shift in the focus of development strategy, from an inward import-substituting industrialization to export-led growth. The process was wide-ranging and deep, liberalizing all sectors (Acharya *et al.* 1998).

However, global market integration is not only an economic process. It is a multidimensional development encompassing all aspects of life, involving economic processes, the concentration of political power in global centres and corporations, mass media advocacy of unlimited consumerism, and United Nations (UN) advocacy of human rights and democracy, including the reduction of social inequalities along the lines of gender, caste, and race, with less attention to class inequality. Many authors have called it the 'new constitutionalism' (e.g. Chapter 1, this volume).

In Nepal, together with the liberalization of the economy, policies were accelerated to reshape gender roles to fit the needs of the globalizing economy and the new rhetoric of gender equality. The emphasis has been on integrating women into the system as new economic agents, to prepare them for industrial employment with minimal literacy and schooling levels, and to maintain the viability of small farm households in the face of male migration by supplementing their incomes through social mobilization and microcredit/ microenterprise promotion. Responding to the demands of globalizing capitalist production, UN organizations, international non-governmental organizations (INGOs), and non-governmental organizations (NGOs) have carried out a concerted campaign for women's social mobilization and individual rights as incorporated in various United Nations charters. Some legal reforms have been implemented to make women's economic rights a little more secure and to ensure women's minimum representation in parliament and in the grassroots institutions of local governance. The mass campaign by the Maoist insurgents (1996–present) that has used the communist rhetoric of women's legal and political equality has further influenced the new social reconstruction of gender roles.

There is an inherent tension between market expansion and the reorganization of gender relations. Molyneux and Razavi (2002) have tried to analyze this tension (Prügl 1999) in the context of developing countries. Prügl (1999) has elaborated on the process by which gender roles in developing countries are being reshaped by advocacy work and the implementation of such policies. I see the emergence of interconnected revolutionary movements around the world also as a part of such contradictions embedded in the process of globalization (Acharya 2003). This tension is felt throughout this book as well. This chapter analyzes one aspect of the broader tensions characteristic of contemporary globalization process, focusing on the tension between women's empowerment and their concomitant disempowerment under globalization. My specific example examines the way in which globalization is reinforcing traditional oppressive practices such as *tilak* (roughly, dowry)[2] and converting social divisions into class divisions despite the apparent empowerment of women in terms of the indicators commonly used by international and multilateral development institutions.

Objectives and methodology

The objective of this paper is to investigate whether the ways in which women are being positioned in the emerging system of material and social reproduction are conducive to their actual empowerment in any significant way. I try to connect the changing system of material production and the new constitutionalism with changing constructions of gender, bringing out both the positive and the negative aspects of the whole process in terms of the empowerment and disempowerment of women. I highlight the tension between the generally accepted indicators of women's individual empowerment and women's actual social positions embedded in social systems. My focus is on marriage and the subsequent bearing of children as the most important mechanisms that institutionalize control over women's sexuality and hence their life options.

Social reproduction, as discussed in the Introduction and Chapter 1 of this book, includes both biological reproduction and the reproduction of labour power, a process that involves provisioning, caring, socializing, education, emotional support, etc. In addition it includes institutions and mechanisms through which this reproduction is ensured. These institutions and mechanisms evolve through time in intensive interaction with the system of material production, and they lay out the ground rules according to which sexual relations are legitimated for procreation and family, and gender relations are organized to care for, nurture, and socialize the future generation. Almost universally, marriage and family are used to control female sexuality and legitimate procreation, although they have taken different forms in different cultures and have changed over time. As such they have been subject of intense debate in feminism (see Meyers 1997 and Cranny-Francis *et al.* 2003 for representative collections of essays on this debate). Much of the discussion, however, is on an abstract level, focusing on the exchange of domestic labour and childcare services and sexuality

On a more concrete level, Bakker and Gill (2003c) and Nancy Folbre (2001) focus on the current political economy of the whole process of material and social reproduction in their full interaction. But as they deal mostly with advanced countries and the more advanced of the developing countries, they have tended to be concerned largely with the withdrawal of the state from support for social reproduction.

In countries like Nepal with many remote and difficult-to-reach regions, where the state was never there as a service provider anyway, this withdrawal is an issue of less concern. What is of more concern is how accelerated market penetration is dichotomizing the material and social reproduction processes and affecting women. This chapter tries to assess this impact, going beyond the indicators of empowerment usually used in the development literature, such as household divisions of labour, power in household or community decision-making, group membership, or access to microcredit (World Bank 2003; UNDP 2004). The focus here is on socialization and marriage itself, around which social reproduction is organized.

In order to accomplish these objectives, I explore three topics: (a) the precise processes by which the capitalist production system is interacting with the local economy in two villages, one in Terai and one in the hills,[3] both of which were also studied in detail in 1978; (b) the impact of these developments on gender relations; and (c) the comparative status of women who have remained in the rural hill areas versus urban women factory workers in Terai and Kathmandu.

I have used micro-level (1978 and current field survey) case studies to highlight the processes of transformation, while using macro-level information to contextualize them. At the micro level, I have compared household and individual data for 25 households, 25 individual men, and 25 women from two villages with data from the 1978 studies. I have also collected information on a total of 50 men and 50 women factory workers from Kathmandu to examine the impact of women's move to factory work on their gender status. At the macro level, data from censuses and family budget and living standard surveys (1984–85,[4] 1996–97, and 2003–4) have been used to illustrate the shifting spheres of work, from self-employment to wage employment, from agriculture to non-agricultural sectors, and to various occupations. Macro-level data also provide background information on social and human development indicators.

The emerging pattern of women's incorporation into the system of global material reproduction

In 1985, when the structural adjustment policies were initiated in Nepal, the country's economy was still dominated by subsistence agriculture. In 1978, more than 70 per cent of the rural household income was home produced in rural areas of Nepal; less than one third of the total rural household income passed through market transactions, i.e. was either exchanged for money or bartered for other goods (Acharya and Bennett 1981). Another study (NRB 1988) showed that about 67 per cent of the income was derived from household enterprises: 61 per cent from agricultural enterprises, and the rest from other sectors. Wages and salaries constituted only 26 per cent of the household income. The majority of workers, men and women, were self-employed.

Liberalization greatly increased the exposure of the economy to external factors. Foreign trade increased from 24 per cent of the gross domestic product (GDP) in the period 1985–89 to 40 per cent in 2000–3. The contribution of agriculture to GDP came down substantially, from about 65 per cent in 1981 to 47 per cent in 1991, and fell again to 38 per cent in 2001 (Acharya *et al.* 2003). But the reduction in the contribution of agriculture to GDP was not matched by a concomitant reduction of its role as employment provider, which remained at 66 per cent in 2001 (ibid.). Nevertheless, income from migrants has kept the economy going, and the overall poverty level is estimated to have declined from 42 per cent in 1996 to 31 per cent in 2004, in spite of the insurgency. But gains in income have been distributed very unevenly and disparities of income have increased (World Bank 2005) – between men and women, between urban and rural areas, between the hills and Terai areas, between migrant and non-migrant households, between well educated and uneducated people, and among people of various castes/ethnicities (see NPC/UNDP 2004; DFID and World Bank 2005; TPAMF 2005).

With the changes in the structure and organization of material production from household-based to market-, factory- and export-based, the nature of women's role in material production is changing also. Four distinct trends are apparent: increasing dependency on women's labour for farm production, and women workers' relative concentration in agriculture; transfer of women workers from home-based, local-market-oriented production to factory-based, export-oriented production and tourism-oriented service sectors; conversion of a large group of women into pure consumers and housewives, as illustrated by lower economic activity rates of urban women (38 per cent) as compared to rural women (58 per cent);[5] and increasing international migration of both men and women in search of better employment and income-earning opportunities (NPC/UNDP 2004; DFID and World Bank 2005; TPAMF 2005).

In 2001, women constituted 43 per cent of the total labour force, about 48 per cent in agriculture and 34 per cent in the non-agricultural sectors, nearly

10 percentage points higher than in 1991.[6] In the same period women workers' representation in agricultural wage employment has increased dramatically, from 25 per cent to 50 per cent, indicating the deteriorating situation of small farm households. However, in the better paid non-agricultural wage employment, their proportion has remained at about 18 per cent since 1991, despite expanding carpet and garment industries and services, the main sectors of their current non-agricultural employment (TPAMF 2005).

The majority of women in both agricultural and non-agricultural sectors are employed in the informal sectors (CBS 1999). Even in the formal labour market, they have access to only low-status employment. They are concentrated in low-paying and less productive, low-capital-intensity jobs, as is clearly illustrated below by the current survey of factory workers. In terms of daily wages, women earn about three quarters of what men earn in both agricultural and non-agricultural sectors (CBS 2004). In agriculture this ratio has declined in the last 10 years. Moreover, in this sector, average real wages have also declined, while in the non-agricultural sector they increased by 20 per cent.

There are complex dynamics involved in the transformation of an economy based primarily on household production into a market economy. The political economy of marketization is particularly problematic in the current context of globalization. Under new constitutionalism (Gill 1998; 2002), unlike post-World War II welfare statism, government interventions are aimed at facilitating the market, not limiting its scope. This involves privatizing major public resources and activities (in Nepal, for example, forestry, transport, and other public enterprises); withdrawing subsidies to agriculture and even social sectors; opening all sectors, including education and health, to private and foreign investment; and lifting all constraints on use of resources and labour by foreign and local capital. This process usually accentuates existing inequalities along with creating new ones. The following case studies from Nepal illustrate amply this complex process of unequal development.

The shifting structure of the economy, the erosion of village livelihood systems, and women's options

Table 3.1, presenting a comparative picture of two villages from different ecological regions of the country in 1978 and 2005, tries to capture the process of change to some extent. It presents a contrasting picture of the household economy in two villages. In terms of 1977–78 prices, the average household income had almost doubled in 2005 in the Terai village but declined slightly in the hill case. But per-household assets have increased in the hills and decreased in the Terai village. The percentage of land in the asset structure has declined in Terai and increased in the hills. This can be attributed primarily to the stagnation of agriculture and its decline as a

Table 3.1 Changes in the village: assets and income in Nepalese rupees*

	Sirsia (Terai)		Katarche (Hill)	
Selected indicators	*1978*	*2005*	*1978*	*2005*
Per household assets (at 1977–78 prices)	67,871	38,573	22,111	25,692
Percent land	*91.4*	*80.7*	*77.8*	*91.9*
Percent livestock	*6.4*	*5.9*	*20.6*	*7.9*
Percent other	*2.2*	*13.4*	*11.6*	*0.2*
Per capita income (at 1977–78 prices)	898	1,676	588	554
Percent Agriculture	*69.7*	*55.4*	*56.5*	*56.7*
Percent Salary and Wages	*8.4*	*44.5*	*22.4*	*13.4*
Percent sales of agricultural production	11.8	34.8	3.6	7.7
Percent cash income (sale + all other cash income)	23.4	48.1	31.2	46.8

Note: *Exchange rate as of July 2006: NRs74 = US$1
Source: Field data

source of employment in the hills. Relatively better off hill people and migrant workers are shifting their residence to Terai or urban areas and putting their land to alternative uses, leaving their land to those who remain in the village or selling it. The Maoist insurgency in the hills has accelerated this process. On the other hand, there is little permanent migration from the Terai village, and land is successively divided and subdivided among brothers, resulting in reduced assets per household. But remittances in some households have raised average household income.

However, the penetration of markets into the household economy has increased in both villages, as is indicated by the increased proportion of agricultural products sold and the increased proportion of cash in household incomes. On the other hand, the contribution of wage/salary incomes has increased in the Terai but declined in the hills, indicating a decline in local employment opportunities in the hill villages. Men migrate to urban areas for higher paying wage work, rather than seek such work in the village.

Another change has been the decline of the *perma* system. In 1978 in the hills, the prevailing system was the *perma* system, which was based on labour exchange with no direct calculation of who owed how many days. Older men and women benefited from this system, as their farms could also be cultivated. Today the system is also changing: each household has to pay, if not in days of labour, then in cash, indicating a move towards a free wage-labour market. In the Terai areas also, in-kind payments were slowly being replaced by cash. This commodification of labour has increased visible wage incomes, but the system that allowed children to eat along with their parents in the field at the expense of the landlord has disappeared. The net gain or loss to the labourers is not calculable.

Liberalization has also severely reduced the viability of commercial agriculture. Agricultural production has stagnated, as subsidies on fertilizer and other inputs have been withdrawn, and subsidized products from India have out-competed those made locally. Another reason that the role of agriculture in the economy has declined is the diminishing availability of free land for new cultivation. Better protection of national forest land and the introduction of community and lease forestry since the early 1980s has also reduced the availability of land for grazing animals and gathering fuel and fodder.

From an environmental perspective, it was good for the country to protect its forests, as the land and forest resources were being exhausted at a rapid rate. But for poor women, it represented a loss of supplementary livelihood avenues. Small livestock raising had been the main activity of the poor in all microcredit programmes, but its viability has rapidly eroded. The problem has been aggravated by the fact that the large-scale and middle-range landowning peasants, instead of investing in land, are selling their land and shifting capital to more lucrative businesses in urban areas, and investing their incomes in sending their children abroad. Or they are converting land to forestry, fruit orchards, or some other plantation with a long gestation period, eroding the food security system and narrowing the agricultural labour market in the villages. The poor are left with no access to resources or alternative employment.

Moreover, the progressive penetration of the hinterlands by roads and mass-produced factory products has destroyed the traditional local labour market for the service castes in rural areas. This process was accelerated by liberalization, which destroyed the protection of cottage and small industries. The substantial reduction in the level of protection forced domestic industries to close or reduce their scale of operation, even in urban areas (Acharya *et al.* 2003). Among the industries that closed or were downsized, textiles, bidi, and bricks and tiles employed a substantial number of women workers. Although the recent growth in export-based industries, such as carpets and knitwear, has opened up new employment opportunities for women, whether these new opportunities are adequate to compensate for those that have been lost has yet to be evaluated.

Women's direct incorporation into the global production chain

The erosion of the traditional livelihood systems has created streams of migration to urban areas within the country, to India, and overseas. But, lacking educational qualifications and money to pay the agents for overseas and Indian employment, and facing the threat of violence in public arenas, comparatively few poor women go overseas or to India. Instead, they take whatever employment they can find within the urban areas of their own country. Many are employed in the export sector, particularly in carpet and garment manufacturing, both of which are sectors that have extremely unfavourable work conditions.

The carpet industry employs primarily rural–urban migrants with low educational levels and high carpet weaving skills. According to the current survey, 100 per cent of female and 80 per cent of male carpet weavers earned less than US$40 a month. Nobody earned more than US$80 a month in carpets or garments, the major export industries of Nepal. All women and 80 per cent of men in carpets were paid on a piecework basis. Garment industry conditions and pay scales seem to be only slightly better for women than those in carpets. In carpets and garments combined, about 70 per cent of workers were paid on a piecework basis, which means that for this large segment of the labour force there was no job security or provision of leave or other benefits. Other studies (GDS/FES 1997; GEFONT 2001) have also found that these industries bypass most standard labour regulations by employing women at piece rates.

Moreover, both pay scale and working conditions in these export industries seemed to be much worse than in either the food industry or hotels, whose products were more oriented to the domestic market and tourism. These industries employed 97 per cent of women on a permanent basis and provided legally required leave and other benefits.

The carpet workers mostly were migrants from rural areas. They came from castes other than Brahmin/Chetri and Newars, and they lived in factory-provided dormitories, four (plus any children) in one room (12 foot square), and took their children to work. They came from landless or near landless families, owning less than 0.05 hectare of land. In other industries workers were more evenly distributed between urban and rural origins, migrants and non-migrants, and castes and ethnicities. In contrast, most Brahamin/Chetri and Newar men and women who worked in factories and hotels had secured positions in institutions with better working conditions. This shows clearly how traditionally discriminatory structures get transferred to the factory space.

In general, a larger proportion of women than of men were in the lowest earning brackets of workers, even though they also had longer work experience. On average, they worked less than men by only one hour per day. On average, those at the lower end of the pay scale, both men and women, worked longer hours.

Generally, women did not fare as well as men. Nevertheless, only 20 per cent of the women carpet workers interviewed and 30 per cent of all women workers interviewed were unhappy with their working conditions, while 44 per cent of male workers expressed dissatisfaction. This may show that women are constrained to express a higher level of "satisfaction" than men because of the lack of alternative work opportunities for women, and/or is representative of women's greater inhibition of negative evaluations of their situations.

Women's working and living conditions in these low-paying export industries may add up to a more exploitative situation than they faced in traditional villages based on subsistence agriculture and personal relations. Still the national government is being pressed by international donors to further liberalize the labour market regulations. This is probably going to be one of the major destabilizing issues in the coming years, particularly given the strengths of leftist politics and the donor community in Nepal.

The social reconstruction of gender

In the introduction I mentioned that there has been a concerted effort to reconstruct gender roles to fit the requirements of the increasingly market-ized economy. Policy-makers and researchers have measured women's "empowerment" in terms of the division of labour, control over one's own mobility, participation in groups, visibility and voice in household and community affairs, and confidence in dealing with service providers, health offices, police, etc., in addition to voting, political representation, and awareness of social and political issues.[7] Elsewhere (in Acharya and Ghimire 2005) I have argued that these indicators measure only initial steps towards women's empowerment and not their real empowerment. Below, on the basis of the two villages and urban studies, I illustrate why this is so.[8]

Visibility and voice

In terms of both women's visibility and voice and social and political awareness levels, the situation in the case study villages was much more positive today than in the late 1970s. The first visible change in the Terai village was the unveiling of women's faces and their participation in group meetings. The village had several savings/credit groups, organized to borrow from institutions that lent primarily to women's groups. The hill villagers, however, were active only in community forestry. Although many NGO/INGO as well as government savings/credit programmes were started in this village 15–20 years ago, no other groups were reported currently active in the hills. There was no continuity in the programmes. While better off households were made aware of the importance of growing and eating vegetables regularly, poor households were never involved in such activities. The two contrasting village cases and the unevenness of the impact within each village illustrate the class differentiation process at work.

Women's voice in household matters[9] had increased in comparison to 1978, except for capital and investment decisions in the hill village, where it had declined. In 1978 in the hill ethnic communities, women made home-spun cloth, brewed alcohol, and cooked food and sold it in the local market. Along with their greater role in trade at this time, women also had a greater role in investment decisions. Currently all these activities have ceased, owing to competition from factory-produced or imported goods – and, in the case of brewing, outright prohibition by the state, despite the fact that factory production of alcohol is permitted and the factory-pro-duced alcohol is sold widely. So women have a lesser role in investment decisions and trade opportunities. In addition, in domestic matters joint decisions now predominate, representing quite a change since 1978, when decision-making by the most senior women within households pre-dominated.[10]

Concerning women's voice in community matters, a mixed picture emerges. While women in the Terai village had given up the visible symbol of their seclusion, veiling, and were participating in groups, their participation was limited to attending meetings, and even all-women groups were still controlled by men, particularly among the women of better-off households. Moreover, even the single female political representative, an appointed member of the outgoing executive body of the village-level local government, complained that men did not listen to her. This has been a constant complaint of both appointed and elected women in local government (see MWCSW/MGEP/UNDP and SAHAVAGI 2004). But in this village merely having a woman from an elite household as a member of this public body was progress as compared to 1978. In 1978 there was a mandatory provision that the village body include at least one woman member. But no "respectable" household was willing to nominate a member, so a woman who was considered to be a commercial sex worker was appointed, and everybody laughed at her (Acharya 1981).

Awareness and attitudes

As a consequence of government, INGO, and NGO campaigns and Maoist propaganda, awareness about women's rights has increased among both men and women over the last three decades. In 1978, depending on the village, only 1.5–3.1 per cent of women were aware of the then existing women-related political institutions, the Nepal Women's Organization and Women's Social Services Council. In 2005, 31–37 per cent of women were aware of issues and institutions related to women. But awareness of district and national politics, measured in terms of knowledge about the prime minister, parties in power, the legislative representative from the area, and the district chairman, had increased only marginally since 1978. Moreover, women's awareness of such politics was not anywhere near male awareness (see Table 3.2). Women's participation in voting, however, has always been high in Nepal, as parties and male relatives have tried to use women's votes to their own advantage.

There has been a noticeable change in attitudes towards gender roles over the three decades since the first study. First, people now favour literacy and education for both boys and girls. For example, despite the current discriminatory behaviour towards girls, in the field survey an overwhelming majority of men and women factory workers wanted to educate their male and female children as much as the children wanted or the parents could afford. Many rural parents also said this. The largest proportion of respondents, in both urban and rural areas, named education as the first priority in the list of qualities they wanted for their children, both sons and daughters. For both urban factory workers and hill village residents, their

Table 3.2 Political awareness and attitudes to change, 2005 (as percentage of total responses)

	Rural				Urban	
	Sirsia		Katarche			
Selected indicators	Men	Women	Men	Women	Men	Women
I Awareness and contact	42	16	35	30	44	42
(a) Local politics/community affairs	76	11	57	26	46	34
(b) National politics	41	4	37	22	41	28
(c) Women's representation	–	3	–	15	–	22
(d) Laws about women.	46	37	54	31	80	79
II Positive attitudes	69	77	72	79	85	86
(a) Social issues*	53	73	69	78	93	96
(b) Women's rights*	50	60	70	65	68	64
(c) Reserving places for women	100	88	82	100	90	98
(d) Reserving places for *Dalits*	88	88	68	84	94	98
(e) Reserving places for ethnic groups	100	100	76	88	94	100

Source: Field survey; see text for description.

children's ability to earn a living and work hard was secondary to their interest in seeing their children educated. But in the Terai village prettiness still figured as the second most desired quality for daughters. In 1978, among the qualities wanted in a bride, prettiness was the most desired in the Terai village, while a majority of hill villagers had accorded first priority to hard work. For bridegrooms in 1978, in both villages, the first desired quality was wealth and the second education.[11]

Another group of questions administered to test attitudes to social change included whether it was all right for a husband to slap/beat his wife sometimes, to use shamans against witches, to observe the caste system, or to take money for sending girls to employment via agents.[12] The majority of both male and female respondents in both rural and urban areas said no, but it is revealing that proportionately more men than women thought that it was all right to use a little violence against their wives or against witches.

A series of questions was also asked to test the social environment for change towards a more equitable society. Questions included in this group concerned divorce, daughter's inheritance, widow remarriage, equal and full citizenship rights, and abortion. Responses were generally positive in terms of the social environment's support for more equitable social relations. An overwhelming majority everywhere responded in favour of reserving places in educational institutions, political office, and the civil service for all three groups mentioned: women, ethnic groups, and *dalits*. Nevertheless, proportionately more urban women and men factory workers were aware of both political and social concerns. Both men and women in the Terai village scored lowest in terms of such awareness

Role in social reproduction

Despite these positive indicators, women's roles in social reproduction and the way they are integrated into the social system has hardly changed since 1978. The global system is reinforcing the traditional forms of gender inequality.

Although Nepal's population is multi-ethnic, two features of Nepalese society that are structurally detrimental to women's equality are common to almost all groups – gender inequality in access to property and resources, and the importance accorded to marriage in women's lives (Acharya and Bennett 1981; Gurung 1999). Both of these barriers to improving women's equality are being reinforced by the kind of development currently promoted.

Traditionally a woman's economic rights have been constructed so that she is dependent on her marriage and sexual subordination to men, and these views and associated practices have remained intact. A married woman has rights only to her husband's property; on marriage a girl forfeits any right to her parents' property. There has not been much change in this system in the last 20–25 years. Changes in this present decade have made it a bit easier for unmarried daughters to inherit parental property and to claim material support for survival on an equal footing with their brothers, and have made a woman's right to property more secure in her affinal household, removing the conditions that she must be 35 years of age or have been married for 15 years (FWLD 2003). However, the institution of marriage is still the major determining factor for a woman's right to own, use, and control property, linking her property rights to her sexual loyalty to the husband even after his death.

As a consequence, generally very few women own property independently. According to the 2001 census, almost 83 per cent of Nepalese households had no property whatsoever under women's legal ownership, even though 88 per cent of the households owned their own house and 76 per cent owned a farm in their district of residence. On average, female-headed households had only 0.50 hectares of farm land, compared to 0.78 hectares for male-headed households.

In spite of various credit programmes, women's access to institutional credit is also still marginal, at both individual and household enterprise levels (Acharya 2000). Even in mid-July 2004, women did not share more than 2 per cent of the total outstanding credit from banks and financial institutions (SAHAVAGI 2006).

Second, the legally instituted dependency of women on marriage for any access to the generational transfer of property is reinforced by the religious/ideological/social priority accorded to the institution of marriage and fertility. The continuing primacy of marriage and children in a woman's life governs all her life options, including education. Marriage and children are still the first priority for women in almost all communities, but to a much higher degree in the Indo-Aryan groups, where the ideology of purity of the female body as described by Bennett in 1983 continues to rule very strongly.

It compares well with the image of mother and wife described by Prügl (1999) for Western countries in the period immediately after the Industrial Revolution. For women, besides the social need to produce progeny, marriage is also seen as a primary means of securing a livelihood in almost all communities, since land and property are inherited along the patriline, from father to son. This gendered land inheritance pattern results in a high proportion of married people in the population and high fertility rates nationally. Even in 2001, 78 per cent of women and 48 per cent of men were married before they reached age 25. Nearly 2 per cent of girls aged 10–14 and 33 per cent of those aged 15–19 were already married. As a result the mean age of marriage for Nepalese women is still quite low at 19.5. The country's total fertility rate, at 4.2 in 2001, was one of the highest in the region (CBS 2001).

The implications for women's equality are vividly exemplified by the situation of the Terai village in my field survey. In this village the marriageable age for girls seemed to be improving, to 16 or 17, but 20 was the maximum limit permitted in the village. Neither men nor women had much choice in selecting marriage partners there, while in the hill village and among the Kathmandu factory workers women and men seemed to have some say on such issues. But most of the women who answered positively to this question in either Katarche or Kathmandu belonged to the Tibeto-Burman groups, which traditionally have had much more freedom in these matters (see Acharya and Bennett 1981). Nevertheless, even in these communities greater proportions of men than women had such choice.

Further, generally dowry has acquired new dimensions, as prospective husbands have started to view it as seed capital for new businesses or for their own overseas trips, motorbikes, cars, TVs, and other consumer durables. Although this is more of a middle- and educated-class phenomenon, it is putting much social pressure on the lower middle class as well. While searching for bridegrooms for their daughters, parents may be outbid in the marriage market. As not being able to marry off daughters is still considered a disgrace for the natal family, especially in the Indo-Aryan communities, parents may have to spend all their savings and accumulated capital in marrying off their daughters. Moreover, my current survey suggests that dowry is spreading even among communities that did not have it before. Thus, globalization and the consumer culture have not done away with the onerous system of dowry/*tilak,* but converted it into a vehicle for the promotion of consumerism and capital for new business, and made it more onerous for families to have daughters than sons.

The impact of this system is most visible in women's unequal access to education (Table 3.3), especially beyond secondary school. While literacy is widely appreciated throughout the country, and its rate among the cohort aged six years and above has more than trebled, from 12.0 per cent in 1981 to 42.5 per cent in 2001, the male/female disparity persists. There were only 66 literate women per 100 literate men in 2001. The higher the education level, the lower the number of women with comparable educational degrees. Because of this inequality in education, even in 2001 women constituted only 17 per cent in the combined categories of professional and technical workers, senior administrators, managers, lawyers, judges, legislators, politicians, etc. Women's education remains distinctly limited as a result of the primacy placed on marriage as a life goal (for similar findings on India see also Chanana 2003).

Girls face substantial discrimination in access to quality education also. The current field study reflects the situation very well. Boys in both villages and in urban areas were sent to private schools and/or to cities, while girls, particularly from villages, had few such opportunities. Daughters of factory workers had much better chances of quality education, but still less than sons from those families.

Gender plays a major role in this unequal access to education. First, upon marriage a girl is compulsorily transferred to the affinal household, and the natal household may no longer use or claim her earnings. Thus the opportunity cost of forgoing a girl's labour at home, plus the financial expenses involved in her education, costs parents in the end much more than it does for boys, who are expected to take up household maintenance responsibilities upon reaching adulthood.

Although male education has helped somewhat to increase girls' schooling, as educated grooms want brides also with some minimal education, at higher levels it has become an impediment to female education because of the practice of dowry/*tilak*, particularly in Terai communities. For educated girls, parents have to find grooms with even higher education, and the higher the groom's degree, the greater the *tilak* demanded.

Thus traditional mechanisms of social reproduction hinder women's advancement in education, career jobs, or politics. This problem is being worsened by globalization. Banerjee (2002), analyzing why the female/male ratio of the population is declining fast in India, highlights how globalization is reducing economic opportunities for women and hence their economic worth as wives.

Table 3.3 Educational achievements, 2001

Indicators	1981	1991	2001
Literate 6 years +	33.8	46.3	65.8
Female percentage among full-time students	27.2	34.7	43.1
Number of women per 100 men			
(a) With primary education	41.5	53.5	76.8
(b) SLC and above*	21.0	28.2	43.6
(c) Graduates** and above	18.4	22.5	22.9

Note: *Secondary schooling ("high school") and above
** Equivalent to undergraduate university education in the USA
Sources: (1) CBS: population census, 2001; (2) CBS: population monograph, 1995.

Conclusions

Nepal's integration into the global economy is changing the conditions of both material and social reproduction in the country. On the economic front, the expansion of markets into the hinterlands and development programmes directed to women and men have opened up new opportunities for women and men. But men of traditionally powerful groups are moving much faster to take advantage of the diversified opportunities provided by such developments. Poor women are relegated to low-paying agricultural jobs and intensely exploitative labour-intensive industries. The relative disadvantage of women vis-à-vis men is declining only slowly or even increasing in many arenas, such as education. Gender-specific differences in the opportunity spectrum are accentuated by caste and ethnic disadvantages, although women uniformly fare worse than men in all groups. In terms of purchasing power parity calculated on the basis of earned income, the female/male earned income ratio in the country was 1:2, with incomes of PPP\$1,868 for men and \$949 for women (UNDP 2005).[13]

Market penetration has accelerated under globalization, creating havoc in people's lives by upsetting the traditional organization of production, labour markets, and food security systems in the hinterlands of Nepal, and not providing viable alternatives.

The rapidity with which the Maoist insurgency spread in Nepal is partly a result of this impoverishment of the country's hinterlands (Acharya 2003). In the contemporary era, it is often automatically assumed that production for the market universally increases productivity and people's incomes. Yet many cases do not fit this picture, at least in the short run, as is illustrated by the hill village described here and many other cases evaluated by North and Cameron (2003).

In the manufacturing sector, the survey results described here confirm the findings of many other authors who have studied similar processes in other countries or the global cities.[14] What this paper has added to this literature is to draw a picture of how, in the South Asian context of caste and ethnic diversity, the old discriminatory structures have combined with international competition to keep poor women from traditionally oppressed groups at the bottom of the labour hierarchy. Although human rights rhetoric has helped to raise women's political awareness as measured by the conventional indicators, in reality the traditional discriminatory social structures have been shifted to the modern jobs as well.

In spite of extensive government and donor programmes aimed at reshaping gender relations to women's benefit, women's roles in the social reproduction process have not changed a bit. As the new expectations dictate, women are getting some minimal education; supplementing the household income by wage work, subsistence agriculture, and household-based microenterprises; and participating in local community affairs to raise programme efficiency. But their primary role as mothers and caretakers is not changing much. They are expected to get married on schedule, remain chaste and loyal to the affinal household and clan, fulfil their primary responsibility as caretakers of the household, and raise the children. Marriage remains the most important avenue towards livelihood security for a woman, as her property rights and social honour remain tied to her marriage. Globalization is reducing women's economic worth, and this effect, together with globally advocated consumerism, has intensified the onerous dowry/*tilak* system rather than doing away with it or reducing its impacts. As a consequence of the progressive deterioration in their economic opportunities vis-à-vis men, women may even be losing whatever bargaining power they previously had.

Notes

1 I would like to express my thanks to Fulbright for giving me this opportunity to be part of this very fruitful and rich experience of interactions and collaboration with international scholars. I learnt a great deal from these interactions. I would also like to thank the people of the two villages and urban workers who spent their valuable time on responding to my questions. Last but not least, my thanks also go to Asmita Publishing House and Worec for helping with my field work.
2 The difference between dowry and *tilak* is that *tilak* is given to the groom's family and the girl has no claim to it, while theoretically dowry is the bride's property.
3 Nepal has three ecological belts: the high mountains, the hills, and the Terai plains; and five development regions, which are inhabited by people of different ethnic/cultural groups. While analyzing these groups in 1981, we (Acharya and Bennett 1981) classified them in two major groups, Indo-Aryan and Tibeto Burman, on the basis of their "racial"/ethnic origin and the socio-cultural space accorded to women. On the basis of women's participation in the labour market, decision-making roles within the household, and greater freedom in marriage and sexual matters, we concluded that the Tibeto-Burman group was more egalitarian towards women as compared to Indo-Aryan groups, who idealized the seclusion of women. According to the 2001 census, there were 100 ethnic/caste groups and sub-groups in the country, of which Indo-Aryan groups constituted 57 per cent and Janajatis (Tibeto-Burman and Terai ethnic groups) about 37 per cent. The religious minorities – Muslims, Sikhs, Christians, and others – accounted for 4 per cent. About 1 per cent did not report their ethnicity/caste or religion. All three groups are divided into multiple sub-groups. Traditionally the Hindu high castes – Brahmin and Chetris and Newars – have exercised power in Nepal and have the greatest access to resources and education, while the Dalits and certain tribal groups have been most disadvantaged, with least access to power structures, resources, and education.
4 Nepal's fiscal year is mid-July to mid-July. For example, 1978 means these figures are for the period from mid-July 1977 to mid-July 1978.
5 Rogers (1983) has called this process, along with the emerging gender roles, the "domestication of women."
6 The census figures on economic activity rates are slightly problematic because of changing definitions; nevertheless they correctly represent trends (see TPAMF 2005). However, the wage employment figures are comparable.
7 For example, Bennett and Gajurel (2004), using such indicators in their interview of 2,000 men and women in a nationwide survey, concluded that women were

more empowered today than in the late 1970s, although they recognized that higher-caste men were far more empowered than women and/or other men. Creevey (1996), Harper *et al.* (1998), Fisher and Sriram (2002) and Datta and Kornberg (2005) also draw similar conclusions on women's increased empowerment in other countries, using similar indicators.

8 Only a few more indicators of empowerment are analyzed here. The data on hours of work, collected by recall, are not comparable to the 1978 data, collected by one year of observation of frequency of activities.

9 Domestic decisions include purchase of daily needs such as food, keeping of household money, lending and borrowing small amounts, etc., as well as education-related questions: whether to send the children to school or buy educational accessories for them.

10 There may be several reasons of this change, a major one being the nuclearization of families, which needs to be further explored. Further, while in the 1978 data, women answering this question were the most senior ones, current data may relate to any woman in the household.

11 These two items are not exactly comparable. Nevertheless, I think the overwhelming change does show a trend. Because marrying off one's daughter is of paramount importance (see the next section), people want their daughters to be marriageable.

12 This question was phrased in this way because the word *sale* or the phrase *purchase of human beings* would have been too leading. In the practice referred to, traffickers tell the relatives that they are taking sisters/daughters/daughters-in-law/sisters-in-law – generally girls or women – for various kinds of employment and induce the family members to send them, for which they give the family members money.

13 The Purchasing Power Parity dollar (PPP$) is a unit specifically devised and used by the World Bank for measuring comparative actual incomes of various countries. It is not equal to the US dollar. While income in US dollars is simply Nepalese Rupee income converted at the prevailing exchange rate, the PPP$ compares the purchasing power of each currency in its own country with the purchasing power of the US dollar in the US.

14 For example Salaff (1981); Banerjee (1991); Sassen (1998); Kabeer and Subrahmanian (1999); Rai (1999); Kapadia (2002); Wichterich (2002); North and Cameroon (2003); Ahmed (2004).

4 Limits to empowerment

Women in microcredit programs, south India

Lakshmi Lingam[1]

Increasingly, women are being considered a "resource" for globalizing capital, which simultaneously incorporates women's work but undermines its significance. A mutual accommodation of markets and gender ideology in service to each other is evident. Countries that are undergoing structural adjustment programs and adopting neoliberal policies are witnessing the loss of livelihoods, growing impoverishment, and declining support for social reproduction. Women's income-earning work is at precarious levels, and while they remain responsible for social provisioning, they receive less public support than they did previously, and are experiencing further shrinking of public space available to them as citizens or as contributors to the economy (Lingam 2006).

Many of the solutions proposed to deal with the negative impacts of structural adjustment have focused on "microcredit" and "self-help groups" as support for women in poverty. Early experiments by the Grameen Bank Bangladesh Rural Advancement Committee (BRAC) in Bangladesh, and the Self Employed Women's Association (SEWA) and Working Women's Forum in India, established the need to link women collectively to formal credit and provide support for their microenterprises. Development planning, which had viewed women from a "welfare" perspective, moved on to a view that investing in women improves both human capital and the performance of development programs. A "new poverty agenda" surfaced in the World Bank's 1990 *World Development Report*, as a counterpart to the "Washington Consensus" on structural reforms. Within this new agenda market-led growth is seen as the most effective means of overcoming poverty. Microcredit – or small loans to the poor for the purpose of promoting small-scale enterprises – is seen as a veritable panacea for poverty worldwide. The justification for including women in microcredit programs has highlighted the threefold purpose of reducing household poverty, providing space and means for the empowerment of women clients, and enabling the lending institution to remain viable. The term "empowerment," used by feminists of the South engaged with grassroots women to indicate a change in power relations in favor of women, has increasingly come to be used in the microcredit and microfinance sector.

As part of the global trend towards the state's diminishing role in basic health care, education, and welfare, the current official endorsement of microcredit and the appropriation of feminist notions of empowerment can be understood as elements of the global consolidation of neoliberalism worldwide. The declines in state support to the social sector, and the concomitant increases in women's social provisioning roles and responsibility for social reproduction, have been referred to as the "privatisation of the economic crises" (Benería 1992; Rocha 1995; 2001). Women are disciplined to fit markets' need for cheap and docile labor. Weber notes that, though microcredit is implemented at the local community level, it is a policy crafted at the global financial institutional level (Weber 2002). According to Weber:

> microcredit, via its implications for policy, facilitates financial sector liberalization, and extends the policy of trade in financial services to the local level. Secondly, microcredit has a disciplinary potential that renders it particularly conducive to functioning as a political safety net which "dampens or contains resistance to the implementation of neoliberal policies at the national and local levels.
>
> (Weber 2002: 541)

Feminist and critical writings that expose the "instrumentality" embedded in focusing on women's participation in microcredit and self-help groups highlight the point that "money proves an inadequate currency for changing gender relations" (Jackson 1996: 491). Microcredit programs that are successful in terms of loan repayment rates and growing membership seem to be not challenging the existing social hierarchies along lines of caste, class, ethnicity, and gender. On the contrary, according to some research (Fernando and Heston 1997), they seem to be legitimating these hierarchies. However, other research emerging from some innovative initiatives in India and Bangladesh has challenged earlier skepticism about the potential benefits of microcredit (Carr *et al.* 1996; Antony 2001; Kelkar *et al.* 2004). This research, contradictory at times, seems to indicate that women in microcredit programs are able to negotiate for better status within their households. But it remains unclear how this empowerment can be sustained within a local and global context of women's exclusion, marginalization, and impoverishment resulting from trade regimes and macroeconomic policies.

Given the competing claims of success that are made by non-governmental organizations (NGOs) and government agencies about microcredit programs and their impacts on women's empowerment, the present chapter, based on a study conducted in select villages in Andhra Pradesh, south India, attempts to capture the different grounded practices in programs that mobilize women for welfare, efficiency/equity, or consciousness-building. The paper highlights the limited gains that women make by being members of self-help groups, and directs attention to two questions: (1) Can women's empowerment happen within a larger context that is disempowering? and (2) Can an exclusive program focus on women help change inequalities based on gender and caste?

In order to elucidate the processes contributing to the limits to women's empowerment in microcredit programs, the chapter first briefly reviews microcredit and empowerment linkages. Second, the chapter provides background information on the study locations, Andhra Pradesh and the Mehbubnagar district. Third, it presents the study's findings on women's experiences with microcredit at the household and community levels, as well as in the context of broad village processes

Linkages between microcredit and empowerment

Empowerment changes power relations in favor of those who have exercised little power over their own lives, and it is both a process and an outcome. Definitions therefore place value upon transformation of consciousness, in addition to control of material resources (Batliwala 1993).

The terms "autonomy," "control," and "agency" are widely used to signify empowerment. However, there is no unitary definition of empowerment or consensus on how to measure it. So some studies focus on "outcome" indicators and others on "process" (Malhotra *et al.* 2002). Access to material resources is considered a significant precondition for women's making "strategic life choices," which in turn may be observed in various outcomes such as improvements in child survival, acceptance of contraception, decline in domestic violence, increase in physical mobility, improvements in living standards, and property ownership. Studies have at times arrived at contradictory results and interpretations, depending on the indicators adopted to represent "autonomy," "agency," and "control." It is not clear through what pathways gender relations and many other inequitable structures have changed or are being challenged by women, nor how sustainable changes might be. Researchers have also brought into question the cultural specificity of ways in which women choose to make or not make choices and the difficulty of measuring culture-specific choices with external parameters. Reviewing research on women in microcredit groups, Kabeer (1999) highlighted the importance of capturing subjective explanations given by women themselves to understand women's negotiations of gender relations within the household and their significance for evaluating empowerment.

Much of the literature on microcredit defines the success of women's groups (Self-Help Groups [SHGs]) in terms of effective group savings, regularity of meetings, maintenance of record books, loan repayments without defaults, building of capital, and setting up of microenterprises. Such measures of success are used as a proxy for empowerment. Mayoux (2000) identified three approaches to women's empowerment: (i) the financial sustainability paradigm; (ii) the poverty alleviation paradigm; and (iii) the feminist paradigm. Each of these paradigms assumes that increasing women's access to microfinance will set off mutually reinforcing "virtuous spirals" that will increase women's economic, social, legal, and political empowerment. However, each of these paradigms has a different approach to addressing gender relations within the program. In a recent paper, Mayoux (2006) challenges assumptions about the automatic benefits of microfinance for women. For example, high repayment levels do not necessarily indicate that women have used the loans themselves, nor that they have necessarily benefited from the loans. Men may take the loans from women, or women may choose to invest loans according to men's priorities. Likewise, high demand for loans by women may be a sign of social pressure to obtain resources for in-laws or husbands rather than an indicator of empowerment. Kabeer (2005) similarly observes that there are no magic bullets, no panaceas, no readymade formulas, and no blueprints for meaningful gendered structural transformation. According to her, "micro-credit may at most provide a safety net for the poor rather than a ladder out of poverty" (Kabeer 2005: 4718).

The study background

Andhra Pradesh

Andhra Pradesh (AP) is known as a significant information technology hub. The state has unambiguously been used a laboratory for neoliberal World Bank policies over the past 10 years under the close management of a former chief minister, Narla Chandra Babu Naidu of the Telugu Desam Party (TDP). Minister Naidu was popularly known in the business media as the "CEO of Andhra Pradesh."[2] Under his aegis, the state's goal of becoming the national leader in terms of growth, equity, and quality of life were engraved in a "Vision 2020"[3] state document. Along with several economic restructuring policies the state also introduced innovative governance initiatives aimed at democratic decentralization, e-governance, and campaign-based approaches to development initiatives. Women's and girls' development needs were high on the agenda, and women were positioned in the forefront of all social sector government programs. The government has pursued microcredit programs for women as a development panacea aimed at poverty alleviation in particular (Mooij 2002). Over 4.8 million poor women are mobilized through this activity, and there is an accumulated capital fund of Rs.7500 million (about $165 million). The government claims that this initiative is the "largest organized anti-poverty initiative in the world" (see www.andhrapradesh.com).

The cumulative impact of agricultural policies and recurrent droughts have set the stage for long drawn-out agrarian crises and rural indebtedness. Farmers (especially male) from the states of Andhra Pradesh, Karnataka, and Maharashtra among others are committing suicide on an unprecedented scale (Mishra 2006; Narasimha Rao and Suri 2006; Suri 2006). Despite heightened hopes of winning the assembly elections in the year 2004, the Telugu Desam Party (TDP) government was routed in all of the state's rural districts. The major reasons for the party's loss are considered to be drought-related discontent in the countryside, privatization of the power sector, lack of subsidies to the agricultural sector, declining access to credit for male farmers (as opposed to women in SHGs), and "women-friendly" policies. The National Congress Party, which won the elections, actively campaigned to reinstate the state's focus on agriculture, provide free power to farmers, and in essence reinstate also the "male pride" lost under the earlier regime. The present study was carried out during August-December 2004, immediately after the election. Hence the impacts of political change on program implementation and people's perceptions of women's programs were visible. Nevertheless, in my recent visits to Andhra Pradesh, I have noticed that the focus on women has not really changed. In fact, practically all departments of the government enlist the support of women's SHGs to implement or monitor programs or introduce new initiatives. Women continue to be seen and mobilized as enthusiastic and reliable grassroots workers.

Mehbubnagar district

Mehbubnagar is one of the poorest districts in AP, with small and marginal landholding farming households. Several coarse food grains have always been produced in this region as dryland rain-fed crops. The past few decades have witnessed a steady shift to rice, a marketable crop, which requires irrigation. In the absence of canals and other sources of irrigation, all the villages in this district tap underground water sources to raise wet crops. At the time of the study, scanty rainfall for the third consecutive year had placed considerable strain on the farming community. For generations, seasonal migration to Mumbai, Hyderabad, and different parts of the country has been an important survival strategy for landless households in this and neighboring districts. In recent years, deaths due to HIV/AIDS, associated with increased male migration, have been on the rise. Over the years, the district has been one of the national government's high priority districts for poverty alleviation programs and new initiatives in addressing poverty.[4]

The programs studied

Three villages from three *Mandals* (administrative clusters consisting of 10–20 villages or more), each of which has taken a different approach to women's programs, were chosen for the study.

Village 1 has a *women's empowerment* program called "Mahila Samata" (women's equality) managed by an autonomous government-supported body called the Andhra Pradesh Mahila Samata Society (APMSS). This program, which is more than 10 years old, is supported by funding from the Dutch government, and is managed by the Ministry of Human Resources Development of the central government of India. The program that began in 1988 in the state of Karnataka presently exists in several other states in India and is closely monitored through a National Resource Group. In this village women from the lowest castes are members of *sanghas* (collectives). The membership fee of 10 rupees a month goes toward the collective's administrative, travel, and communication expenses.

Village 2 has *poverty-reduction* women's self-help groups, popularly known as *Velugu* (light) but renamed after the change of the party in power as "Indira Kranti Padam"[5] (IKP). This program is managed by the Society for the Elimination of Rural Poverty (SERP), a semi-autonomous government-supported body funded by the World Bank. The program's priority in the initial years was to form SHGs of women from among the Scheduled Castes and Scheduled Tribes (SC and ST).[6] At present, it includes within its ambit SHGs formed by women of other caste groups as well. Here women contribute to their savings at the rate of 1 rupee a day. Each village also has a village organization (VO) made up of two representatives from each SHG. They in turn elect a president, a vice-president, and a treasurer, and hire a bookkeeper (an educated youth who can keep accounts and minutes of meetings).

Village 3 has a *welfare-oriented program*, Development of Women and Children in Rural Areas (DWCRA) popularly known as *Podupu Lakshmi* (*podupu* means savings and *lakshmi* is the name of the goddess of wealth) managed by the Department of Rural Development (DRDA). The women's savings and credit movement in AP can be said to have really begun in 1995, in Nellore district as a *Podupu Lakshmi* anti-liquor campaign by women. This led to large-scale promotion of SHGs in every district of AP. Women generally form neighborhood savings groups of 18–20 and save on either a weekly or a monthly basis. They meet once a fortnight to update their accounts and decide on lending, borrowing, and saving. In most of the villages *Podupu Lakshmi* groups have often been made up of semiliterate Other Backward Caste (OBC) women who can make savings either by maneuvering their household budgets or through some home-based activity like managing milch cattle or petty lending.

In each village, the program described above had commenced during the last five years, and each village also had several other ongoing government initiatives. Since early 2004, SERP and DRDA have been in the process of administrative convergence. So the SHGs mobilized by the welfare and poverty alleviation approaches at the village level are seen as belonging to a single program by the officials but not by the women. In Village 1, despite the existence of *Podupu Lakshmi* self-help groups, women drew their primary identity from the *sangham*; also, several members of the *sangham* were not in any savings group. The demand to save, borrow, repay, and comply with group norms is often not possible for old women who do not have regular work, property, or income to fall back upon. Therefore, the *sanghas* were more inclusive than the savings and credit groups (SHGs), which create group compulsions around money.

The women

The study used both quantitative and qualitative methods to collect information from various segments of the program machinery, the village people, and women in the SHGs. The data were collected in August and September 2004, when I stayed in the three villages with a team of field investigators. Focus group discussions and village meetings were conducted during a follow-up trip in January 2005.

A total of 300 women from three villages were interviewed, 88 percent from SHGs and 12 percent non-SHG women. Of the total, 69 percent were below age 40; 85 percent were currently married; 92 percent were illiterate; and the majority belonged to Hindu "backward castes" and "scheduled castes." The respondents came predominantly from landless households and were dependent on agricultural and non-agricultural wage work (see Table 4.1).

Findings

Despite the different modes of mobilization that the three programs use, the responses to several questions pertaining to gender relations and household division of work (elaborated in the following sections) were not very different. There were, however, differences in women's awareness of gender issues and what they saw as their public role in changing these. Women from Village 1 were far more aware of gender issues than those from Villages 2 and 3, where women were more focused on savings, credit, and repayment.

Newfound public domain visibility

Women expressed the changes they experienced from being part of collectives as increases in *dhairyam* (self-confidence) and *thelivi* (awareness). The ability to interact with and question unsatisfactory government officials, whether hospital staff or school teachers, was explained by the women as a reflection of their *dhairyam*. In a context where women previously had seldom expressed their rights as citizens beyond casting a vote as per the will of their men or caste collective, this shift is palpable. Women say they have discovered their voices. They often reveal their identity as *sangha* members in their conversations with government staff or officials. Many of them are well aware that they can make a written complaint to the district collector if they perceive that bureaucratic red tape is stalling responses to their demands. This practice was part of the *Janmabhoomi* (land of birth) campaigns of the TDP government, which introduced the concepts of people's participation in governance and accountability of the bureaucracy

Table 4.1 Profile of women interviewed

	Village 1 100(N)*		Village 2 95(N)*		Village 3 104(N)*	
	No.	%	No.	%	No.	%
Age						
Lowest through 30	31	31.0	37	38.9	28	26.9
31–40	36	36.0	39	41.1	36	34.6
41–50	23	23.0	17	17.9	27	26.0
51–60	7	7.0	2	2.1	10	9.6
61+	3	3.0	–	–	3	2.9
Caste						
Forward caste	1	1.0	2	2.1	4	3.8
Other backward castes	73	73.0	37	38.9	59	56.7
Scheduled castes	26	26.0	42	44.2	34	32.7
Scheduled tribes	–	–	12	12.6	–	–
Others	–	–	2	2.1	7	6.7
Religion						
Hindu	100	100.0	89	93.6	92	88.5
Muslim	–	–	2	2.1	7	6.7
Christian	–	–	4	4.2	5	4.8
Marital status						
Unmarried	2	2.0	–	–	1	1.0
Married	85	85.0	88	92.6	83	79.8
Widowed	12	12.0	7	7.4	20	19.2
Divorced/separated	1	1.0	–	–	–	–
Education						
Primary	–	–	3	3.2	–	–
Secondary	2	2.0	7	7.4	4	3.8
High school	1	1.0	1	1.1	6	5.8
University	–	–	–	–	1	1.0
Not literate	97	97.0	84	88.4	93	89.4
Work details						
Farming	23	23.0	5	5.2	7	6.7
Agriculture/wage labour	63	63.0	69	72.5	55	52.8
Farming and small business	–	–	1	1.1	–	–
Seasonal migration	1	1.0	–	–	4	3.8
Cattle grazing	–	–	1	1.1	–	–
Non-agricultural occupations in the village	5	5.0	13	12.8	14	6.7
Non-agricultural occupations outside the village	–	–	–	–	4	3.8
Small business	3	3.0	8	8.5	2	1.9
Government job	1	1.0	–	–	3	2.9
Teacher (private)	–	–	–	–	2	1.9
Student	–	–	1	1.1	1	1.0
No occupation	8	8.0	6	6.3	19	18.3
SHG member						
Yes	81	81.0	93	97.9	91	87.5
No	19	19.0	2	2.1	13	12.5

*(N): Number of respondents

to the people.[7] The populist *Janmabhoomi* program subverted decentralization, undermined representational politics, and drew a set of parameters for governance that delinked democracy from development (Reddy 2002).

Women's SHGs along with community based users' committees were/are identified as community-based oversight committees to monitor various government programs. Despite the 73rd and the 74th amendments to the Constitution which had opened the doors for women in general and SC/ST women in particular to participate in democratic decentralization, it is ironically the membership in SHGs, VOs and SHG Federations (called *Mahila Samakhya*) that provide spaces for women to make their voices heard.[8] On the one hand, this has opened new avenues of negotiation with the *sarkar*[9] and the emergence of women's political agency outside the framework of democratic representational politics. On the other hand, it has contributed to the undermining of democratic institutions and the negotiations of women with ongoing democratic processes (Powis 2003). As will be revealed in one of the later sections, the associations of women are being actively politicized to contest the legitimacy of democratic institutions.

In Village 1, the village women mentioned that they had collectively demanded that their *panchayat* (village council) provide amenities like drinking water and street lighting. The *panchayat* had arranged for the digging of a bore-well and the laying of pipelines for drinking water. Households pay a small fee for the service. Women are proud of their achievement and often invoke collective protest as a strategy to resolve their problems. Women mentioned that men in the village seek their help to approach government officials for village-related development works or for community mobilization, for example, for fund raising to construct a temple. In response to questions regarding "instrumentality," women mentioned that they were aware of getting overburdened with public domain roles, but at this point they wished to put to good use the newfound legitimacy within and outside the village that emerges from their collective strength.

SHGs and the household

Experiences from India and other parts of the world show steady changes in gender norms and gender relations in the public and private domains in response to women's mobilization. To questions on perceived changes in gender relations, women gave the responses presented below. It should be noted that unlike several parts of north India, south India does not practice strict seclusion. Women from the lower and the middle range caste groups are visible in public and work on their own farms or as agricultural laborers.[10] Further, Mehbubnagar district is part of a historical region that had strong peasant revolts against the *Nizam* rulers immediately after India's independence. Women participated actively in this armed struggle (*Stree Shakti Sanghatana* 1989).

In rural areas men and women express the measure of an event (like rainfall) in terms of paise to the rupee (1/100), or a measure equivalent to cents on the dollar). During my field study, in response to a question about the adequacy of rains during the season, most people said they had had only 50 paise rain (or 50 percent of what was needed) and at all the wrong times. While this looks like evidence of a monetized idiom, it is not clear when this expression began. Similar expressions were reported by Integrated Health Management (IHM), Pachod, Maharashtra, which statistically validated the use of what it calls *Pachod Paisa* in place of Likert's scale (Kapadia-Kundu and Dyalchand 2005).

My survey asked women to use this idiom to measure changes in their husbands' attitudes toward their contribution to the household and their participation in social/community activities, their husbands' facilitation of their attendance at meetings, and actual sharing of household work, including male children's learning to do domestic work. The attempt was to understand changes in gender relations and division of labor within households that can contribute to sustainable change. The data are presented in Table 4.2.

The majority of women reported a 50 paise change in men's appreciating their contributions to the household; a 25 paise change in men facilitating women's participation in SHG activities; a 50 paise increase in actual sharing of domestic work; and a 25 or 50 paise reduction of anger/irritation. One woman commented, "In the beginning he used to do lot of *lolli* (petty quarreling and nagging); now he does not." Another said, "If I leave the house after informing him with the rice still cooking on the stove, he will tend it and also feed the children. That is a big change." On the question about husband's anger and irritation, one woman reported that now she

Table 4.2 Women's perceptions of changes in gender relations: rupee ratio

	25ps	50ps	75ps	Total
A How many paise in a rupee is your husband...	%	%	%	%
1 Willing to share work in the family?	13	79	8	100
2 Actually doing domestic work?	31	65	4	100
3 Giving a larger share of earnings for the household?	12	77	11	100
4 Appreciating your contribution to the family?	17	76	7	100
5 Appreciating your participation insocial/community activities?	36	65	4	100
6 Facilitating your attending of meetings and trips outside the village?	56	37	7	100
7 Not expressing anger and irritation towards you?	38	40	22	100
B How many paise in a rupee are male children learning household work?	64	31	5	100
C How many paise in a rupee do you attribute these changes to the SHG/sangha?	24	70	6	100

argues and fights back. In Village 1, women have collectively constructed a *sangha* office. One woman said that if her husband quarrels too much she will threaten to go and stay in the *sangha* office; she also has the support of the other women. Her husband is afraid that all the women will quarrel with him. All of them mentioned that men are afraid to oppose them as a group. Also they see that women are talking sense and are doing good work instead of "gossiping."

Mobility patterns

The women from all three villages reported experiencing increases in their mobility outside the village for meeting government officials, transacting business at the bank, and attending training programs. A small group of women takes turns carrying out tasks for the SHG, such as visiting the bank, depositing money, getting passbooks updated, and discussing the possibility of bank loans; negotiating for government schemes; and attending training programs, village cluster meetings, and so on. Trips related to family activities such as visiting places, purchasing small assets, or traveling to hospitals are undertaken along with other family members or with the husband. Though women also travel alone or with children, this does not emerge as a major pattern in all the villages.

Household decision-making

There was a typical pattern of decision-making observed in the three villages. Decision-making within households is linked to the family type. With regard to domestic work, women reported almost complete independence in their decision-making. This also translates into sole responsibility for domestic work and the ensuing drudgery. In households that have older female members, like the mother-in-law, decisions about what to cook are either made by her or influenced by her. However, women see this as a routine task that does not require a lot of decision-making. Most of the time, it is limited to and dependent on the provisions available at home or what the day's wage can buy. On special occasions like festivals, cooking caters to the desires of men and children. In cash-strapped poor households choices are few and decision-making is limited.

Responses to several questions about purchases of assets (small/large, agricultural/non-agricultural) indicated that decisions are taken by men or by men and women together. Women's autonomous decisions on most family matters are rare. Where senior members like a mother-in-law are present in the family, they, rather than their daughters-in-law make the decisions. Even younger men have to abide by authority or negotiate their way. I have observed that when a mother-in-law and daughter-in-law are both members of an SHG, it is the mother-in-law rather than the daughter-in-law who attends the meetings. The daughter-in-law has the responsibility of cooking and caring for children, a set of tasks that the mother-in-law has graduated out of. In the case of decisions pertaining to children's education, women mostly said that they would like their boys and girls to study "as much as they want" or "as long as we can afford." Yet in practice, the education of most girls is discontinued after primary or secondary schooling owing to economic concerns. All the respondents are aware of the legal age for marriage and the government's focus on girls' education; hence responses to such questions are given in the context of such formal state discourses. In all the villages my research team and I observed that few young girls traveled by bus or bicycle to larger neighboring villages or towns for higher studies. Women reported that decisions about marriage and gifts/dowry were often made by community elders who were consulted to settle marriage liaisons. They also mentioned that the practice of dowry is not changing as a result of women's mobilization (on similar patterns in Nepal, see Acharya, Chapter 3, this volume).

Women's participation in farming-related decisions is generally limited. In farming households, farming decisions are seen as routine activities, because the same crops are grown each year and what is grown is linked to land quality, availability of water for irrigation, and, at times, the predicted market. Women contribute labor for cultivation, crop processing, and storage. They are more likely to intervene to influence how many bags of food grains are retained for domestic consumption. Giving priority to liquid cash would mean the sale of food grains in the short term and purchase of food grains in the open market at higher prices in the long term.

The limits to empowerment

Despite all these data and observations, I argue that there are distinct limits to "empowerment" in terms of decision-making, control over resources (specifically income and occasionally access to land), mobility, and changes in the gender division of labor. Below, I attempt to explain what I see as these limitations.

Domains of empowerment

Definitions of empowerment encompass change within the material and ideological arenas and women's collective "power to" bring about these changes externally as well as their "power within" to believe in their own ability to do so. However, empowerment programs with different entry points, for example those addressing access to material resources *or* ideological issues, seem to be creating limits to women's empowerment or only partially addressing issues. For example, poverty alleviation and welfare-oriented programs expect women to individually renegotiate the ideological arena. Meanwhile, women-oriented mobilizations that address selected ideological issues like girls' education, early age at marriage, and domestic violence barely address gender relations within the domestic domain, caste-based inequalities, or official policies of marginalization.

Women's collective interventions and agency are, at this point, limited to public domain negotiations with institutions. Though men in private poke fun at women's newfound visibility, at a collective level they see women's mobilization "within certain limits" as not really threatening. In certain villages in the Mehbubnagar district, *sangha* women directly confronted upper-caste interests in maintaining cultural practices like dedicating young girls as *joginis*.[11] In this case, because their empowerment *was* considered threatening, the women were roughed up by upper caste men and were told that the party in power had changed so they would have to close their *sanghas*; it was men's turn to rule. In Villages 2 and 3 men maintain a close watch on the proceedings of the women's meetings. Men not only support women's activities, accompany them to the bank if necessary, and carry out some errands for the SHGs, but also indirectly intervene in the outcomes of the meetings through the women members of the household. Key informant interviews with men (of lower- and middle-caste groups) who were considered to be opinion leaders revealed a lot of skepticism about government strategies to empower women at the cost of neglecting male farmers in terms of access to credit, support through agricultural extension services, and market support by the government. Both men and women pointed out that the government has to generate employment to occupy the youth. Educated and uneducated youth migrate to distant cities to work on construction sites for lack of avenues for work within or close to the village.

At the household level, women seem to be striving for shared male/female decision-making rather than autonomy and control. Women consider being part of the SHG a household strategy rather than an opportunity to claim a share in household power. When older women are part of these mobilizations (as in Village 1), they are much more likely to support raising the age of marriage for girls to 18 years, accept a small family size, and favor institutional deliveries for their daughters and daughters-in-law. In many villages, my field observations indicate that women who take up leadership roles in the SHG or in the affairs of the village are more likely to be older women past procreative and caring commitments, or single/widow women, or women who have adult daughters or daughters-in-law to take care of domestic work. So women who manage to negotiate for public domain power are also women who have better bargaining power within the family and have alternative persons to deliver social reproduction work for them and their families.

The state's class-based mobilization as opposed to women's caste-based affiliation

While gender relations are going through nominal changes, caste hierarchies, differences, and hostilities among the poor are resistant to change.

All the village-level SHG meetings that were held as a preamble to the study involved women from all caste groups. While in Village 1 we did not notice any overt physical distance being maintained by OBC women from the lower castes, in Villages 2 and 3 all the OBC women tended to cluster together. Further, in introductions, while women from the lower castes stood up, put their palms together (to indicate reverence), gave their name and the name of their *sangha,* and conveyed their greetings, the OBC women sat in their places and gave their names and the names of their *sangha.* After the meeting one OBC woman explained, "How can we fold our hands in front of people who are lower caste and work for wages on our fields?" Women come into these meetings with a caste and family identity that constitutes a more overtly and self-consciously defining set of characteristics than their gender identity.

Self-help groups of women in the DWCRA program were comprised of women from one neighborhood who also belonged to similar caste groupings. Most groups were predominantly made up of women from "other backward castes." The DRDA had introduced several criteria for moving up the spiral of state subsidies to receive large matching grants for women's savings. One of these criteria was that the SHG, regardless of its existing membership's caste status, must include women from SC/ST. This had mixed success.

The convergence of poverty-reduction and welfare approaches over the last two years in Villages 2 and 3 is producing palpable tensions in these villages. Resistance has been expressed in response to the move from multiple departments addressing issues linked to welfare toward the development of the IKP as a single uniform program. In earlier time periods, women were not only mobilized through different programs with differing program goals but were also mobilized as different caste groups. The DWCRA had by default focused on OBC women, and the IKP had clearly focused on SC/ST women. Now the convergence of these programs at the administrative and executive levels has created a situation of contrived social cohesion for different caste groups of women who had historically tended to adhere to caste-based social distance.

In Villages 2 and 3 the formation and functioning of the village organization, the disbursement of funds, and other SHG activities have come to a standstill. In Village 2, there were caste conflicts focused on the location of a community building, the funds for which were sanctioned under the DWCRA program. The old claimants to the program belonged to the OBC groups and the new claimants are SC groups. There were physical fights and serious tensions in the village that lasted two days. Police came in to dispel tensions. Several men and women were badly bruised, physically and emotionally. Cases of alleged sexual abuse were also filed. It is well known that caste conflicts often use women and their bodies to reinforce demarcations and also to send signals of punishment and retribution. "Empowered" women are now being actively punished for playing a role in these caste conflicts. However, nobody – neither men, women, nor the community coordinators – can afford a continued conflict or deadlock on this issue. Thus my visit to the village a day after the violence was used by both of the feuding groups to make their case to a third person. The community coordinator and person in charge of recovering loans were the most worried about the implications for the functioning of the program. In the village meeting, the community coordinator said that he had nothing to do with politics or with the DWCRA program so he would not take sides with any community in the village. If village women wanted more loans and grants coming to the village, they would have to come together, hold meetings, and continue with their savings and repayments. Such selective involvement in local struggles on the part of program leaders reveals their interest in "disciplining women and communities" and functionally cobbling together "social cohesion" among the poor as a class, as well as their lack of capacity to work on the deep-seated caste differences and contestations around development politics.

In many villages in Andhra Pradesh, caste conflicts also erupted around the Mid-day Meal Scheme, with serious differences of opinion about who should cook the meals for children. The purity-pollution principle of the caste system regulates inter-caste commensal practices and thereby requires social distance. Accepting or rejecting cooked food is directly linked to the caste status of the individual. According to secular democratic values there must be no caste-based discrimination in public programs. Therefore, the government pressured people to agree that OBC and SC women should form a team and cook food at the school premises.

Thus building cross-caste solidarity within the SHGs is proving difficult. Further, discontent that originates in relation to development politics is mediated through identity and caste-based politics and vice-versa. So the dissonance in the villages reflects the political struggles in the macroenvironment. Women's experiences of being part of these SHG programs have to be understood in the context of the broader economic and political climate. Poor women are not a homogeneous group, and sisterhood among the poor is neither simple nor straightforward. The expectation that women can be mobilized as a class ignores the reality that gender is embedded within multiple social stratifications including caste, ethnicity, religion and race. Addressing these inequalities is a monumental challenge that is not amenable to a quick fix via microcredit programs.

Women's empowerment in the midst of growing agrarian crises

Among the several descriptors of the agrarian crises, those that stand out are the declining share of agriculture in the gross state domestic product (GSDP) since the 1980s;[12] the high cost of cultivation, diminishing productivity, and low returns; weak support from government; growing underemployment; increasing indebtedness of farm households; and numerous farmers' suicides. Research on farmers' suicides points to the growing distress among the agrarian classes, an effect of individualization, a process of socioeconomic "estrangement" in the context of rapid economic transformation (Mohanty 2005). Access to loans and small capital is seen to be providing elbow room for women and households, but it is not seen as a solution to deal with poverty or agrarian crises (see Table 4.3).

Most of the women who took loans from the SHG used them to raise crops and drill bore-wells, but if the water table drops and crops cannot be grown, such investments lose their value. Loans taken for consumption and health expenditure, often referred to in literature as "consumption smoothing" loans, are also examples of how these loans represent no more than a straw on which to stay afloat in a cash-strapped situation. Migration out of the villages for purposes of earning a living is still a major strategy in all the three villages. In the context of declining state support in the provision of public goods, SHG spaces are claimed and vigorously contested. Because access to credit is "better" for women than men, men are expressing some support for women's public domain participation in the SHGs. However, men's shrinking loan opportunities for agriculture and allied activities are leading to male resentment of government policies and some backlash against women's programs in several villages. While microcredit can reduce women's poverty and improve women's status within households, it is crucial not to ignore the simultaneous disempowerment, loss of livelihoods, and lack of life options that low-income men face. The severity of farming men's problems is reflected in the growing numbers of farmers' suicides in this region.

Table 4.3 Purpose of loans taken from the SHG

Purpose of loan	Village 1	Village 2	Village 3	Total
Agricultural investment (crop)	21	14	7	42 (22.6%)
Consumption	–	17	10	27 (14.5%)
Health expenditure	1	13	8	22 (12%)
Purchase milch cattle/sheep/goats	5	11	5	21 (11.5%)
Purchase consumer assets	3	7	5	15 (6.4%)
Start small business	2	3	7	12 (6.5%)
Dowry/wedding	–	4	3	7 (3.8%)
Purchase land	3	2	1	6 (3.3%)
Purchase agricultural assets	3	1	1	5 (2.7%)
Given on re-lending	1	3	–	4 (2%)
Bore-well digging	1	1	1	3 (1.6%)
Consumption assets and agricultural investment	1	2	1	4 (2%)
Repay another loan and agricultural investment	2	1	–	3 (1.6%)
Agricultural assets and bore-well	–	1	–	1 (0.5%)
Don't know	4	4	3	11 (6%)
Total	47	84	52	186 (100)

The discourse of women's empowerment through microcredit and self-help groups provides a glimmer of hope in the midst of growing poverty and declines in livelihood in the context of globalization. Women are creatively mobilizing solidarity despite the context of extreme economic adversity and growing urban–rural inequalities. Participation in microcredit is giving women a glimpse into the world of expanding markets and commodification, and it is enabling them in limited ways. This is a world that is accentuating women's poverty in the first place and then devising minimal means of mitigating it through the supposed encouragement of their human agency. This is a world that evokes hope and despair at the same time.

Notes

1 I would like to sincerely thank the Fulbright Program, the United States Educational Foundation in India (USEFI) and the Council for International Exchange of Scholars (CIES) for giving me the opportunity to conduct this study and interact with scholars as part of the Fulbright New Century Scholar Program (2004–5). I would like to thank the Tata Institute of Social Sciences for giving me all the requisite official support. Special thanks to Dr. Jayati Lal and the Institute for Research on Women and Gender, University of Michigan (UMICH) for inviting me to spend time as a visiting scholar at Ann Arbor. The time at UMICH was valuable in many ways. This study would not have been possible without the support of the village women, field staff, my research assistant and organizations like Andhra Pradesh Mahila Samata Society, Society for the Elimination of Rural Poverty, Department of Rural Development and the Naandi Foundation, Hyderabad. I would like to thank Ms. Ramani Murty, who painstakingly analyzed the data. I owe deep gratitude to Professor Neera Desai for giving valuable suggestions for this study. Most importantly I would like to thank the team of women who formed the Gender, Globalization and Governance group (the 3Gs sisters) for the wonderful sisterhood.
2 This is the second state after Bangalore (in Karnataka) that has received maximum IT-related foreign direct investment. The city of Hyderabad, also known as "Cyberabad," is always a favorite stopover for Bill Gates, Bill Clinton, and recently George Bush.
3 AP was one of the first states in India to devise a vision document for the state. There were 14 task force groups that worked on different sectors of development. The final report (January 1999) was crafted by Mckinsey and Co. Inc., a private multinational think tank.
4 Mehbubnagar and a few other districts that belong to the Telengana region of AP have been agitating for separate state status to meet the development aspirations of the people. The Telengana region has a history of revolt and rebellion against feudal lords. Women were active in these uprisings.
5 "Indira" stands for the former prime minister of India, Indira Gandhi. Her name and those of her deceased sons Rajiv Gandhi and Sanjay Gandhi are given to programs, buildings, airports, etc., whenever the Congress Party comes to power.
6 The bottom caste groups in the Hindu caste hierarchy have faced centuries of discrimination and marginalization. In independent India these caste groups as well as the tribal groups have found special mention in the Indian Constitution as Scheduled Castes and Tribes deserving affirmative action.
7 The Janmabhoomi program borrows its inspiration from a South Korean program called *Saemoul Undong* and a Malaysian program called *Bhoomiputra*.

8 In April 1993, the Parliament of India ratified the introduction of decentralization policies through the 73rd and 74th amendments to the Indian Constitution. By April 1994 all states of India had ratified the two amendments. These amendments had introduced the 33 percent representation for women and proportional representation for marginalized groups like the Scheduled Castes and Tribes in the rural and urban governance, i.e. the *Panchayati Raj* Institutions (PRIs) and urban Municipalities and Corporations, respectively.

9 The term *sarkar* is used to denote state, bureaucracy, authority or officials.

10 The all-India female work participation rate as per 2001 census is 25.68 percent and for Andhra Pradesh it is 34.93 percent.

11 The practice of dedicating girls as *joginis* exists in the border districts of Andhra Pradesh and Karnataka. Young girls under 15 are dedicated in service to God in a ritual in which they are married to a local deity. Generally an upper-caste man will patronize the dedication and in return will claim physical rights, sexual and labor, over the girl, with no commitment to the children that are born through such a liaison. The girl continues to stay with her parents and contributes to the economic survival of the family. Indirectly the family seeks economic support from upper-caste men through such practices.

12 The share of the agriculture sector in the GSDP, which was 53 percent in 1960–61, has dwindled to about 13 per cent in 2002–3. The most rapid declines were after the 1980s (Narasimha Rao and Suri 2006).

Part III

Social reproduction and transnational migrations

5 States, work, and social reproduction through the lens of migrant experience

Ecuadorian domestic workers in Madrid

Gioconda Herrera[1]

The relationship between the feminization of migrations and the new global order has been analyzed through the interpretative framework of feminist political economy and illustrates the ways in which social inequality has increased with globalization. Female migrant work has become a privatized response to the global crisis of social reproduction in which the neoliberal economic and political order has placed many families in the Western world (Sassen 2004; Bakker and Gill 2003c). Within this framework of structural constraints, analyses of gender and migration also show that processes of empowerment may take place and affect women's lives and their families. Changing gender relations with migration may affect the meanings attributed to social reproduction too (Levitt 2001; Hondagneu-Sotelo 1994; 2001). This article explores the relationship between the global crisis of social reproduction and immigrant domestic work through an analysis of the trajectories of Ecuadorian migrant women in Madrid. It connects the informalization of social reproduction in both Ecuador and Spain with the increasing mobility of Ecuadorian women and the growth of transnational strategies of care, and looks at how these structural processes intersect in women's everyday lives.

By looking at the way in which Ecuadorian domestic workers deploy transnational work trajectories as well as transnational social arrangements around care, I wish to illustrate how these women have to negotiate with multiple settings of belonging and multiple class, gender, and race hierarchies. The location in a transnational field produces contradictory ways of constructing one's identity: both empowerment and structural subordination take place in female migrant experience and has destabilizing consequences social reproduction. While social networks are crucial to sustain the transnational experience, this case illustrates that the role of states, social policies, and regimes of power, in both origin and destination, affect women's transnational experience and everyday lives.

After a short discussion on how to connect social reproduction with transnational fields, I look at the crisis of social reproduction in both the Ecuadorian and the Spanish states and how this is connected to the emigration of Ecuadorians and the rapid formation of an Ecuadorian community in Spain in the late 1990s, a community mainly pioneered by female domestic workers. Then I examine women's migrant experience, focusing on two issues: contradictory perceptions of work, and the complex organization of work and social arrangements of care in both immigrant and transnational settings.[2]

Immigrant domestic work, social reproduction, and transnational fields

Feminist scholars have argued that gender inequalities are constitutive of contemporary patterns of intensified globalization (Bakker and Gill 2003b: 23; Sassen 1998), and that gender differences in migration flows often reflect the way in which gender divisions of labour are incorporated into uneven economic development processes (UNRISD 2005: 109). Accordingly, immigrant domestic work, which in Western countries is mainly accomplished by women and/or is feminized, is one of the activities at the heart of the contradiction between the expanded power of state-protected capital and sustainable forms of social reproduction (Bakker and Gill 2003c). Indeed, immigrant domestic work is considered a domain where the expansion of capital is undertaken at the expense of greater insecurity for those at the bottom of the global class and racial hierarchies (Young 2003).

My understanding of social reproduction draws on feminist contributions to economics that define it as any activity that involves biological reproduction, the reproduction of the labour force and of goods, and the reproduction of relations of production. It refers to the social processes associated with the daily sustenance of people, the reproduction of the labour force, and the maintenance of communities and may involve material provision of health, education, and welfare (Bakker and Gill 2003c). My interest here is to grasp such processes within the experience of migration.

The connection between immigrant domestic work, globalization, and the informalization of social reproduction has been variously designated – the new domestic world order (Hondagneu-Sotelo 2001), the new international division of reproductive labour (Parreñas 2004), or the transnational economy of domestic labour (Young 2003). These terms all refer to the rapid increase in the number of immigrant women performing domestic work in both developing and industrialized countries, and the consequences of this situation for global inequality. First of all, access of immigrant women to domestic work in developed countries coincides with deterioration in the terms and conditions of work for many at the global level (UNRISD 2005; Martínez 2004). Second, precarious and increasingly transnational frameworks have become important elements in the social reproduction of many poor communities around the globe through remittances and other social arrangements (Young 2003). Third, domestic work is subsidizing the work of more privileged women; consequently, male privilege within homes and families remains uncontested and new inequalities are formed (Ehrenreich and Hochschild 2004; Hondagneu-Sotelo 2001). In sum, "the activities, tasks and resources involved in the daily sustenance of people, homes and communities are more and more organized on the basis of the immigrant labour force and produce unequal social arrangements at different levels" (Hondagneu-Sotelo 2001: 24). Moreover, distinctly positioned motherhoods involved in transnational arrangements of care can elucidate the racialized character of the international divisions of gendered labour and show how specific definitions of motherhood are made possible by the labour of others (Ehrenreich and Hochschild 2004).

While the structural constraints and inequalities described above are the mandatory global context to which the Ecuadorian women's experience belongs, my analysis is also informed by Levitt and Glick Schiller's understanding of transnationalism as a social field: a "set of multiple interlocking networks of social relationships through which ideas, practices and resources are unequally exchanged, organized and transformed" (2004: 1009). This concept underscores two factors useful for interpreting social reproduction within immigrant experience. First, when people belong to multiple settings, they also experience multiple layers of power. That is, they come into contact with the regulatory powers and hegemonic culture of more than one state (2004: 1013). Second, these multiple legal and political institutions organize and legitimate gender, race, and class status. "Individuals occupy different gender, racial and class positions within different states at the same time. Thus, migrant behaviour is the product of these simultaneous multiple statuses of race, class and gender" (2004: 1015). In sum, an examination of women's migrant experience through its connection with social reproduction should take into account how the regulatory powers and social policies of two states shape their lives and determine the scope of their negotiations.

Immigrant domestic workers are not a homogeneous social group. The literature demonstrates that the occupation includes women from poor as well as "middle" status backgrounds in their country of origin. Ecuadorian immigrant domestic workers are not an exception and come from a wide range of social, economic, and cultural backgrounds that reflect the diversity and social inequality of the country of origin. Their heterogeneous backgrounds shape the diversity of stories they narrate, revealing different ways of reacting to and accommodating state policies, as well as diverse understandings of social reproduction. How are women from many different social backgrounds drawn into the experience of international migration and domestic work? In the following section I look at how the crisis of social reproduction of both the Ecuadorian and the Spanish states determines this phenomenon.

The crisis of social reproduction of the Ecuadorian state

At the end of 1990 there was a sudden and massive emigration of Ecuadorians to Europe and the United States. Because of problems with registration no one really knows how many Ecuadorians left the country, but according to the *Dirección Nacional de Migración* (DMN 2004), which keeps the official data on entries and exits, between 1997 and 2004, 837,062 people left the country and did not come back. This was an unprecedented number in the history of Ecuadorian international migration and represented about 8 per cent of Ecuador's population.[3]

This exodus has been explained in different ways. Some argue that it was the acute financial and economic crisis of 1999 that pushed so many Ecuadorians out of the country (Acosta 2004).[4] Others have stressed the role of social networks and pioneer migrants (Ramirez and Ramirez 2005; Pedone 2003). My purpose here is to demonstrate that the 1990s emigration process is associated with a more profound and long-lasting crisis of social reproduction of the Ecuadorian state that started with the implementation of structural adjustment policies in the 1980s, and is connected to growing social inequality in the country.

According to the 2001 Ecuadorian census, women represented 47 per cent of this new emigrant flow. They outnumber Ecuadorian men in Italy and other European countries, except for Spain, where men and women were found in approximately equal numbers. Only in the United States does immigration of Ecuadorians still seem to be a predominantly masculine phenomenon, although even there women accounted for 37.6 per cent of the Ecuadorian immigrant community. In terms of socio-economic background, although 60 per cent are classified as not poor, 27 per cent are classified as poor and 13 per cent as extremely poor (Ramirez and Ramirez 2005), which shows that people from very heterogeneous backgrounds decided to migrate.[5]

While the 1999 economic crisis provoked this massive emigration, there were other structural elements before the crisis that prepared the way. These are directly related to the inadequate role of the state in social reproduction and to sharpening social inequality. Indeed, Ecuadorian social expenditure is one of the lowest in Latin America and has been decreasing since 1982, when structural adjustment policies were first implemented. Public expenditure on education dropped from 4.8 per cent in 1981 to 1.7 of gross domestic product (GDP) in 2000, and health spending went from 1.3 per cent of GDP in 1981 to 0.6 per cent in 2000. In 1996, the state allocated US $285 per student for education, whereas in 2000 it provided a mere US$130 (Vos 2003).

The consequences, in terms of human capital, are devastating. Analyses report stagnant enrolments in primary and secondary schools between 1990 and 2001, and very poor achievement levels. The situation is similar with respect to health: Ecuador reports one of the highest rates of child mortality in the region, and in 1999 immunizations covered only 70 per cent of the population under one year of age (Vos 2003). According to the World Bank, in 2001 the number of Ecuadorians who could not satisfy their basic needs increased by 5 per cent and represented more than 5 million people. While the rural sector is the most affected, urban poverty has increased dramatically in recent years.

In sum, while the financial crisis of 1999 provoked an unprecedented drop of GDP per inhabitant, the numbers regarding the role of the state in education and health, both pillars of social reproduction, had been less than satisfactory for the last 20 years. Consequently, people's expectations about social reproduction did not take into account the role of the state. On the contrary, neoliberal reforms and fiscal policies, among others, involved privatizing the few services offered to the citizens and unintentionally promoted the informalization of social reproduction by compelling people to seek on their own for viable strategies, of which emigration was one.

One consequence can be grasped by looking at the growing importance of remittances in the Ecuadorian economy. Several reports (Herrera 2005b; FLACSO and Banco Central de Ecuador 2004; Bendixen and Associates 2003) have called attention to the significant role of remittances in poverty reduction and indicate that they are used mainly to meet social and basic needs, including welfare, education, and health. Thus, remittances from Ecuadorian men and, increasingly, women, have filled the void left by the diminishing role of the state in social expenditure, while emigration has contributed to a drop in unemployment rates. No wonder some international organizations, such as the World Bank and the Interamerican Development Bank, view remittances and emigration as a much more efficient anti-poverty programme than any of the schemes launched to date in developing countries as compensation for structural adjustment policies. Moreover, there is a consensus among analysts that an important part of the recent macroeconomic recovery is due to remittances, which increased from US$794,000,000 in 1997 to US$1,750,000,000 in 2005, representing approximately 5.6 per cent of GDP. In other words, emigrants are currently one of the most important sources of foreign earnings for the Ecuadorian economy (Acosta *et al.* 2005). This process has been accompanied by an increasing concentration of wealth. In 2000, the wealthiest 10 per cent of the Ecuadorian population possessed 46 per cent of total income, a huge increase over the 35.4 per cent they controlled in 1990. While economic growth experienced ups and downs over the last 20 years, inequality has grown steadily in the same period and has accompanied the crisis of social reproduction. Currently, Ecuador ranks third in Latin America, after Brazil and Paraguay, in unequal concentration of wealth (0.57 on the Gini index) (Acosta *et al.* 2005).

The crisis of social reproduction of the Spanish state

Over the past twenty years Spain has become a country of immigration. As is well known, one of the reasons why Spain has attracted so many immigrants in recent times is that the population is aging because of a drop in the fertility rate, and this makes labour shortages more difficult to avert without substantial immigration (Cornelius 2004). The country's total fertility rate has dropped to 1.2 children per woman, the lowest in the world after Italy and Japan. It has been projected that, at the current fertility rate, Spain's population will decrease by 9,408,000 between 1999 and 2050 (Cornelius 2004: 403). A 1999 survey found that 47 per cent of Spanish women were childless, while 42 per cent of Latin American immigrant women had two or more children, and 30 per cent of African immigrant women had three or more (Cornelius 2004).

Analyses of the character of the Spanish welfare state associate this low fertility rate with insufficient welfare provisions in education, health, and family support. Social expenditure is well below the European Union (EU) average. In 2002 public expenditure on social protection reached 19.7 per cent of GDP, compared to 26.9 per cent in the EU and 31.3 per cent in Sweden (Navarro 2006: 35). Spain was the country with the lowest spending on social protection after Ireland. Moreover, the gap between Spain and the rest of the EU countries increased from 1993 on. The rapid economic growth of the country translated not into social expenditure but rather into a diminishing fiscal deficit, which became one of the lowest in the EU (Navarro 2006: 37). Indeed, in 2002 Spain reached 86.5 per cent of EU average economic development, but it scored only 67.6 per cent of the average of EU health public spending, and spent 21,723 million euros less than what it should have spent according to its level of wealth. The same situation is observed in education. The percentage of GDP devoted to public education in Spain (4.4 per cent) is lower than in many EU newcomers such as Poland, Estonia, or Lithuania (Navarro 2006: 67). But data on public support for families even better illustrate how social reproduction has been a private matter in Spain and has been put in mainly on the shoulders of women. Only 8 per cent of children between 0 and 3 years go to a publicly supported daycare programme, as compared to 40 per cent in Sweden, 23 per cent in France, and 30 per cent in Belgium, and only 3 per cent of the elderly (over 65 years) receive some kind of assistance at home (Navarro 2006: 83). Moreover, 28 per cent of fathers and 32 per cent of mothers older than 60 years of age live with their adult children (Martínez 2004).

In sum, insufficient welfare provisions despite economic growth illustrate a different crisis of social reproduction from the one described in the Ecuadorian case. However, in both cases, the role of the state has been crucial in reproducing such deficiencies. Fiscal austerity and conservative ideologies on the role of women and families in activities of care complemented each other to create a fertile ground for the increasing migration of women, and transnational social reproduction became a partial solution to both crises.

Indeed, immigration policies regarding domestic work in Spain seem to be connected to this situation and partially explain the rapid growth of immigrant domestic labour. As Cornelius (2004) argues, in one of the strongest informal economies of Europe, domestic workers belong to a minority of immigrants who are able to obtain work contracts that include social security payments by employers. After five years of legal work, non-EU workers can apply for permanent resident status. According to Brian Gratton,

> between 1992 and 1998 permits to work in domestic service expanded for Ecuadorian women more rapidly than any other foreign group. Data from social security registers reveal that Ecuadorian women in domestic service account for 84 percent, a higher number than any other foreign group.
>
> (Gratton 2004)[6]

Ecuadorians have benefited from the seven regularization programmes launched by the Spanish government since 1986, and from the tailor-made programme of regularization of 2001.[7] Currently, with respect to the regularization programme launched by Rodríguez Zapatero, Ecuadorians account for 21 per cent of the approved applications, followed by Romanians (16.55 per cent) and Moroccans (11.5 per cent). This programme benefited 70,964 women and 64,819 men. Domestic work accounts for 31.7 per cent of applications (18.7 per cent represent workers with one employer only, and 13 per cent workers with several employers).

The parallel between a crisis of social reproduction provoked by structural adjustment policies in Ecuador and unresolved deficits in health, education, and family support in Spain illustrates the privatization and informalization of social reproduction and explains the growth of Ecuadorian women's migration to Spain. At the same time, this is what frames transnational arrangements of social reproduction among immigrants' families.

Work and social reproduction in the lives of Ecuadorian domestic workers in Madrid

Domestic work is still one of the most common occupations open to poor women, especially rural migrants to Ecuador's cities. Although the majority of domestic employees no longer live in the homes of their employers, most middle- and upper-class families employ one or more women to do the housework and care for their children. While labour legislation provides some protection for domestic workers, these regulations are widely ignored by employers, and neither the labour movement nor the state has taken measures to correct this situation.[8] In 2003, only 12 per cent of domestic workers were protected by social security (Vásconez 2005).

Emigration of Latin American women to other Latin American countries as domestic workers is not a new phenomenon either, although it has been poorly documented. The situation of Colombian women in Venezuela, of

Bolivians and Paraguayans in Argentina before the crisis of 2002, and of Peruvians in Chile, is part of Latin American domestic workers' transnational experience during the 1980s and 1990s. Ecuadorian women, however, did not enter these intra-regional circuits. Internal migration of women from rural areas to the cities predominated. There was an important influx of Ecuadorian migrants to Venezuela, but it was mostly headed by men.

Domestic work still constitutes one of the most important markers of social inequality in Latin America, a marker that sharply divides women on the basis of class and ethnicity, and is deeply ingrained in the imagination of the population. This is an important consideration for understanding the fate of women entering domestic work abroad; the idea of domestic work with which these women left their country of origin is based on their experiences in a hierarchical and exclusionary society (Radcliffe 1999).

In the case of Spain, domestic work has been traditionally done by Spanish women from the southern rural regions of the country, a phenomenon still rather common in the late 1970s among middle- and upper-class families. According to Martínez, the category included 400,000 women in the late 1970s. By 1985, however, only 7 per cent of Spanish domestic workers worked as live-in maids (Martínez 2004: 145). By the early 1990s, their place had been taken by Dominican, Peruvian, Filipina, and Polish women (Cornelius 2004). Other Latin American groups started to arrive in the same period, basically from Peru, Colombia, and Ecuador.

A common trend, mentioned in every interview, is that, compared with the women's activities in Ecuador, whether they were school teachers, domestic workers, housewives, or students, work (domestic work) now occupies a much more important place in their lives than before. Some aspects of this salience are positive, such as the feeling of being more autonomous and less economically dependant, but others are rather negative, and have to do with tensions related to the difficult juggling of care and work. Class and ethnic backgrounds shape both the meanings and the practices of these women's immigrant experience.

The meaning of "work"

Ecuadorian domestic workers tend to value in positive terms the fact of earning money. Besides material gains, which are strongly valued, especially by women coming from very poor backgrounds, one additional advantage is that work opens the possibility of life without a partner or husband, an option they had not contemplated before leaving Ecuador. Even though most of them had a job at home, their salaries were not sufficient to live alone. As one of my interviewees put it, "I am not afraid anymore of being left alone." However, this feeling is hardly grounded in reality. An immigrant working mother cannot live adequately on the salary earned by a domestic worker in Madrid, unless she leaves her children back home. Besides, even though women have tended to lead the migration process in many families, gender gaps in earnings are striking. The salary of a man in the construction sector, the most frequent occupation of Ecuadorian men in the cities, is double, and sometimes even triple, the earnings of a domestic worker. Hence, the sense of autonomy comes more from the availability of jobs and the possibility of working than from actual earnings. None of the women I talked to was afraid of changing or losing her job, not even those with rather unstable work records, something that is unthinkable in Ecuador, where the scarcity of jobs dissuades workers from quitting the job. What keeps immigrants in Spain from changing jobs is usually the regularization process. When employers offer a work contract with social security, workers remain on the job until they complete the regularization process. Flexibility under neoliberalism produces strategies to cope with precariousness.

Perceptions of work differ among generations and women from different social backgrounds. For working daughters it may mean more independence from parents. Even if they still live with their parents, they have more autonomy in taking decisions about their own lives on various matters, from economic to sexual. But this process of individualization is perceived as having certain costs related to status downgrading with respect to their former occupation or identity at home. Some young women who were students in Ecuador have gained more autonomy in sexual matters but do not find the opportunity to continue with their studies.

Enduring domestic work is frequently related to care responsibilities, particularly in downgrading situations. Matilde proudly told me that she had managed to bring over her five children, one by one, in the last 10 years, because she "works." Matilde has a high school diploma and worked as an accountant's assistant in Ecuador. In Spain, she has gone through different jobs, from live-in domestic worker to working for a cleaning company where she is paid by the hour. She said that it was her determination to have her children with her that helped her to endure jobs for which she is overqualified and where working conditions are difficult. In contrast, her younger daughter, whom she left when the girl was eight years old, is not happy with her new life in Spain. While in Ecuador, the girl went to school, thanks in part to the remittances that she received from her mother; now she has to work, caring for an elderly person, and she finds the job extremely unpleasant. Matilde believes that her daughter does not understand the situation and needs to experience "work" in order to appreciate what her mother has gone through on behalf of her children. While Matilde deals with feelings of frustration by convincing herself of the importance of "providing for" her children, the loss of status is not experienced in the same manner by her daughter.

Other women construct their domestic worker identity as a state of transition, as is evident in the following statement:

> You have to have a project and stick to that. Whether you decide to stay for five or ten years, you have to stick to that. I know I won't clean

floors all my life. I will go back home after saving some money. I want to have nice clothes, put on some make-up, look pretty. Here you don't even care about how you dress. Why would you care if all you're doing is cleaning floors?

(Magdalena, age 28)

Social mobility will not take place in Spain, but at home. As many other studies, as well as the statistics, indicate, very few immigrants go home, and the project of immigration tends to change dramatically over time. However, the dream of "returning home" is always present in the way they organize and justify their lives (Sayad 2004).

Downgrading situations may also bring ambiguities and blur the private/public divide. "I feel useful and useless at the same time," says Natalia (age 29), a live-in domestic worker who takes care of a four-year-old boy:

I feed him, I dress him, I take him to the school bus stop. ... I know he needs me, I know they (her employers) need me. But I also feel useless. In Ecuador, I supervised 20 people. Here my only worries are to get his clothes ready on time, to prepare the meals, to look after him.

Natalia grew up in a peasant household near a small town in the Ecuadorian highlands. Her parents owned a little bit of land and managed to give her and her sister a high-school education. Then she went to the state university in Quito and studied agronomy for a year. While at the university, she started working at a flower plantation near her home town, one of the many plantations that sprang up in the country in the 1990s as the result of state incentives meant to shift the economy to export-oriented intensive agriculture. Natalia quit her studies and accepted a full-time job. She soon went from being a simple worker to the role of supervisor. But the nation's financial crisis affected the plantation. Natalia was not fired, but she knew that she had no future there.

Natalia's feelings of ambiguity stem from her awareness that the job is unsatisfying in relation to her skills, and, at the same time, the sense of being trapped by the strong personal relationship that she has developed with the child and her employer. This ambiguity also comes into play in the way she sees her future. She wants to go back to school, but in spite of working with the same family for two years, she has not been able to obtain a work contract, so she remains undocumented.

Domestic work may represent not descending the ladder of social status, but the opposite. This is the case of immigrant women who were domestic workers at home. They moved from live-in situations in Ecuador to non-live-in jobs in Spain. Their current income is many times what they earned back home, and although they talk nostalgically about their former employers, with whom they developed maternalistic relationships, they have no doubt they have made the right decision. Domestic work in Spain represents for them entry into the public domain and a clear differentiation between private, family life and their job.

In sum, transnational strategies of social reproduction in globalization channelled women with heterogeneous social and occupational backgrounds into a single activity: domestic work. A sense of ambiguity prevails in their perception and experience of work. The public/private divide is not clear, nor do the women establish a clear positive balance of their experience in terms of social or economic mobility. Such ambiguity is due in part to class and generational difference, but also to the transforming gender roles that bring the migrant experience to women, and to mothers in particular. The centrality of work, the availability of jobs within a precarious setting, and the feeling of being a provider are some of the changes in women's lives that transform both the way they look at the future and the meaning of social reproduction. Besides work and connected to it, the different ways that migrant women and their families solve social arrangements around care, both transnationally and locally, are crucial components of the new migration experience. Ambiguous evaluation of the migrant experience is sometimes strongly connected with degrees of vulnerability concerning the care of children left behind, and doubts regarding the convenience of the new immigrant environment for those brought along.

Arrangements around care through women's stories

Unlike the Dominican, Filipina, or Peruvian women who came before them, Ecuadorian domestic workers do not seem to experience transnational motherhood for long periods, or as a unique form of social reproduction. Instead, social arrangements around reproduction are a mixture of complex family relations that usually include some children left behind with grandmothers and aunts, new children born in the community in which they are working, and husbands and other relatives in one or the other or both. Conceptions of the family and of the private/public divide not only differ from one site to another, but are transformed by the immigrant experience itself.

Estrella is a non-live-in domestic worker in Madrid. From a very poor rural background, she was a live-in domestic worker in Quito before coming to Madrid five years ago, one year after the arrival of her husband, a construction worker who had also worked in construction in Ecuador. When I asked Estrella to describe her day, she said that it starts at 7.30 in the morning and that she gets home every night at around 9 o'clock and is in bed by about midnight. Her eighteen-month-old daughter goes with her to two of the houses she cleans twice a week, and then to Estrella's sister's apartment, where the baby stays with Estrella's ten-year-old daughter, who goes there after school. Under the supervision of her aunt, Estrella's older daughter takes care of her little sister. Estrella cleans a school every day from five to eight in the evening. That is the job through which she obtained her work contract and her regular status. She meets her husband at her sister's place after work, and the family takes the "metro" home every day after nine.

This kind of childcare arrangement with a relative is very common among immigrant women. These are paid arrangements that usually represent a supplementary income for the relative. However, when the caretaker herself has very young children or is a grandmother, it is the only source of income. This kind of job is usually poorly paid and is perceived as the lowest level in the scale of domestic work.

Estrella feels lucky to have her daughter with her, especially as she has witnessed the suffering of her sister, who left three children behind. Indeed, Lisa, Estrella's sister, is a transnational mother. She started as a live-in domestic worker near Madrid. When she managed to bring her husband and two children, she moved to an apartment that the family currently shares with Lisa's brother. She now works as a non-live-in and supplements her earnings by taking care of Estrella's and another friend's children in the afternoons. Lisa feels very guilty not to have been able to bring her older child. On the other hand, Lisa has had many problems with her other two children, who complain about the lack of space and about being locked in the apartment all day.

The reproductive activities of these two women do not end with their children. They each take care of younger brothers who, though they are now working adults, live with their older sisters. Estrella feels she needs to protect her brother because the environment for newcomers is always problematic. Men without women tend to drink too much, she says, a possibility she finds particularly worrisome because in Spain Ecuadorian men are popularly believed to have drinking problems. She mentions that her brother has a girlfriend, also from Ecuador, and she hopes he will leave soon to live with her so that she can stop looking after him. Estrella is a guardian of sorts for her entire family, a situation that exhausts her.

Transnational arrangements and the children left behind

Many of the women I interviewed in Madrid have, or had, their children at home in Ecuador at some point in the migration project. A 2000 Ecuadorian national survey found that the number of children left behind by emigrant parents went from 17,000 in 1990 to 150,000 in 2000 (INEC/SIISE/ EMEDHINO 2000). Although family reunification has taken place quite rapidly in some cases, changes in immigration policies and current visa requirements for Ecuadorians entering Spain may have delayed this process and increased the number of children left behind. This situation has received extensive play in the Ecuadorian media, and this has frequently led to the stigmatization of the children and their mothers. A moral and psychological view that stresses the destruction of families and the loss of family values prevails over social, economic, and cultural considerations.

Educators and social workers have joined the media in reproducing these stigmas. Stereotypes of abandoned kids, potential gang members, teen pregnancies, selfish mothers, and broken families are in sharp contrast to the widely varying situations of emigrants and, above all, to the radically different views of the children about their situation (Herrera 2005b).

Social arrangements around reproductive activities are diverse, and vulnerability is a factor in varying degrees. Some children are left with their fathers and others with grandmothers and aunts; some children are cared for by paid domestic workers; and finally, some, the most vulnerable, are left on their own. The solution an emigrant mother opts for usually depends on two factors: the availability of remittances to pay a relative for care, and the degree of communication the women maintain with their children and their families. Both factors are the basis for reworking family ties transnationally. When remittances are sufficient to pay for education, clothes, and health care on a regular basis, and the carer receives a modest compensation, the emotional costs are somewhat counterbalanced. When economic and social reproduction are not guaranteed, the emotional costs rise. Besides, remittances are frequently the source of disputes among relatives, and this has negative repercussions for the children.

The perceptions of the children also vary. Some of them have a positive view of their mother's and father's project, but others express anger and frustration. A common feature in every situation is that neither mothers nor fathers discuss their decision to migrate with their children. For instance, most children learn of their mother's trip only a week, or even a day, before she leaves. They feel that it delays coming to terms with the situation because of the shock of the abrupt separation. In general, the process of reorganizing household activities after the mother's departure is very painful for them, especially for elder sisters, who, like grandmothers, feel they are not prepared to assume so much responsibility.

A second common feature is the development of a sense of guilt. Children are constantly told that their parents have migrated because they want a better future for them. Failure at school or misbehaviour is seen as a betrayal of the sacrifice of their parents. They carry on their shoulders their parent's migration. This feeling is frequently aggravated by a very negative view of their parent's experience abroad. Spain is identified with hard work, difficult housing, discrimination, racism, and loose moral values. This perception reflects the migration experience as constructed by the media in Ecuador, but it also has to do with the negative messages sent by their own parents, in part as a justification for why they did not take the children with them.

Finally, transnational ties are maintained through remittances. They are fundamental for the children's material reproduction, and frequently highly valued by them. But they also represent a symbolic tie with their mothers. Cellphones, computers, toys, and, above all, clothes are important signs of the presence of their parents in their lives.

Despite the different ways parents and children maintain family ties, reunions with their parents, either in Ecuador or in the country of destination, are experienced as strange, and sometimes painful, moments. Constrained transnational social reproduction brings separation to families, and it activates strategies to maintain family ties, and by doing so it also transforms "family" – both its practices and the meanings attributed to it. In that sense, reunions may tell us as many things as separations about changes in migrant families, parent-child relationships, and transnational motherhood.

Concluding remarks

The astonishing growth of the Ecuadorian community in Spain, which passed from 13,000 legal residents in 1999 to about 500,000 after the regularization process in 2006, is connected to the consequences of the informalization and privatization of social reproduction in two different settings. In spite of evident economic differences between the two countries, Ecuador and Spain share a crisis of social reproduction that puts migrant women and mothers at the centre of globalization. Such crises have been aggravated since the 1980s as a result of the intensification of economic globalization, fiscal austerity, and state reforms. These processes have direct consequences in the lives of an important proportion of the Ecuadorian population, and also in the lives of many families in Spain who are enabled to deal with the care of children and the elderly by the work of the immigrant labour force. Women and families at both ends of the transnational experience are being dramatically transformed. Changes in social arrangements of care as well as the meanings of domestic work are not determined by economic forces alone; states are crucial in reconfiguring social and economic policies and redefining people's frame of action in the transnational field. The experiences of Ecuadorian immigrant domestic workers in Madrid illustrate how structural and global processes of privatization of social reproduction affect different dimensions of women's lives and produce contradictory and unstable situations that can be both empowering and oppressive at the same time.

Notes

1 Field work for this paper was done in 2004 and 2005 under a New Century Scholar Grant from the Fulbright Commission. I thank María Fernanda Moscoso, Almudena Cortés, Fernando Barbosa, María del Mar Correa, and Noellia who were extremely helpful during my stay in Madrid. I also thank my colleagues, María Cristina Carrillo and Alicia Torres, at FLACSO Ecuador, with whom I discussed many of these issues, and each one of the members of the Gender, Globalization, and Governance team of the NCS, from whom I have learned so much.
2 The data for this paper come from 20 in-depth interviews of immigrant women in Spain (November and December 2004 and May 2005) and 35 interviews with

children and relatives of immigrant women in Ecuador (June–December 2004). The latter were done in conjunction with María Cristina Carrillo.

3 This number does not include persons who left the country by sea, en route for the coast of Guatemala and from there by land into Mexico and, finally, the United States, where the final destination is mostly Queens, New York City.

4 In 1999, as a result of the conjunction of three main phenomena – the dramatic consequences for agriculture and infrastructure of the "El Niño" phenomenon, the drop in oil prices on the international market (from US$18 in 1996 to US $9.20 in 1997), and the collapse of Asian markets provoking a worldwide financial crisis – Ecuador experienced one of the most acute economic crises in its history. Income per inhabitant dropped by 9 per cent, after having declined by 1 per cent in 1998. Unemployment went from 8 per cent to 17 per cent in the three main cities of the country, and urban poverty increased from 36 per cent to 65 per cent (Larrea and Sánchez 2002). By 2002, GDP per inhabitant was the same as in 1980, around US$1800 (Larrea and Sánchez 2002).

5 The category "poor" is used here following the parameters of the *Sistema Integrado de Indicadores Socioeocnómicos* (SIISE-Ecuador) to describe a person who has one unsatisfied basic need; "extremely poor" describes a person with two or more unsatisfied basic needs.

6 As Gratton noted, these data do not account for undocumented workers. Since Ecuadorian immigration has grown spectacularly over the past ten years, new data are needed for a more reliable analysis of the situation of immigrants.

7 This programme was negotiated with the PP after a traffic accident in Lorca involving the deaths of 12 undocumented Ecuadorian males. Immigrant associations organized a march and launched a series of protests that ended in negotiations between the Spanish and Ecuadorian governments which led to the regularization programme.

8 In this respect the Ecuadorian situation differs from that of other Latin American countries, such as Brazil and Colombia, that witnessed strong movements of domestic workers defending their rights during the 1970s and 1980s (Chaney and Castro 1989).

6 Managing migration

Reproducing gendered insecurity at the Indonesian border

Rachel Silvey[1]

Since the 1980s, as growing numbers of Indonesian women have migrated to work abroad (Hugo 2005), efforts have proliferated to monitor, regulate, protect, and govern these migrants. Noteworthy among these was the Indonesian government's opening of "Terminal 3" at the Soekarno-Hatta International Airport in Jakarta in 1999. The government founded the terminal as a site set aside to provide protection to Indonesian nationals travelling home after completion of their overseas work contracts. Non-governmental organizations and the news media had called for the creation of such protection in response to widespread reports of abuse faced by returning migrants at the airport and on their journeys home from the airport. However, rather than improving the airport's safety for migrants, the terminal has become a site of concentrated violence, harassment, and abuse. In this chapter I examine the question of how, in contrast to the stated aims of the terminal, crimes against women haven been normalized in the space, and I explore the repercussions for women migrants of the norms reproduced in this space.

The heightened insecurity that women face in Terminal 3 is not coincidental. Rather, government officials, as well as others involved in the "migration industry," participate actively in producing the terminal as a space where the subordination and abuse of women migrants are made to seem normal. Terminal 3 segregates returning workers from all other travellers entering or re-entering the country through the airport.[2] It is a stand-alone building located approximately 500 metres from the airport's other main terminals. In separating returning workers from other travellers, the terminal reinforces workers' and women workers' social difference. Government officials in the terminal practice a variety of management techniques that serve to reproduce social hierarchies of gender and class. The everyday social practices of state actors in the terminal both reflect and constitute the subordination of the gendered transnational labouring class. The purpose of this chapter is to examine the processes of gendered social reproduction that lay behind the creation of the terminal, as well as the socially reproductive effects of the terminal in reinforcing low-income women's social subordination. The chapter applies the disciplinary lens of geography to the examination of the terminal as a social space.

The discussion is organized into four main sections. The first section relates the theory of "social reproduction" to research on gendered transnational migration. This section identifies the specific contributions that geography as a discipline aims to make to studies of social reproduction. The second section provides some background on the Indonesian government's gender politics, overseas migration programme, and the overseas migration flows from Indonesia. The third section presents an empirical ethnographic analysis of Terminal 3, and reviews the findings of migrant rights non-governmental organizations (NGOs) on the consequences of the terminal. The conclusion discusses the implications of the practices in Terminal 3 for conceptualizing the changing spatialities of gendered social reproduction in "transnational" Indonesia.

Theorizing social reproduction in transnational migration research

Transnational migration is centrally tied to processes of social reproduction, both conceptually and in practice. In relation to migration, the concept of "transnationalism" emerged in the late 1980s primarily as a way to understand the relationships between migrants' incorporation and resettlement into new societies and the ties that migrants build and maintain with their homelands. Scholars had observed immigrants whose lives, actions, and points of reference spanned national borders (Glick Schiller *et al.* 1992). This work argued that research on migration should pay more attention to the relationships that migrants maintain with their origin societies. Glick Schiller (1999) defined transnational migration as:

> a pattern of migration in which persons, although they move across international borders and settle and establish *social* relations in a new state, maintain *social* connections within the polity from which they originated. In transnational migration, persons literally *live their lives* across international borders. That is to say, they establish transnational *social* fields.
>
> (1999: 96, italics added by author)

The emphasis on the "social" aspects of migration, and the focus on *lives lived*, are key to this early definition. It was through paying attention to migrants' everyday social and lived expressions – that is, the social reproduction – of their multiple national affiliations that these researchers came to identify transnational migration as distinct from previous forms of immigration. In particular, the emphasis on migrants' maintenance of social linkages between two nation-states differed substantially from earlier unifocal analyses of immigrant incorporation or assimilation into the receiving nation-state.

In addition to the conceptual linkages between social reproduction and transnational migration, there are also a number of practical ways in which transnational migration is socially reproductive. Katz (2001b) defines social reproduction as:

> the fleshy, messy, and indeterminate stuff of everyday life. ... Social reproduction encompasses daily and long term reproduction, both of the means of production and the labor power to make them work. At its most basic, it hinges upon the biological reproduction of the labor force. ... According to Marxist theory, social reproduction is much more than this; it also encompasses the reproduction of the labor force at a certain (and fluid) level of differentiation and expertise. This differentiated and skilled labor force is socially constituted.
>
> (2001b: 711)

For feminist theorists, social reproduction goes beyond the standard social science foci of state and market to include attention to biological reproduction, the reproduction of the labour force, and the cleaning, caring, and socialization work tied to the fulfilment of basic human needs (Bakker and Gill 2003a: 4). Transnational migrants are the embodied subjects of global flows and contradictions. Their labour and their mobility often support the social reproduction of workers in both origin and destination sites simultaneously (see Herrera, Chapter 5, this volume). For instance, many women who migrate as nurses, childcare workers, or domestic workers from low-to high-income countries leave their own children at home to be cared for by other relatives (Parreñas 2005). The costs of migrant women's own social reproduction from early in life have thus been borne by their own families and their countries of origin, thereby constituting a net subsidization by low-income countries of the costs of social reproduction for higher-income countries. Similarly, the women who carry out the cleaning and caring work in destination countries are themselves providing the social reproduction labour for the families of their employers while also often sending remittances home to support their own children's or other relatives' basic needs.

Recent transnational migration scholarship has paid increasing attention to the everyday mediations of exclusion/inclusion by the various actors involved in governing global circuits of migration. Attention to social reproduction is a subset of such theoretical efforts (Bakker and Gill 2003a). As global capitalist production has accelerated in recent decades, a parallel reorganization of social reproduction (Mitchell *et al.* 2003) has been associated with the feminization of the global labour force and international migration flows (Kofman and Raghuram 2004). Women, immigrants, and racialized minorities have carried out much of the labour necessary for socially reproducing the global labour force, and they have been located disproportionately in unpaid or underpaid, temporary, insecure, and informal labour market positions (Ehrenreich and Hochschild 2004; Yeoh *et al.*

2005). Lower-income sending nations promote the outmigration of their nationals in order to earn remittances, while higher income countries welcome the arrival of low-cost labour for short periods of time (ibid.).

Low-income women migrant workers are multiply marginalized along the lines of nationality, race/ethnicity, and gender, and they are vulnerable to a wide range of abuses before they go to work overseas (KOMNAS Perempuan 2003). Their marginality is then reproduced at multiple points along their journey, including the point at which they seek re-entry into the nation. Immigration gates in international airports are sites where states exert multiple overt forms of discipline and regulation. Attention to the socially reproductive practices of officials and official discourses in airport terminals can elucidate a key arena within which migrant women come to be discriminated against even in a space that was founded explicitly for their protection. I am interested in how the state participates, often at cross-purposes with its expressed agenda, in reinforcing long-standing gender and class hierarchies among citizens as they travel transnationally.

I argue that attention to the social practices at Terminal 3 can reveal a great deal about the ways in which the Indonesian state seeks to manage the social boundaries of the nation. The terminal serves to discriminate between those who can enter the nation's territory relatively smoothly and those whose entry is more actively governed. The terminal is similar to other borders, which Sparke refers to as "consequential condensation points where wider changes in state-making and the nature of citizenship are worked out on the ground" (2006: 152). Approaching the terminal in this way reflects several geographic emphases that are specific to my disciplinary reading of social reproduction. First, geographers have a long history of highlighting the social production (and reproduction) of space and place, as well as the spatial and place-based production of social relations (Mitchell *et al.* 2003). Rather than taking place as a backdrop or a container for social practices, geographers analyze the mutual constitution of the social and the spatial. For the present project, such a commitment entails focusing on the space of the terminal itself as a site of social reproduction, one which is both affecting and affected by the social actors in it and associated with it. Second, geography as a discipline is most interested in the *spatial components* of various processes, rather than, for example the primarily "cultural" or the "political/institutional" components. As a geographer, then, I am interested in how social reproduction occurs in and through space, how space and place contribute to particular forms of social reproduction, and in particular how the specific space of the terminal reveals the broader socio-spatial regulation of migrant workers in relation to the Indonesian nation-state.

Social space, according to feminist geographers (e.g. Rose 1993; Pratt 2004) is experienced bodily. Spatial mobility is circumscribed by gender, such that women's travel becomes the object of greater surveillance and policing than does men's, and women face the threat of bodily violence, both implicitly and explicitly, if we step "out of place" either socially or spatially. The norms that define women's "proper place" shift over time and according to multiple axes of social difference that are refracted in particular spatial practices. To understand this specificity for low-income Indonesian women who have worked overseas, I am interested in tracing the micropolitics and minutiae of the everyday in Terminal 3 in the context of broader state policies and discourses on women's overseas migration. Bringing these foci together pushes standard political economic approaches to migration to attend more thoroughly to the differences in migration across social groups, and to acknowledge the socially and politically constructed nature of categories such as "migration" and "the migrant" (Silvey and Lawson 1999; Leitner 2000). Rather than conceptualizing migrants primarily in terms of theories of rational economic behaviour, a feminist political economy of migration pays attention to the ways in which multiply differentiated gendered power relations shape migration processes and experiences. A feminist political economic *geography* of migration, then, examines such gendered power relations in relation to the gendered production of space and place.

The Indonesian state and the gendering of the overseas migration programme

The Indonesian government has been centrally involved in promoting and managing the movement of female domestic workers overseas (Hugo 1995). Beginning in the mid-1980s, the state's Department of Manpower (DEP-NAKER, *Departemen Tenaga Kerja*) developed programmes to improve overseas perceptions of Indonesian labour. It began to register and monitor Indonesian human resource companies (*perusahaan jasa tenaga kerja Indonesia*) that have been largely oriented towards training women in domestic service skills – how to use a vacuum, a blender, a dishwasher, or a dryer, and how to look busy (Rudnyckyj 2004). Also in the mid-1980s the government formed a unit within the Department of Manpower, named *Pusat AKAN* (*Antar Kerja Antar Negara*, Centre of Overseas Employment), whose mandate was to monitor and regulate overseas workers. The *Pusat AKAN* was charged with expanding the number of employment opportunities open to Indonesian workers abroad, and enhancing the capacities of workers to earn foreign exchange for the national economy. In order to reach these goals, the *Pusat AKAN* was expected "to foster closer relationships between Indonesia and other countries" (Adi 1995: 131, as cited in Spaan 1999: 159). Each year since it began sending workers abroad, the Department of Manpower aimed to send them in increasing numbers.

In 1983, the government began permitting private agents from Middle Eastern and East Asian countries to recruit Indonesian nationals to work abroad (Robinson 1991). The Ministry of Manpower promoted overseas employment to benefit the national economy in order to alleviate unemployment and generate remittances (Robinson 1991). The numbers of documented overseas migrants rose quickly in each successive five-year development period, beginning at a total of 5,624 in the first five-year plan (1969–74) and rising to 1,461,236 by the sixth five-year plan (1994–99; see Hugo 2005: 57). In the most recent period (1999–2004), the numbers of registered overseas migrants reached the highest level yet at 1,886,972 (DEPNAKERTRANS 2006). Approximately two thirds of the migrants have been women, and the majority of these have worked abroad as domestic workers (Hugo 2005).

The New Order government of Indonesia (1966–98) and the post-Suharto governments of B. J. Habibie, Abdurahman Wahid, Megawati Sukarnoputri, and Susilo Bambang Yudhoyono have all promoted low-income women's multiple domestic and transnational roles. They have all framed remittance-sending migrants as "heroes of national development" (Robinson 2000). Yet these same administrations have also, and perhaps increasingly, focused on women's piety and morality as a cornerstone of the nation's future development (Brenner 2005). While the emphasis on women as culture bearers is commonplace in national discourses around the world, when women migrate beyond the nation's territorial boundaries, their role in relation to national identity becomes more fraught. The state encourages them to migrate for the sake of their families and the nation, but migration removes them physically from both their families and the nation. This basic contradiction has been reflected in the government's ambivalence towards women migrants and in official practices at Terminal 3.

On the one hand, the state has framed itself as the paternalist protector of the citizenry. The New Order (1966–98) promoted the ideology of *azas kekeluargaan* (family principle), which located the ideal feminine subject within the domestic sphere. According to overt state gender policies, programmes, and discourses, women have been expected to sacrifice their own individual interests to the greater good of familial harmony and to thereby contribute to national economic development (Brenner 1998; Jones 2004). For example, the New Order state's gender ideologies defined women "as appendages and companions to their husbands, as procreators of the nation, as mothers and educators of children, as housekeepers, and as members of Indonesian society – in that order" (Suryakusuma 1996: 101). The New Order cast women in the roles of wives and mothers in order to contain both women and the family itself (ibid.). Yet the government has also aimed to include women actively in national economic development as both labourers and consumers.

Hundreds of thousands of Indonesian women have completed contracts as domestic workers in countries across East Asia and the Gulf States since the 1970s (Hugo 2005). Their work experiences vary depending on the laws and norms of the country in which they work and the particular employer who hires them. Most migrants who work abroad complete their contracts and return home with substantial savings to pay for their families' basic needs or to invest in land (Hugo 2005). Indeed, the landscapes of major migrant sending areas have witnessed profound transformations as a result of the income generated by migrants. Homes that were previously dilapidated have been remodelled, freshly painted, and adorned with new satellite dishes. Successful returned migrants bring home new appliances and electronics, new clothing, and in some cases enough money to buy agricultural land for their families. Growing numbers of potential migrants learn about these success stories and want to follow suit. Local non-governmental organizations are working in rural areas to harness the development potential of migrants' remittances for local economic investment.

Alongside the financial success stories, however, migrant rights NGOs have raised grave concerns about the lack of protections available to migrants. Reports have focused on the multiple abuses migrants have confronted, including widespread underpayment of wages, overwork, and physical and sexual harassment and violence. High rates of suicide and many mysterious deaths have also been reported (Hugo 2005).

In response to the stories of abuse, women migrants have faced intensified scrutiny from various sectors seeking to both protect and regulate them (Brenner 2005; Tsing 2005). Governmental and non-governmental organizations have focused on migrant women's rights and protection as key policy issues for the new millennium. The Indonesian government has itself begun to develop a growing number of new monitoring, policy, and support initiatives geared specifically towards improving the protections available to migrant women abroad (Silvey 2007). Terminal 3 is one of these new initiatives, and its social effects have mirrored the contradictory gender agendas underlying it.

Terminal 3: the social reproduction of gender subordination

This study grew out of my previous work on gender and development in a locale I call 'Sunda' (in Rancaekek, West Java, outside Bandung), where I have been working during a series of return fieldwork trips between 1995 and 2004. In 2000, in a survey (n = 85 for Sunda, based on random sampling via village registers) that I carried out to identify recent changes in migration patterns and the demographic composition of households, residents began to report growing numbers of villagers migrating overseas to work as domestic labourers. In 2002 I re-interviewed a sub-sample of respondents to analyze further the politics of transnational migration. Finally, in 2004 I worked with non-governmental migrant rights organizations based in Jakarta for two months and returned to Sunda to conduct an additional round of interviews with migrants. In Jakarta I interviewed some key political actors involved in Indonesian women migrants' rights struggles, as well as government officials and religious leaders.

All stakeholders in the "migrant industry" in Indonesia have focused in some manner on the airport and the immigration gate as a key site of regulation of and access to returning migrants. The establishment of Terminal 3 is only the most recent in a series of bids by the Indonesian government to monitor migrants and those who seek to profit from them.[3] The opening of Terminal 3 at the Soekarno-Hatta International Airport in Jakarta, Indonesia, was part of the heightened surveillance. The government designed the terminal, which opened on 31 August 1999, to provide state-regulated re-entry and vans for migrants returning to their villages. As mentioned above, reports by the news media and NGOs have detailed cases of rape, sexual harassment, and extortion faced by returning migrants both at the airport and during their journeys home (Tagaroa and Sofia 2002). The perpetrators of crimes against returning migrants are both members of organized criminal networks, individual criminals, and corrupt state officials (Wahyudi 2002).

The government claimed that building the terminal would enhance its capacity to protect women from the violence and harassment that migrants had commonly faced upon repatriation (Krisnawaty *et al.* 2003). As a group, migrants arc particularly vulnerable to these sorts of crimes for several reasons. In particular, overseas labour migrants, most of whom come from low-income farming families, are commonly visiting Jakarta for the first time when they fly abroad, and their limited knowledge makes them vulnerable to those who wish to take advantage of them. In addition, returning migrants often carry large sums of money with them, which makes them attractive targets for criminals. Finally, women travelling without male relatives are perceived as easy targets for other crimes as well, including sexual violence and harassment. In the terminal it was not uncommon for men to make sexually suggestive comments to returning women migrants.

The terminal segregates overseas workers from the other travellers passing through the airport. The bureaucratic procedures – for which President Suharto's New Order (1966–98) state was well known – have intensified over time at the airport. On 4 October 2001, the Ministry of Manpower and Transmigration put forward a decision to formalize a "Coordination Team for Tackling the Set of Problems Tied to the Placement of Indonesian Manpower" (*Tim Koordinasi Penanggulangan Permasalahan Penempatan Tenaga Kerja Indonesia*) (Wahyudi 2002). The team supported the continued operation of Terminal 3 as a site set aside for the exclusive processing of returning workers, effectively isolating and separating overseas workers from the other travellers passing through the airport.

Upon arrival from abroad at the airport in Jakarta, all international travellers, including approximately 600 returning overseas workers per day (Wahyudi 2002), are directed first to the immigration counter, where they have their passports inspected. Then, all passengers are directed to the baggage claim together. After retrieving their luggage, the "general passengers" (*penumpang umum*) are directed to customs and then permitted to leave through the regular exit doors of the airport. Returning migrant workers, however, are directed by airport staff to follow a "Special Lane for Indonesian Manpower" (*Jalur Khusus TKI*), which directs them to a holding area adjacent to the parked airplanes. Here they wait for the buses that will transport them to Terminal 3.

At the end of the five-minute ride, before the migrants disembark, a policewoman boards their bus. She stands at the front of the bus and delivers a scripted speech warning the passengers of the various dangers they are likely to face on their way home. She says, "There are many people who will try to steal your money. There are also organized crime networks that will try to take advantage of you. If you are a woman, they will bother you. We can help you avoid these problems." Then she shouts a series of drills at them:

POLICE: What will you do with your money? "I will put my money in the bank!" Repeat!
PASSENGERS: I will put my money in the bank!
POLICE: How much money will you carry with you? "I will only carry the money I need!" Repeat!
PASSENGERS: I will only carry the money I need!
POLICE: From whom will you accept a ride home? "I will only accept a ride from a formal agency!" Repeat!
PASSENGERS: "I will only accept a ride from a formal agency!"

After approximately ten minutes of such call-and-response exercises, the migrants are told to climb off the bus and walk on the painted lines on the ground into the terminal.

As the migrants enter the terminal, they are met with a government banner that reads: "Welcome, Indonesian Workers. Bring only the money that you need. The rest you can save or send via the bank. ... " Several messages are thus delivered. First, migrant workers are hailed by the banner that categorizes them as "Indonesian workers," and this differentiates them from other travelling citizens. Second, they are instructed against carrying their money with them. The implication is that migrants cannot take care of their own money; rather, they should trust the bank – which is, not coincidentally, the official government bank (BNI, *Bank Nasional Indonesia*). There is a branch of this bank, but no other banks, in the terminal, open and ready to accept deposits from returning migrants prior to their exit from the terminal. Through its messages about the bank, the government produces an image of itself as the legitimate provider of the guidance, information, and assistance that migrants are presumed to need.

In the terminal's large lobby, migrants sit on worn wooden benches waiting for the various monitoring tasks to be completed. Their wait prior to leaving the terminal tends to be between two and twelve hours longer than the wait for regular terminal passengers. At the various monitoring desks, migrants are asked a series of questions that probe their personal details (age, education, marital status, origin village), earnings, reasons for return, problems while abroad, health status, and location and details of employment. Migrants are expected to provide a higher level of detail and answer a broader range of questions than are "regular passengers." If they claim to have a health problem, or if an official suspects them of having one, they are sent immediately to the medical examiner, who is charged with providing a report on their health status. During the time I observed practices in the terminal, the women who were taken to the medical examiner's office went only reluctantly. They were not given a choice as to whether they wanted to be examined, nor were they offered treatment for their medical problems. Such practices again distinguish the treatment of migrants from other passengers, who are only taken to the airport's medic if and when they request treatment.

In the terminal, hung high on the wall is another large government banner, aimed at the porters, state officials, and vehicle drivers whose job it is to serve the migrants: "Let us make this arrival terminal safe, pleasant, and humane for the Indonesian workers." The implication is that safety, pleasantness, and humanity cannot be assumed. Rather, these are qualities that the terminal employees are expected to produce. By contrast, in the main terminal, the signs that are hung on walls for the staff merely remind them to be *rapi* (neatly groomed and "tucked in"). The Terminal 3 banner re-inscribes the difference between "the Indonesian workers" and other travelling citizens by marking migrant workers as in need of humane treatment, which the banner's subtext indicates they might not otherwise be granted. Finally, the banner distinguishes the terminal from other places where the guarantee of state protection does not apply. Similar to the policewoman's drill discussed above, the banner reminds workers that they are in danger of extortion, robbery, and sexual harassment if they do not abide by the state's prescriptions about when, where and how they should travel and what to do with their money.

Most migrants, both at the airport and in the sending village, had either sought an informal ("illegal") middleman to support their journey, or they had ended up with an unlicensed broker at some point along the way. It was almost impossible for potential migrants to know the difference between a formal, "legal" broker and the many illegal unlicensed free agents operating throughout the countryside. Indeed, often formally licensed front offices hired unlicensed recruiters as subcontractors. In addition, many individuals who worked during part of the day as formal government officials would also "moonlight" on the side to earn money recruiting, processing, and servicing the visa needs of migrants. Finally, even when migrants did register all of their information accurately and formally (a very difficult, expensive, time-consuming, and detailed series of tasks), they could not expect that government officials would treat them fairly. Rather, the rent-seeking behaviour of government officials was rife at every step of the migration journey, and a completely formal set of papers did not protect migrants from those officials working through formal channels to profit off of them.

Migrants were also faced with multiple other forms of abuse by both state and non-state actors involved in managing their migration and their employment abroad. Many returning migrants reported that their visas had been taken from them and kept by their employers (a common practice in several major receiving states), so that their in-country mobility had been restricted while they were abroad. If migrants in this situation tried to escape cruel treatment, for example, they would have to travel without papers, putting them in a particularly vulnerable position. Despite the dangers of travelling without papers, many found their conditions abroad sufficiently intolerable, terrifying, lonely, or brutal to prompt risking escape and attempting early return to Indonesia. At Terminal 3, these women were recorded as "having problems," and they were sent to wait in a room where "problem cases" were to be recorded. This small room had dirty walls; stacks of crumpled papers were strewn about in no apparent order; civil servants only wore parts of their official uniforms, and these were not clean or freshly pressed; and one very old computer was printing out reports about the migrants' problems onto the floor. While in practice this office may operate in a similar fashion to "the state" that "regular passengers" face at the immigration counter in the main terminal, there were few efforts made to produce even the appearance of formality, regularity, consistency, or legitimacy for these "problem" returning migrants or their peers. The arbitrary, disorganized practices of officials in Terminal 3 reflect the state's limited interest in providing regular protection or services to returning migrants.

After passing the various steps in the monitoring process, returning migrants then wait in line to be processed before their release from the terminal. The banner at the exit, adorned with official state seals (one presidential and one representing the government's "Team for the Protection of Indonesian Workers at Terminal 3"), reads: " ... IT IS FORBIDDEN to give money or goods of any kind whatsoever to the officials helping you, whatever the reason." The rule is aimed at controlling corruption, but its additional effect is to further differentiate migrants from other travellers. At the main terminal, tipping of porters and taxi drivers is commonplace. Because only migrant workers are so overtly forbidden to tip or bribe airport employees, the prohibition in effect reproduces the social difference and subordination of migrant workers relative to the "regular passengers."

Prior to the construction of Terminal 3, migrants had been processed at the regular immigration gates along with other passengers. Some migrants reported maltreatment and abuse by officials in these situations, and reports of robbery, disappearance, and rape were commonplace before the terminal was built. Indeed, knowledge of such problems and public pressure to address them lay behind the creation of the terminal at the outset. Yet segregating the migrants into a separate terminal has codified their difference from other passengers and other citizens. It also locates them as a group in an isolated space where maltreatment can and is directed at them en masse.

During the time I observed the terminal, officials detained, pushed, harassed, and yelled at migrants as a matter of course. And criminals waited at the edges of the terminal's gates, aware that everyone who is exiting is a returning migrant, potentially carrying large sums of cash. There is consensus among researchers and NGOs (KOMNAS Perempuan 2003) that crimes against returning migrants have increased since the opening of the terminal.

Upon leaving the terminal, migrants are required to ride home to their origin village in a vehicle registered by the government. Regardless of their capacity to pay for private transportation, they are not permitted to choose a vehicle or a driver, nor are they formally permitted to tip the drivers to whom they are assigned. Private taxi and van operators expressed frustration at this policy, viewing it as the government's method for funnelling the migrants' transportation funds into the coffers of a handful of select companies. Several drivers who were sitting outside the gates of the terminal said that they were waiting for passengers who managed to slip by the formal system. In contrast, in the general terminal passengers are permitted to choose whatever means of transportation they can afford.

Outside the gates of the terminal, families wait for days and sometimes weeks for the arrival of their migrant son, daughter, mother, or father. They camp out in tents and sometimes in family vans. The family members I interviewed had received one letter or a phone call from their migrant family member letting them know the flight's approximate arrival time, but usually there had been no follow-up communication. Their wait lies in sharp contrast to that of families in the regular terminal. The first difference is reflected in the information about arriving flights available at the two terminals. In the regular terminal, flight arrival information is posted on digital electronic boards that are updated with every incoming flight. The waiting area is comfortable, air-conditioned, and indoors, and food vendors have formal kiosks with refrigerators and stoves. In contrast, families waiting at Terminal 3 are required to wait outside the building, exposed to the Jakartan heat. When a flight arrives, the origin and flight number are announced once over a microphone, inaudible to many families who are waiting beyond earshot. Then, the name of each passenger is read aloud over the microphone. The waiting families do not know which day, much less which hour, they can expect the arrival of their family members. Their exclusion from the terminal serves to delimit the population for whom the state plans to provide space or resources for waiting. Separating out the families of the workers from the airport space codes the waiting families as different from and less worthy of service or comfort than those who come to meet the "general" passengers.

The overall socio-spatial segregation of the terminal is also gendered in several specific ways. First, the majority of the migrants being processed are women. In the autumn of 2004 when I observed the terminal, I estimated that there were approximately 10 women for every man passing through the terminal. In contrast, the majority of the employees, both civil servants and private sector employees, were male. The staff working at the immigration desk, the people monitoring the processing desks, and the van drivers were almost all men. Second, while the lead official in the terminal was a woman and had hired an all-woman police force to control the entrance doors and collect data from migrants, the policewomen were subordinate in rank to the mostly male terminal workers. The state had worked to provide a place where women in particular would be protected from criminal activity, but the terminal became instead a place where masculine privilege was reasserted and women's vulnerability was reproduced.

Gendered social reproduction

Terminal 3 does cultural work. As a space, it reproduces the distinction between returning migrant workers and the "general passengers." The everyday practices of the staff, and the banners hung by the government in the terminal, reproduce the subordinate status of the workers forced to file through the processing lines. The workers are segregated, drilled, and monitored in myriad ways that further reify their difference. As most of the workers are women, the reproduction of workers' marginality takes on a gender-specific aspect. The vulnerability of women migrants to extortion and sexual violence has intensified in the context of their spatial separation in the terminal.

Though this reproduction of gendered and classed inequalities is carried out in the name of protecting migrant workers, and women in particular, from crime, the securitization has, paradoxically perhaps, opened new doors to abuse. For scholars sceptical of the state's interest in protecting its nationals, much less protecting them equally, this heightened insecurity will come as little surprise. But for those interested in the ways in which the state produces particular spaces, the social reproduction of inequality in and through Terminal 3 may prove more compelling. The state has planned, built, and managed the terminal as a funnel through which the bodies and incomes of mostly female returning overseas workers are re-nationalized and re-territorialized. As workers file through the various monitoring procedures, their labour power is reclaimed by Indonesia. Yet they are simultaneously actively reminded that they do not represent the national norm.

Both sending and receiving states benefit from the reproductive labour of transnational domestic workers. Migrant workers clean and care for the families of their employers abroad, and their remittances often contribute to covering the basic living expenses of family members back home. All of their reproductive labour subsidizes both sending and receiving states' economic development. Terminal 3 represents one site within which the state participates in the social reproduction of inequality. The terminal is a local node in the network of technologies aimed at extracting surplus value from women workers who migrate transnationally. The terminal provides an illustration of the ways in which the territorialized nation-state manages to re-colonize migrant subjects who have temporarily moved beyond their nationally scripted spaces. The terminal puts migrants back "in their place."

But the contradictions that have played out in Terminal 3 also provide an entry point for thinking about geographies of social reproduction. Katz (2001b: 724) has argued that "space carries and reinforces uneven social relations." The terminal has perpetuated the national, classed and gendered inequalities entrenched in the transnational labour economy. Yet reorganizing space can potentially prompt the reworking of social hierarchies. If the goal of state officials and migrant rights activists is to ensure that migrants receive protection that is equal to those of "regular passengers," then the spaces of regulation and management should not be separate. Socio-spatial re-integration of migrant workers with other travellers will not of course alleviate the problems of abuse that migrants in particular face, but dismantling Terminal 3 will at least interrupt the social reproduction of inequality through that segregated space.

Notes

1 This research was supported in part by the US National Science Foundation, BCS-0422976. That support is greatly appreciated. I am also grateful to the Lembaga Ilmu Pengetahuan Indonesia (LIPI) for permission to conduct this project, and to the Fulbright New Century Scholars Program and the Rockefeller Bellagio Conference Center for further support of this research. My heartfelt appreciation goes to each of the New Century Scholars for their contributions to this work, and to Carla June Natan and Maria Hartiningsih for their input, without which this project would not have been possible.
2 See Silvey (2007) for further discussion of the history of the terminal and the practices of officials in the terminal.
3 The empirical ethnographic material here also forms the substantive basis of Silvey (2007).

7 Human trafficking as the shadow of globalization

A new challenge for Ukraine

Olga Pyshchulina[1]

Economic globalization and privatization have increasingly feminized poverty, forcing greater numbers of women worldwide to migrate in search of work (Aman 1993; Stone 1995: 987, 989). At the same time, as economic, political, and social transnational linkages expand beyond local and state control, globalization has fostered the growth of shadow economies and transnational criminal networks in newly independent states, including Ukraine (Hughes 2000). As a result, many transnational women migrants end up as victims of human trafficking, which "involves one or more forms of kidnapping, false imprisonment, rape, battering, forced labor, or slavery-like practices which violate fundamental human rights" (US Senate Resolution 82 on Trafficking, 1998). Increased migration allows members of organized crime rings to establish contacts with willing collaborators in diaspora communities throughout the world, and work within migrating populations to build transnational criminal networks. Increased migration also serves as a cover for traffickers transporting women to destinations in the sex industry.

The volume of trafficking has increased rapidly over the last 10 years. There are two plausible explanations: first, the demand for prostitution and other sexual services has increased in Western Europe; and second, because of their current economic and social problems, the former socialist countries in Eastern Europe form a source area from which the traffic in humans can be organized far more easily and more economically than from the old source areas (Anderson and Davidson 2004). This modern slave market is an extraordinarily complex problem because it is at once an issue of economic and cultural disparities, technological progress and sophistication, enhanced labour mobility, human rights, and the expansion of criminal networks. The monetarization of social and personal relationships in conditions of economic and social crisis leads objectively to the treatment of women as goods, to the growth of prostitution, and to trafficking in women.

One of the areas of the world where trafficking is growing fastest is the former Soviet Union (Levchenko 1999; Shelley 1999). Weak border controls and surveillance mechanisms at the newly created border lines between former Soviet countries, as well as partly insufficient visa regimes, attract traffickers. For example, Belarusian borders are highly vulnerable to illegal migration and trafficking in women because the border guards lack professional skills and appropriate technical equipment such as reliable transportation, communications, and computer networks. Ukraine's location at the crossroads of East and West and its transparent border with Russia have long made it a transit country for migrant flows from Asia to Western and Central Europe. In addition, because of strict control at the western border and the absence of any real mechanism for repatriating detainees, Ukraine has steadily been accumulating illegal migrants. Ukraine is a primary source country for men, women, and children trafficked internationally for the purposes of sexual exploitation and forced labour. The number of destination countries increased in 2005, with almost 50 countries serving as destination points throughout Europe and eastward, including China (US Department of State 2006). Primary destination countries include Turkey, Russia, and Poland. Other major destinations include the Czech Republic, Italy, Israel, Greece, Serbia and Montenegro, the United Kingdom, Lithuania, and Portugal.

Because most Western countries have imposed strict limits on the numbers of legal migrants who can enter their territories, many women are forced to accept the service of traffickers and/or to accept legal work in the entertainment sector as "artists" or "dancers" – in practice, often as sex workers. According to the Ukrainian Embassy in Greece, there are 3,000 young Ukrainian women working in legal or illegal sex businesses in Athens and Saloniki alone, and 5,000 in Turkey (Druz' and Hryshynska 1999: 88). Evidence exists from a wide variety of sources including police, non-governmental organizations (NGOs), health care providers, prosecutors, and international organizations of the widespread and increasing nature of the problem (US Department of State 2006; Minnesota Advocates Group 2000: 16). The International Helsinki Federation for Human Rights in its *Women 2000* report cites the figure of 100,000 having been transported across the border illegally since 1991 from Ukraine (2000: 491). Current estimates, however, appear much higher.

Human trafficking harms society in various ways:

- Injury to individual women victims. Trafficking networks may recruit and transport women legally or illegally for slavery-like work, including forced prostitution, sweatshop labour, and exploitative domestic servitude.
- Injury to communities. Trafficking in women as a shadow economy does not bring financial prosperity to local communities. The women often end up with nothing, or any money they earn comes at great cost to their health, emotional well-being, and standing in the community. Even the money made by the criminal networks does not stay in poor communities or countries, but is laundered through bank accounts of criminal

bosses in financial centres, such as the USA, Western European countries, or offshore accounts.
• Injury to the governments whose officials are either complicit in trafficking or unable to combat it effectively. Trafficking helps perpetuate systemic government corruption.[2] And its quick and continuous profits help fund the expansion of other organized criminal activities, as traffickers in humans are often also engaged in trafficking arms and drugs (Shelley 1999).

Causes of human trafficking in Ukraine

Many factors have contributed to human trafficking: rapid and varying economic and political developments; gender relations; improvements in transport infrastructure across borders; and widening disparities both within and across countries, accentuated by economic crisis. Economic and political reform has been slow in Ukraine compared to some other former Soviet Union (FSU) countries. Today, whereas some FSU countries are showing remarkable political, social, and economic progress towards stability and democracy, Ukraine is lagging behind in its transition. The most notable reason is governance. Ukraine has been hesitant to embark on the political, economic, and social reforms essential to democratization. The prolonged political and socio-economic transition has had severe implications, including the marginalization and, to some extent, exclusion of some groups from the social and political forefront. One of those groups is women, who have been marginalized through discriminatory policies practised by political parties, governments, and individual employers (Pyshchulina 2004).

Structural changes in post-communist countries have affected the everyday life and gender identities of both women and men in ways that have either predisposed or triggered violence against women. British sociologist Kevin Bales shows that such violence flourishes in societies under stress and in extreme poverty. Bales posits that

> existing power structures are overturned and a battle breaks out to fill the power vacuum. Economies that had been stable, though perhaps poor, are replaced by haphazard development and exploitation. And, as we have seen, in the absence of law, greed can overwhelm human rights.
> (Bales 1999: 245)

One of the main consequences of social change is the sharpening of social differentiation between a small number of very rich and a large number of poor people, with an almost disappearing middle class. This has important consequences in the creation of new masculinities and femininities, as well as in the emergence of different models of family and class relations (Hagan 1988: 171).

It is well known that contemporary population movements cumulate from individuals seeking, through migration, either to escape war, persecution, poverty, or human rights violations, or simply to find better economic opportunities (von Struensee 2000). With the collapse of communism, as Eastern European livelihoods were destroyed systematically by unregulated market forces and inefficient government policies, cheap labour became available to wealthier, West European nations. According to unofficial data, about 40 million people in Eastern Europe, the majority of them women, live below the poverty line. With the increase in poverty, food insecurity, and insecurity of livelihoods, people, in particular women, have been forced to migrate out of their villages into neighbouring towns, cities, and countries.

Increasing numbers of East Europeans are migrating legally or illegally, both internally and to other countries, in search of employment. Such migration has also taken the form of trafficking. The example of Ukraine very tellingly shows how a combination of economic transition and globalization-related factors pushes women into sex trafficking. Traffickers make use of the existing market demand and the women's need to find jobs. In this process, development of a market (neoliberal) economy plays a major role both by enhancing disparity and inequality between countries and by creating demand for women as sex objects. Disparities and inequalities influence the channels of migration in general, and the channels of trafficking in particular: they are the consequence of "the world economic order, of the distribution of wealth among nations and the exploitation of persons by others" (Konig 1997: 17). Thus trafficking channels go from developing countries to the industrialized nations and not vice versa. Trafficking in women and children cannot therefore be separated from globalization and livelihood issues.

There are both internal and external reasons for the increase of trafficking in women in Ukraine. The most important factors are the low standard of living and the practical impossibility for women to get employment in Ukraine. It is no surprise that the results of survey show that 80 per cent of women expressed the wish to work abroad. The restrictive migrant policy in the destination countries, the high level of internal unemployment there, and the Ukrainian women's lack of knowledge of foreign languages restrict official job possibilities, leaving them the "choices" of domestic labour and the sex industry, in its legal and illegal forms.

Internal reasons include first of all economic ones. In Ukraine the transition to a market economy has resulted in huge job losses and an increase in poverty. Recent studies and discussions in Ukraine on the subject of women's situation confirm that the political and economic changes have not been gender neutral. Women were the first to lose their jobs, and the possibilities of finding a new position are, to say the least, not promising, especially outside the big cities. Migration is especially popular among young women from small, underdeveloped cities and the countryside, where jobs are very scarce. In those areas, women cannot find positions in their own professions, as salespersons, teachers, or nurses, for example. Even if they do, those occupations are very low-paid and cannot assure economic independence. Women make up 54 per cent of the population of Ukraine and 45 per cent of its labour force. Over 60 per cent of all Ukrainian women have higher education (college level and above). However, the unemployment rate of women is very high compared to men with the same educational background (80 per cent of all unemployed in Ukraine are women), not to mention the extensive hidden unemployment among women. Given this context, it is not surprising that many young women are keen to find employment in the West and to travel to countries that for years have been inaccessible to them.

Numerous studies conducted in Ukraine during the last decade confirm this connection. According to the results of the all-nation sociological monitoring performed by the Institute of Sociology of the National Academy of Science of Ukraine, 10.2 per cent of members belonging to Ukrainian households have experience of temporary labour migration (Pribytkova 2002: 159). There are about 13 million households in Ukraine, which means that at least 1.5 million people went abroad with the purpose of gaining an income. In reality the number of labour-migrants is even larger, since in each household there could be several persons who participate in labour migration. According to the parliament's human rights commissioner Nina Karpachova, more than 7 million Ukrainians have to leave their country in search of jobs abroad, primarily because of poverty and unemployment. According to the commissioner, 27 per cent of Ukraine residents live in poverty. This figure is even bigger in the Crimea, Trans-Carpathia, and the Khmelnitsky, Kherson, Volynskaya, and Lugansk regions, where 33–40 per cent of the people are destitute.

Another motivation for Ukrainian women to migrate to the West is the disappearance of the state social security system.

The probability of becoming a victim of trafficking is greater for younger women, since young women are more often identified by themselves and by potential recruiters as sex objects. This is connected with changes in gender images about sexuality, which are mirrored in the explosion of beauty/fashion magazines and pornography in post-communist societies. Under communism, suppression of sexuality delayed the sexual revolution, so that post-communist social changes were seen as an opportunity to compensate for all that had been missed for so long, as well as to achieve individual instead of collective identity. As noted Bulgarian feminist historian Krassimira Daskalova says, "the message conveyed is that beauty is the most valuable female 'asset' and that every woman should try to make herself sexually attractive to men and to become a source of men's pleasure" (Daskalova 2001: 249). Media have reconstructed the traditional opposition between men's sexual needs and women as passive sexual objects and men's property, which is further used to justify violence and blame the victim (see www.globalizacija.com/doc_en/e0058sim.htm-_edn35#_edn35). Global mass media reinforced this trend through the circulation of stereotyped gender images "deliberately made attractive for marketing purposes" (Connell 2001: 61). Demonstrably, economic processes connected to globalization, such as rapid liberalization of trade and economies across the world, have increased the role that sexuality plays throughout public culture (Taylor and Jamieson 1999: 264).

The large gap between rich and poor increases the numbers of both prostitutes and their clients. Low income, especially among women, accelerates decline in the standard of living, and the country's gradual integration into the global market of exchange of goods and services.

Internal reasons include legal ones as well. First of all, Ukraine lacks regulations concerning slavery-like practices and the sex business, and lacks protection for the victims. Even those women who are ready to work as voluntary prostitutes within the country cannot bring themselves to effect. In a situation of lack of legal regulation and misunderstanding of the position of trafficked women and their human rights by Ukrainian policemen, women prefer to deal with pimps and traffickers, not with the police. They must find adequate jobs abroad, mostly in the illegal (because they are foreigners) sex business.

An important factor that facilitates sex trafficking is the development of organized crime, which is under significant influence from globalization (Williams 1997: 202). The confluence of these two forces has enabled the development of the sex industry, which is "based on and perpetuated by prevailing unequal socially and culturally defined gender and power relations." Traffickers exploit the fact that many persons are in vulnerable situations, undocumented and separated from their families. Immigration laws and policies in destination countries, including policies on migrant labour, migration, and prostitution, and corrupt officials in sending, transit, and destination countries further contribute to the development of sex trafficking merely by making organized crime possible.

Another reason for spreading of trafficking in women in Ukraine is the low effectiveness of law enforcement bodies directed at counteracting this phenomenon.

Psychological reasons, though insufficiently researched, are also very important. The general crisis has led to lowered self-esteem and worsening of women's psychological state. Assuming that "it cannot be worse," women agree to various dubious proposals without even considering the possible consequences. Both women's desperation and their efforts to find a solution contribute to their inaccurate perception of risks and failure to anticipate danger. The myth of an easy and affluent life in the West and the tradition of migrant workers further draw women in.

Proposals of employment abroad most commonly involve such kinds of jobs as waitressing, striptease dancing, singing or dancing in restaurants, massage, hotel maid work, governessing, cleaning, tutorial work, manicure, or seasonal work. Sometimes, women are explicitly recruited as prostitutes and know that they will work in the sex sector, but do not know they will be held in forced labour or slavery.

External reasons include both "positive" and "negative" ones. The "positive" ones are the opening of state borders and fall of the "Iron Curtain," and the increased opportunity for Ukrainian citizens to travel around the world, both for pleasure and in search of jobs.

The negative reasons are the internationalization of the shadow economy; the emergence of international criminal organizations; corruption among civil servants; and the inability of Ukrainian citizens to migrate legally to work legally abroad, which forces them into situations of illegality and violence.

In discussions on trafficking, particular attention must to be given to the question of the voluntariness of the migrants' movement. A neat line of demarcation between voluntary and consensual, and involuntary and non-consensual migration is widely regarded as deeply problematic with reference to refugees and economic migrants, and it is equally fanciful in relation to the issue of trafficking. If we consider trafficking (or even smuggling) as a process, the idea of "consent" is extremely problematic, since individuals can volunteer to enter the process and then find themselves unable to retract, however much they want to, or conversely, they can be coerced into entering the process but then proceed voluntarily.

In general the main causes of trafficking are as follows:

- Men's wish to buy sex.
- Women's increasing poverty, which drives women and children into situations of sexual exploitation.
- The economic policies of international lending organizations that mandate structural adjustments in developing regions of the world, forcing countries to cut back on social services and employment, thus driving more and more women to seek income abroad.
- Predatory recruiters who take advantage of this poverty to recruit women into the sex industry.
- Repressive immigration policies that cast traffickers in the role of major international players who facilitate global migration.
- A military presence in many parts of the world, which generates sex industries that are tolerated by governments, including our own, as rest and recreation venues for the troops.
- Racial myths and stereotypes that promote sexual exploitation, for example, in tourism brochures and on the internet, advertising "exotic women for sexual pleasures" abroad.
- Globalization of the economy, which allows the sex industry to operate across borders, actively recruiting girls and women, especially from villages, city streets, and transportation centres. Hotels, airlines, and charter companies, often with direct and indirect government collusion and corruption, are involved in the trafficking of women for, for example, sex tourism.

Mechanisms of trafficking: survey results

Research methodology

This study used both qualitative and quantitative methods for gathering information from experts. Our main method was the interview, because even the most advanced questionnaire would not provide us with responses to all our questions.

For experts, we selected specialists from different agencies combating violent crimes – deputy directors of violent crime units in a number of cities of different Ukrainian regions, as well as officers in other law enforcement agencies. For basic data on the structure of trafficking groups and their activities, we turned to police officers specializing in detecting or investigating organized crime, in particular, trafficking in human beings. The following categories of experts were selected for interviewing:

- investigators working for prosecutors;
- prosecutors at different levels, representing different divisions;
- police officers;
- representatives of the security service (SBU);
- representatives of the Ministry of Internal Affairs;
- lawyers;
- scholars.

The number of persons interviewed may be considered not significant enough to support percentage correlations, but such correlations allow us to get a clearer picture of the situation.

In the course of our study we discovered some "taboos." Thus, some prosecutors, investigators and SBU representatives were not enthusiastic while discussing human trafficking, but were much more open while talking about other crimes, such as rapes, kidnapping, etc. Investigators working for prosecutors and middle/high level representatives of the Criminal Investigation Department at the Ministry of Internal Affairs were the most open while being interviewed.

Qualitative study is supplemented by quantitative study in different regions of Ukraine. We surveyed various categories of people, including wholesale and retail businessmen, who were included because of their personal experience in international travel (in so-called shopping tours) and because they often discuss issues that are the focus of our survey. Compared to other social groups, entrepreneurs know more about the criminal transportation of people. At the same time, their opinions should not be considered to be absolute and should be weighed against experts' opinions. In addition, we used information from specialized publications and sources as well as comparative analyses of legal means.

Statistics are used at least for orientation, and when possible, we analyse concrete cases from file materials. Results from public opinion polls, and more technically oriented newspaper advertisements and articles can also be used to a limited extent. For research purposes, in accord with the Ukrainian criminal code, we use the following working criminological definition: Organized crime comprises repeated (systematic) acts of purposefully coordinated criminal activities (and activities supporting these acts), where actors are criminal groups or organizations (largely with a multiple-level vertical organizational structure) whose main goal is to attain the maximum illegal profit while minimizing the risk (via contacts in decisive social structures). Accidental criminal groups or organizations, the majority of white-collar crimes, and terrorism are thus excluded from the scope of organized crime.

Findings

All experts agree that the primary cause of human trafficking is uneven socio-economic development. One law enforcement authority stated:

> The impact on Ukrainian society as a result of human trafficking will be felt for at least two generations, taking into account the breakdown of social structures, depletion of human resources, and the many broken homes and lives in the wake of criminal forces taking advantage of the difficult economic situation in Ukraine.

The experts agreed that females are trafficked from all regions of Ukraine, from large and small cities (see Figure 7.1).

Almost 92 per cent of experts believe trafficking is a serious problem in Ukraine; 70 per cent think that trafficking is widespread; and 44 per cent claim they have personally come across trafficking. Representatives of the

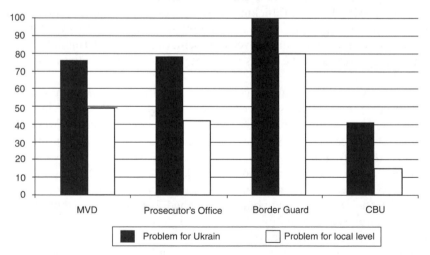

Figure 7.1 Is human trafficking in Ukraine a problem for Ukraine at the national level? At the local level? Opinions of experts interviewed, by category

Ministry of the Interior (MOI), procuracy and border guards all believe that the official statistics far understate the reality. Out of 430 females who participated in the study, 20 per cent claimed they had received job offers to work abroad. Six per cent said they would agree to work as waiters, 4 per cent as housekeepers, and 8 per cent as dancers; only an insignificant number claimed they would agree to work as prostitutes or would take any job.

All people questioned during this study were unanimous: human trafficking will exist in Ukraine until there is better social protection and the economic situation has improved. NGOs believe that the low level of legal awareness is another base for human trafficking (see Figure 7.2).

Our interviewees did not consider well organized criminal groups to be a significant factor influencing human trafficking in Ukraine, but it seems appropriate to treat this last statement as opinion, not as a reflection of the real situation.

In most cases what exists on the ground is individual recruitment, not well organized, which makes the issue even more complicated (see Figure 7.3).

Modelling, employment, and marriage agencies play some role, but individual recruitment obviously is the most significant.

Most experts agree that victims of human trafficking cross the borders of Ukraine using real passports and visas (see Figure 7.4).

When women first meet their recruiters, most do not have passports; in most cases the recruiters themselves process the necessary documents. According to experts, there are usually no or very limited violations involved in the issuing of the documents and some support of corrupt officials of the specialized passport service (see Figure 7.5).

But corruption is not so widespread as has often been claimed and is not often directly related to trafficking. In many cases officials just do not pay appropriate attention to the facts when the situation is obviously suspicious.

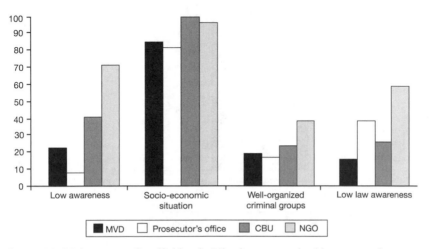

Figure 7.2 Main causes of trafficking in Ukraine as perceived by experts, by category

This suggestion was supported by reports that employees of specialized passport services are involved in trafficking. Thus, there is an obvious need to focus on preventive measures, as giving out passports to third persons may point to human trafficking.

Typical mechanisms of human trafficking

Viewed as a process, trafficking can be said to entail several phases: acquisition/recruitment;[3] transportation/transit, which may be across several

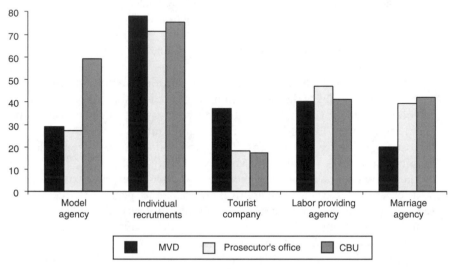

Figure 7.3 Systems of recruitment as perceived by experts, by category

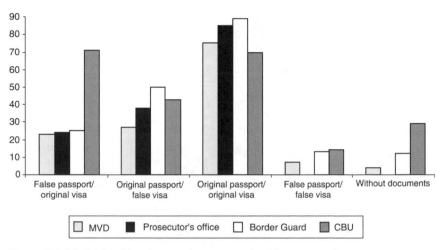

Figure 7.4 Methods of border crossing as perceived by experts, by category

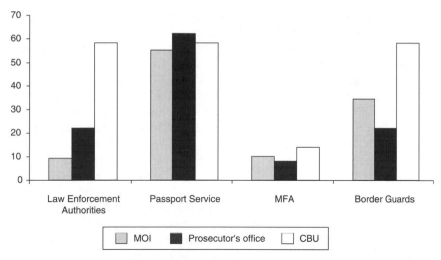

Figure 7.5 Involvement of corrupted authorities in trafficking as perceived by experts, by category

countries; and control/exploitation (illegal use of the physical abilities of a person with the purpose of gaining profit) in the place of destination. Different groups or individuals may be involved in different phases of the process, and can organize recruitment, transportation, and control in a variety of ways.

The first two stages of trafficking are carried out in Ukrainian territory, while exploitation usually occurs in some third country, beyond the jurisdiction of Ukraine. This can be done in a number of ways, which differ according to the purpose of the future exploitation.

Acquiring/recruitment

It is a fact that a majority of Ukrainians aspire to go abroad. They do so on their own initiative and voluntarily, driven by the difficult economic situation in the country. The ways of recruiting women for "employment" are varied and at the same time traditional and specific to this sphere. Of course these means are not being used only for illegal criminal business and trafficking in women (or human beings in general). There are lots of good examples of Ukrainian specialists finding legal jobs abroad or of Ukrainian women making happy marriages with foreign men. But there are some methods of recruitment that lend themselves to illegal migration and trafficking in human beings.

Advertisements for employment abroad are published in all newspapers that offer work to Ukrainian citizens. Content analysis of the newspapers *Robota dlya vas* ("Work for You"), *Aviso, Proponuemo robotu* ("Work

Offers"), *RIO* (Kyiv), and *Gorodskaya gazeta* ("City Newspaper") shows that each of the issues contains 5–20 "suspicious" advertisements addressed to young and good-looking women. Here is a typical example that gives food for thought: "High-paid contractual job in a night club for young good-looking girls. Full subsistence, free lodging. Travel passport required. Pay from US$1,000" (*Robota*), followed by the address where the interviews with the candidates are held. Or consider the following advertisement: "A dancing group is invited to work abroad," with a telephone number. A single newspaper may contain several similar offers.

Such advertisements offering work abroad are copied from national newspapers and local newspapers in large cities to the press in small towns and district centres. Young people there are more naive and accept less reliable information. It is very difficult to check such firms because of the absence of laws and the high level of corruption among police.

The same analysis revealed that generally about 80 per cent of newspaper job offers are for men (mainly within the country, but also abroad, particularly in Russia and the Czech Republic). Even where the job in question is gender indifferent, men are openly preferred. Only 20 per cent of the offers are for women, and the work offered is mostly sewing, housework, and secretarial work. Unfortunately, Ukraine has no laws against gender discrimination to stop such practices. No wonder Ukrainian women try to find their "work happiness" abroad, using every opportunity, even illegal ones. Still, fewer than 20 per cent of women who subsequently become trafficked persons go abroad as the result of answering the advertisements of employment agencies.

Realizing one's plan to find a job abroad is often difficult, because Western consulates impose restrictive visa policies to reduce the number of illegal labour migrants. People then turn to middlemen or agencies that specialize in getting visas. Such individuals and agencies actively advertise their services in mass media, but also resort to more veiled forms of labour recruitment. The criminal activity starts with the registration of travel documents.

According to experts, 84.5 per cent of the victims of trafficking request help from travel agents and visa brokers, whom they pay directly; 13 per cent of the victims refrain from saying how they obtained visas; and only 2.5 per cent receive visas without go-betweens.

We can distinguish five different types of agency:

- agencies providing legal tourist visas, insurance, and other required travel documents;
- agencies providing legal visas but organizing illegal jobs abroad;
- agencies providing false documents or organizing illegal entry to a country;
- agencies specializing in trafficking young women and providing travel documents, transportation, and employment abroad;

- agencies specializing in fraud, which promise to provide travel documents and highly paid work abroad but do not fulfil their obligations.

According to experts, a majority of the illegitimate firms have a "roof," meaning that they are controlled by organized crime. The organizations, especially those that provide clients with legal documents, have close contacts with officials, sometimes with the highest echelons of power. For example, there is evidence that governmental delegations have been used to smuggle people abroad.

A more widespread method of smuggling people is to give them so-called artistic or sports visas, and to include them in a well known arts group, ensemble, or sports team that frequently travels abroad. In some cases, officials have connived to form fictitious groups for the sole purpose of obtaining legal visas. Such frauds are usually executed by highly organized groups of criminals, controlled by "thieves in the law" or other criminal authorities. The cost of such services varies from $1,500 to $10,000 depending on the country of destination. Some agencies specialize in smuggling people to specific countries, such as Greece, where the standard price is $1,500. The Bulgarian/Greek border, the so-called "green corridor," is usually crossed with the assistance of local smugglers.

Some agencies and individuals specialize in manufacturing false passports and other documents. Normally they acquire the passport of a person who has a valid visa for a Western country, and simply replace the photo in the passport with that of another person – an easy change, since the photographs in Ukrainian passports are not affixed by a seal or other means of protection. It is also quite common for passport service officers to help people who have been refused a visa to acquire a new passport under a different surname.

In point of fact there is no clear-cut distinction between human trafficking and other forms of illegal migration from Ukraine. Frequently the same firms are engaged in the organization of trafficking and illegal migration, using the same methods of recruitment and transportation, and the same intermediaries for getting visas. However, the victims of trafficking are somewhat different from other illegal migrants, in that they are disproportionately female; young; unmarried, divorced, or living alone; from rural areas; relatively less educated and less familiar with their rights; with no prior experience of living abroad; and more willing to entrust themselves to dishonest middlemen.

Middlemen tend to prefer trafficking in women to other forms of illegal migration, because it is more profitable. Recruiters may

- contact professional prostitutes working in brothels, and suggest they continue their business abroad;
- invite girls to work as models, waitresses, dancers, or maids, and then uncoercively or violently engage them in prostitution;

- blackmail girls who owe money to commercial organizations or private persons, and force them into prostitution to pay their debts;
- get girls addicted to drugs, take them abroad, and then force them into prostitution in exchange for drugs.

The commission per girl is $2,000 to $5,000, depending on her age and physical appearance.

Transit

A majority of illegal migrants go to the country of destination in the company of other migrants. In 61 per cent of cases, the group is accompanied by its "enlister" or an assistant to the agent. Transit is carried out in different ways, depending on the legality of the migrants' transportation. Studies show that approximately 72 per cent of the migrants cross the border legally and use an optimum means of transport in terms of cost and time. In other cases, the migrants are treated as contraband. Firms that specialize in smuggling people organize the manufacturing of false documents, develop complex routes of transit, and have close ties with international organized crime.

In recent years the amount of human smuggling organized by travel agencies has increased in Ukraine, owing in part to the fact that many consulates have tightened their visa requirements, but also to the increasing number of Ukrainians who have become personae non gratae in different countries for different offences.

In practice, many illegal migrants manage to reach the desired country safely through the ramified network of transnational organized crime to which Ukrainian criminal organizations also belong. Trade in people has become so lucrative that criminal organizations take pains to perfect the chain from recruitment and transportation to safe exploitation of potential slaves in host countries.

Exploitation

A majority of migrants who become victims of trafficking are employed abroad through intermediary travel companies and agencies that operate legally in Ukraine. Usually migrants are accompanied by traffickers all the way to their final place of work. As a rule, the conditions that migrants meet in the destination country do not correspond to the promises given by the travel agency in Ukraine. Research has shown that trafficking is carried out for the purpose of

- acquiring slave labour (physical coercion, psychological coercion);
- sexual exploitation (prostitution and pornography);
- adoption (trade in minors);

- trafficking in organs (obtaining transplants);
- using women as substitute mothers.

Ukrainian governmental response

The government of Ukraine does not condone trafficking; indeed, it has taken a series of concrete measures in order to respond to this severe problem, and can now be said to be in the forefront of the criminalization of human trafficking in Europe. Among international instruments, on 15 November 2001 the Ukrainian government signed the Protocol to Prevent, Suppress and Punish Trafficking in Persons, Especially Women and Children, supplementing the United Nations Conventions Against Transnational Organized Crime, and in May 2004, Ukraine ratified the Protocol to Prevent, Suppress and Punish Trafficking in Persons, Especially Women and Children.

Domestically, in 1998, Ukraine added article 124-1, a law against trafficking in people, to its criminal code, making it one of the first countries in Europe to formally criminalize this offence by adopting a discrete anti-trafficking statute. In May 2000, Ministry of the Interior decree no. 319 created special units to combat crimes related to trafficking in persons within the ministry's main criminal investigation department and in the regional interior affairs departments. Special units for combating trafficking in persons have also been formed in the General Prosecutor's office and security service of Ukraine. In 2001, under the new Code of Criminal Procedure, responsibility for investigation of offences was transferred from prosecutors to police investigators.

The Cabinet of Ministers established the Inter-agency Coordination Council for Prevention of Human Trafficking as well as the National Coordination Council against Human Trafficking in the ombudsman's office. In June 2002, the Cabinet of Ministers of Ukraine adopted the National Ukraine Comprehensive Complex Programme Concerning Prevention of Trafficking in Humans for 2002–2005. Government departments that are involved in programme implementation have adopted specific programmes of activities; for example, in July 2002 the ministry of health adopted "Activities on Realization of the Complex Programme Concerning Prevention of Trafficking in Humans for 2002–2005." Finally, within available resources the government of Ukraine appropriates funds for prevention campaigns (public education, spreading information) aimed at eradicating trafficking.

Ukraine has tried a variety of measures, including education, prevention campaigns, and economic programmes. Among the government strategies, significant attention has been paid to the legal framework. In reviewing and considering legal measures to counter a particular societal problem, the legal and social contexts in which these measures will function are crucial. This is especially important when penal measures are considered. The criminal law is one of the most intrusive instruments in the hands of the state authorities with respect to citizens. The question is first and foremost whether this fits into the rule of law.[4] Moreover, it is important to distinguish between the law in the books and the law in action.

Conclusion

Trafficking out of Ukraine is a consequence of the difficult transition from a centrally controlled and planned economy. Millions have suffered in this transition to a market economy, where the state no longer assumes responsibility for all of its citizens. Trafficking groups have flourished with the decline of police control. Trafficking in people, as one of the most lucrative criminal businesses, spreads quickly in Ukraine, and is practically unpunished.

Low wages and arduous socio-economic problems breed the destitution of a huge mass of people, putting them at risk of exploitation. Women are perhaps the worst off. They are among the first to lose jobs, and they suffer from discrimination in the labour market and lack of social support. All this forces them to migrate abroad, thereby increasing their risk of falling into the hands of modern slave traders.

Trafficking in human beings cannot totally be prevented by developing only anti-trafficking laws and enforcement strategies. A multidisciplinary approach is required, including appropriate social and economic measures that address the root causes of trafficking such as poverty, economic disparities, and unemployment. Collective efforts by origin, transit, and destination countries are also necessary.

Notes

1 This paper is based on research which was made possible due to the Fulbright New Century Scholars Program – "Toward Equality: The Global Empowerment of Women." I am grateful to the Transnational Crime and Corruption Center, American University, Washington DC, for supporting this research. For helpful comments and advice, I thank Louise I. Shelley, founder and director of the TraCCC, Karen Saunders, Dr Sally Stoecker, John T. Picarelli and Kristin Kowalew.

2 Corruption plays a very special role in the reproduction of crime. Foreign experts place Ukraine among the most corrupt states in the world. Corruption of the law enforcement bodies and of the judicial system presents the biggest threat to society. In 1997, the Institute of Economic Development at the World Bank investigated corruption among Ukrainian judges. According to this research, more than 20 per cent of the citizens whose cases had been tried in the courts of first instance (district courts) had bribed judges with either cash or commodities. More than 30 per cent of respondents complained about unjustified delays, and 15 per cent about inappropriate behaviour by judges. Assessment of the current situation leads to the conclusion that corruption is an integral part of Ukrainian society and an independent system of social relations. At the same time it is closely linked with other spheres of social relations. There is an intricate system

of corrupt relationships at different levels of government and law enforcement, making corruption a constituent element of the whole system.

3 Some legal experts prefer the term "acquire" as opposed to "recruit"; see for example A. Repetskaia (2005) "Classifying the Elements of Human Trafficking Crime," in *Human Trafficking and Transnational Crime: Eurasian and American Perspectives*, Lanham MD: Rowman and Littlefield, 47.

4 The term "rule of law" embodies the basic principles of equal treatment of all people before the law, fairness, and both constitutional and actual guarantees of basic human rights. A predictable legal system with fair, transparent, and effective judicial institutions is essential to the protection of citizens against the arbitrary use of state authority and lawless acts of both organizations and individuals. Unfortunately in Ukraine, where the democratic tradition is weak and judicial independence is compromised, individual rights are not truly guaranteed.

Part IV

Social reproduction, health, and biological reproduction

8 Reproduction, re-reform and the reconfigured state

Feminists and neoliberal health reforms in Chile

Christina Ewig[1]

While women have traditionally taken on a large portion of responsibility for social reproduction worldwide, neoliberal policies heightened the costs of such responsibilities and shifted their weight more dramatically from states to markets, families, and women as individuals.[2] The transnational trend towards neoliberalism began in the 1980s, as advanced industrialized countries (especially the USA and Great Britain) sought to strengthen their economies using new economic principles. In contrast to the previous Keynesian economic model, neoliberalism prioritizes markets and market mechanisms over state intervention. It has been promoted on a global level, and especially in the global South, by international financial institutions such as the International Monetary Fund (IMF) and the World Bank as a means to promote economic and social development. In much of the developing world, neoliberal economic adjustment measures, aimed at stabilizing debt-ridden economies, led to high inflation and unemployment while state services were simultaneously cut. In this phase of neoliberalism state policy-makers relied on women to act as "shock absorbers" for community and family survival (see e.g. Tinker 1990; Benería and Feldman 1992; González de la Rocha 1995). Following economic adjustment, these states began to apply neoliberal principles to their social policies, privatizing significant portions of their social policy apparatus, reorganizing their public welfare systems to act more like markets, and transferring substantial responsibilities for social welfare from the state to women, as women became the permanent "volunteer" health and daycare providers for the neoliberal state (Lind 2005; Ewig 2006a). In the case of Chile, the move to market-based social policies shifted the costs of biological reproduction to women as individuals.

In this chapter I examine Chile's neoliberal health reforms, and how in the early 2000s feminists and their allies attempted to roll back neoliberal policies in the health sector "re-reform" process to claim societal, rather than women's responsibility for one aspect of social reproduction: biological reproduction. Chile was a forerunner in implementing neoliberal social policies, and it applied neoliberal principles in a doctrinaire manner compared to other countries. As a forerunner and as a country that has been held up as a model neoliberal reformer, Chile is instructive regarding the effects neoliberal social policies can have on the distribution of responsibility for social reproduction. It is also instructive as to the ways in which women, in order to reclaim the state's responsibility for social reproduction, must strategize in the new political terrain of the neoliberal "reconfigured" state (Banaszak *et al.* 2003).

Whereas scholars have argued that Chilean women's movements declined in influence and activity with the consolidation of democracy (see e.g. Waylen 1994: 353; Frohmann and Valdés 1995; Schild 1998; Baldez 2002: Ch. 8), I demonstrate that their lower visibility is due not only to a return to "politics as usual" but also to the reconfiguration of the Chilean state as a result of neoliberal globalization. In the context of neoliberalism, the Chilean state reconfigured itself by downloading essential social services from the central government to municipalities; by lateral-loading key decision-making to non-elected bodies; and by offloading portions of the welfare state either to private sector actors or to women and families. I focus on the consequences of this reconfiguration of the state for the division of responsibilities for social reproduction among women, families, and the state. I show that the reconfigured state has led to new forms of contestation between women's movements and the state, and that the reconfigured state also has led to gendered contestation within the state itself.

I begin by outlining the ways in which the Chilean state reconfigured itself in a context of neoliberalism. I then examine the consequences of Chile's neoliberal health sector reforms of the early 1980s for women, in which the Chilean state off-loaded responsibility for social reproduction to women in families and to private sector interests, and in so doing privatized responsibility for the costs of biological reproduction. The heart of this chapter focuses on the contestation between the women's movement and the state and contestation within the state to make social reproduction and gender equity a central focus of the re-reform of the Chilean health system during the 2000–6 period of centre-left coalition government under President Ricardo Lagos. I conclude with reflections on how the neoliberal state provides both opportunity and obstacle to advances in socializing the responsibilities for social reproduction.

Reconfigured states and social reproduction

Throughout this chapter I use the typology of shifts in state character developed by Banaszak *et al.* (2003), which they term "state reconfiguration." Banaszak *et al.* argue that European and North American states in the 1980s and 1990s underwent significant changes in structure and responsibilities due to conservative economic shifts inspired by neoliberalism. They argue that these changes are critical to understanding the new ways in which states and social movements interact and the changed character of women's movements from radical, autonomous movements to movements that are more "state-involved and accommodationist" (2003: 2). These authors limited their analysis to women's movements in Western Europe and North America. I apply their framework to Chile, show its importance for questions of social reproduction, and build on it to demonstrate that state reconfiguration also leads to particular forms of gendered contestation within the state itself.

Banaszak *et al.* outline three key structural changes in the state: "uploading," "downloading," and "lateral loading," and they point to a significant change in state–society relations that they term "offloading." *Uploading* refers to a shift in powers from the nation-state to supranational organizations. Unlike much of Latin America, where authority has moved decisively up to the IMF in the financial realm and to the World Bank and Inter-American Development Bank in the social policy realm, Chile has experienced minimal uploading. Chile is an outlier among Latin American countries in that it implemented neoliberal reforms before the hegemony of neoliberal thinking. Chile implemented neoliberal economic liberalization beginning in 1974–75, and neoliberal social policies in 1979–82. In many ways Chile was the poster child upon which the "Washington consensus" was modelled.[3] Chile's tenuous democratization in 1990, in which conservative forces were given disproportionate powers, has meant that Chile has not deviated from the global neoliberal economic consensus despite a lack of uploading.[4]

Downloading means the devolution of national responsibilities to subnational units. Also a forerunner in downloading, Chile transferred responsibility for state health services to municipalities in 1979, under the dictatorship of General Pinochet. But since mayors at that time were appointed, downloading was not a devolution of authority. Rather, it was aimed at diffusing responsibility for state services and thus decreasing claims on the central government. For women's movements, downloading multiplies the terrains where state public policies affect the division of responsibilities for social reproduction and where these policies must be contested.

Lateral loading shifts policy-making power from elected bodies to non-elected ones such as courts, executive agencies, and quasi-governmental organizations (Banaszak *et al.* 2003: 5). Exemplifying lateral loading, the decision to implement neoliberal policies in Chile was made by a small circle of advisors to General Pinochet. Even in contemporary Chile, now considered one of the most democratic countries in the region, lateral loading is commonplace. The danger of lateral loading is that issues become invisible to the public, decisions are insulated from civil society, and political questions may become depoliticized.

Offloading shifts traditional state responsibilities to private actors in the market or in civil society (Banaszak *et al.* 2003: 6). In Chile, common to both phases of neoliberalism was an "offloading" of the burdens of social reproduction more squarely to women as members of families and communities. But other forms of offloading have also been prevalent. Chile offloaded to private sector interests when it introduced private health providers into its previously state-dominated public health system. In addition, following calls from the World Bank for greater participation by civil society (part of the bank's own response to critiques of its top-down approach), Chile offloaded aspects of social service delivery directly to nongovernmental organizations (NGOs).

Discourses regarding the role of the state and state–citizen relations have changed dramatically in Chile as a premise for these state reconfigurations. Calls for universal citizenship rights, once frequent, have been replaced by views of the state as a provider of last resort with only limited responsibilities for maintaining the nation's "human capital." The concept of the citizen has been replaced, at least in those areas where market influences are greatest, with the concept of the consumer.

These changes in states constitute a new terrain for contestation over state policies – both inside and outside the state. While each element of change presents new challenges to women's movements, several also bring opportunities. As states have uploaded to international financial institutions, feminist activists have shifted their focus to these, and have had some success. The movement "Women's Eyes on the World Bank" succeeded in making the bank integrate the agreements made at the Fourth World Conference on Women at Beijing into its policies ("Women's Eyes" 1997). United Nations agreements on women's and human rights have served as crucial points of leverage for women's movements, even as states have sought to hide their politics through lateral loading (Keck and Sikkink 1998; Ewig 2006b). Moreover, women's ministries, gender budgeting, and other mechanisms that may provide access points for pushing the neoliberal state in new directions have been publicized through feminist global networks and facilitated by international bodies like the United Nations (see also the Afterword by Govender in this volume).

As states have downloaded to multiple policy centres, feminists have found it much more complex to pinpoint accountability for state policies. Yet in some instances decentralization has opened spaces for women's local influence (Ewig 2006a). When states offload, often the consequences are a shirking of state responsibility. Yet at other times it is women's NGOs that have been offloaded to, presenting unique opportunities for women and womens' movements to shape social policy from the bottom up (Ewig 1999; della Porta 2003; Valiente 2003). Moreover, shifts in social reproductive responsibilities have at times spurred women to contest state policies related to social reproduction (Brenner and Laslett 1991), making the consequences of offloading a potential spark for broader political change. Finally, concurrently with the new discourse of a minimalist state and citizens as consumers, there have emerged global human and feminist rights languages that have served as a powerful discursive counterpoint to the neoliberal discourse (Petchesky 2003).

The rest of this chapter focuses on Chile's health reforms and feminist responses to these, as an example of how the reconfigured state poses limits, but also new opportunities, for feminist interventions in state policies.

Chilean health reforms of 1979: privatizing reproduction

Before the health reforms begun by the Pinochet dictatorship in 1979, Chile had one of the most universal health systems of the region, with the majority of the population having access to health care services. It was divided, however, into separate but interrelated public systems. The old pay-as-you-go social security health system, the Employee Medical Service (*Servicio Médico Nacional para Empleados*, SERMENA), was designed to serve white-collar workers and civil servants, while the National Health Service (*Servicio Nacional de Salud*, SNS) served blue-collar workers and the poor. Blue-collar workers and the poor relied on the extensive SNS health infrastructure, while SERMENA beneficiaries could choose from SERMENA's limited number of hospitals and clinics, those of SNS, or private providers to whom SERMENA would pay partial subsidies. When created in 1952, SNS was envisioned by its proponents as a universal health system modelled on the British National Health Service (Labra 2002). While this vision was never completely attained, the universal citizen's right to state-provided health care was an important part of political discourse. In the 1970s, SNS supplied health care to about 60 per cent of the population, SERMENA served about 25 per cent of the population, and 15 per cent were either uncovered or covered by the separate medical programmes for the military and police (Cartin 1998: 206).

The major reform of this system took place between 1979 and 1982, a moment in which General Pinochet's regime was most coherent in its advocacy of a neoliberal policy approach (Kurtz 1999; Borzutsky 2002: 166). The reforms involved both downloading and offloading. In 1979 the SNS and SERMENA health systems were fused and restructured to separate their health policy, provision, and insurance functions. The funding portion was split into a new entity called the National Health Fund (*Fondo Nacional de Salud*, FONASA), which was financed by employee payroll contributions and state subsidies. Employer contributions were eliminated. The health provision infrastructure was renamed the National Health Services System (*Sistema Nacional de Servicios de Salud*, SNSS), with its primary care services downloaded via decentralization to municipalities and regional departments. Primary care was financed by municipal funds and fees for services (Titelman 2000).

The separation of the financing from provision cleared the way for greater participation of the private sector in health provision – and the beginning of offloading the most profitable aspects of health care to markets. The top income earners in the state health system were given the option of choosing private providers to whom the state system contracted out (Barrientos 2000:

100). These changes in turn allowed for the legalization in 1981 of Health Provider Institutions (*Instituciones de Salud Previsional*, ISAPREs), for-profit private health insurers with their own private health facilities. Once the ISAPREs were established, individual workers could choose health care coverage from the state through FONASA, or could buy this care through an ISAPRE. (There are two types of ISAPREs, closed ISAPREs that serve one company and are not open to non-employees, and open ISAPREs with whom employees individually negotiate contracts.)

Compared to downloading, offloading via the ISAPREs has caused greater detriment to equity in health care in general, and to gender equity in particular. In general terms, the ISAPREs led to greater segmentation and financial inequity in the health system. Initially, 11 per cent of total state health care beneficiaries moved to the ISAPREs, taking with them 48 per cent of overall health insurance contributions and deepening the financial crisis of the state system (Titelman 1999). As intended, the ISAPREs generated a greater role for the private sector, and in so doing caused greater segmentation along class and gender lines. Beneficiaries can return to FONASA, so Chileans use an ISAPRE during high-earning and low-risk years and return to FONASA when earnings drop and health risks go up. The flight of the best paid workers to ISAPREs at the highest-paying and lowest-risk moments in their lives further impoverished the public system.

The ISAPRE system reflects a strong male breadwinner bias. In order for women to benefit to the same degree that men do from the ISAPRES, women would have to have the same rate of workforce participation and wages equal to those of men. Because this is not the case, women are concentrated in the impoverished public system: 69.1 per cent of women, compared to 63.7 per cent of men, were affiliates of FONASA in 2000 (OPS-Chile 2003). Because only about 34 per cent of women are in the paid Chilean workforce, and even fewer are in the upper earning quintiles, ISAPREs, with presumably better quality of care, are an option for only a small segment of women, unless they are dependents on a spouse's policy. In 2001 women represented 34.4 per cent of ISAPRE beneficiaries (Ramírez Caballero 2001: 1). Women's participation in the ISAPREs drops faster than men's in their later years, signifying women's lesser ability to maintain the cost of the ISAPREs later in life (for figures see Pollack 2002: 26). Moreover, given women's lesser earning power in Chile (on average 40 per cent less than that of men), most women enrolled in ISAPREs are not able to pay for the best quality care, because an increase in quality and coverage requires additional premiums (Ramirez Caballero 2001: 218). The premiums for covering women, even as dependents, are prohibitively expensive.

Dependent entirely on the market, the costs of health care coverage via the ISAPREs are based on the risk factors of sex and age, a policy allowed under Law 19.381 of May 1995 (Casas 1999: 27). Because women experience greater morbidity, have specific reproductive health needs, and live longer than men, their "risk" of needing health care services is higher. But it is childbirth that is the primary reason why ISAPREs charge women more than men (Merino 2005 interview). At age 30, during women's peak childbearing years, Chilean women enrolled in the ISAPREs in the early 2000s paid 3.2 times as much as men for the same health care coverage (Pollack 2002: 20). Initially, ISAPREs were to cover the cost of childbirth, the cost of maternity leave, and family leave to care for sick children under one year of age (each being part of Chile's standard family benefits). In an effort to reduce the costs of leaves to the ISAPREs, the state (through Law 18.418 of 11 July 1985) accepted partial responsibility for maternity leave itself and for leave to care for sick children under one, assigning to the ISAPREs only the responsibility for pre- and post-natal supplementary leaves. Yet, even with this state support, and even if a woman were infertile or had no plans to bear children, she would still be classified as high risk, and thus charged higher premiums (López 1999: 8; Ramírez Caballero 2001: 2).

As a result of complaints that it was unfair to charge high rates to women who could not have children, insurers began to offer plans that did not cover childbirth, colloquially known as *planes sin útero* – literally "no uterus health plans." According to insurers, these plans were a benefit for women who had had hysterectomies (Merino 2005 interview). However, they were not marketed to infertile women, but to young women of fertile age, thus entailing the major risk that if they became pregnant they would not have the necessary health coverage (Casas 1999: 23, 25). Even in these health plans that did not provide maternity benefits, women 30 years of age were charged on average 207 per cent of what men were charged for the same health plan (Pollack 2002: 22). The "no uterus health plans" became a symbol of the discriminatory nature of the ISAPREs and their refusal to shoulder any of the costs of biological reproduction.

More evidence of discrimination against women by the ISAPREs was the fact that the differential rates were not confined to women's childbearing years – women paid more from age 20 until age 60, varying from three times as much as men to 1.2 times the men's rate. Only for males under one year old and over 60 years old was the rate higher than that of women (Pollack 2002: 23). Inequality in the ISAPRE system was also evident in exclusions, which were decided separately by each ISAPRE but tended to bar key services for women such as voluntary sterilizations or treatment of complications from abortions (Ramírez Caballero 2001: 2).

By offloading responsibilities for health care to the market, the Chilean state allowed two important aspects of social reproduction, health and bio-logical reproduction, to become the responsibility of individuals, and in the case of biological reproduction, the responsibility of individual women rather than the state or society. Under the Pinochet reforms, women in Chile were afforded high-quality health care to the extent that they could pay for this as consumers. The majority could not pay the discriminatory cost of the ISAPREs and thus were concentrated in the increasingly under-funded public sector – under-funded in large part because of the "cream-skimming" practices of the ISAPREs (Titleman 1999).

The politics of re-reform, 2000–5

In 1990 Chile underwent a democratic transition, since when it has been ruled in its first four governments by a centre-left coalition, the Coalition of Parties for Democracy (*Concertación de Partidos por la Democracia*), composed of the centrist Christian Democratic party (PDC), the Socialists (PS), the left-leaning Party for Democracy (PPD), the Radical Social Democrats (PRSD), and a handful of independents. Owing to institutional and political constraints on the Concertación governments as a result of the controlled transition to democracy, change in the neoliberal economic model was slow (see note 3). Women's movements in Chile had gained substantial visibility for their role in supporting democratization (Waylen 1994: 353; Frohmann and Valdés 1995; Baldez 2002: ch. 8). As party politics returned to Chile, however, observers argued that women's movements lost strength and visibility with the return to male "politics as usual." In fact, women made advances in traditional politics: voluntary gender quotas by the Concertación political parties raised women's formal role in politics to 15 per cent of congressional representatives, and in December 2005 Chile saw the election of the first female president in Latin America elected on her own merits – President Michelle Bachelet. The low visibility of women's movements was due not just to a return to politics as usual but also to a shift in the terrain of politics itself. As a result, women's movements had to shift their tactics in order to challenge the neoliberal, reconfigured state.

Following Chile's transition to democracy, gender equity in health reform was not a banner of the women's movement as a whole, nor even of the active women's health movement – these were more interested in the specific areas of violence against women and reproductive rights. The relationship between gender equity and health reform was, however, of interest to small groups in civil society, such as sub-groups of the women's health movement, social medicine organizations, and the nursing and midwifery professional organizations (Matamala 2005 interview). When health reform became an agenda item under the government of Ricardo Lagos in 2000, these groups were poised to make gender equity a central issue. By this time, there was a general recognition of a need to regulate the ISAPREs, strengthen the financially weak public sector health system, and better equip the health system to respond to changing epidemiological profiles. The Lagos government promised in particular to overcome the significant inequalities among Chileans with regard to access to care and quality of care.

The discussion and formulation of the health "re-reforms" took place in two parallel spheres: one in public forums and working groups initiated by then minister of health Michelle Bachelet (for a full discussion see Celedón and Orellana 2003), and the other in a closed technical commission led by a personal appointee and friend of President Lagos, Hernán Sandoval. Both the health ministry and the technical commission constituted areas of "lateral loading," in that neither was an elected body. But Bachelet's forums and working groups attempted to open up some space for dialogue, while the technical commission, which ultimately had the most influence over the reform process, remained closed. One women's movement activist described the latter commission as "absolutely technical" and commented that it "never discussed its plans with any type of organization" (Espínola 2005 interview). According to its leader, Sandoval, the commission's role was only to elaborate reform options for policy-makers to consider, and it was subordinate to the minister's authority ("Ministra Bachelet" 2001). In practice, parallel discussions took place and the technical commission had more weight and authority.

Organized feminists and their allies interested in gender equity in health sector reform had access to state health reform discussions via the forums and working groups established by Minister of Health Bachelet, but these were low on the policy reform process hierarchy.[5] Members of women's organizations participated in the civil society working group (Matamala 2005 interview). In addition, Bachelet also created a special commission on gender and health sector reform. In January 2001, this commission published a document that outlined a number of ways to make the existing health system more equitable. The document reflected the long-term interests and issues of the women's movement, such as reproductive health and violence against women, but it also began to move beyond these important issues to recommend financing based on ability to pay rather than risk, and shared responsibility for the costs of social reproduction – including maternity and childcare leaves and the cost of childbirth (MINSAL 2001: 34). The document was an important first attempt to integrate gender into the reform process.

When Bachelet left the health ministry and Dr Osvaldo Artaza took over, the document on gender was pushed to the side and the participatory discussion process was halted (Matamala 2005 interview; Gómez 2005 interview). "Lateral loading" decision-making to ministries leaves input from civil society dependent almost entirely on the goodwill of particular ministers to engage in dialogue and to take gender equity seriously. Bachelet was willing to do both of these, but the new minister was not; as a result, the spaces gained for intervention in the reform process were abruptly closed.

The technical commission was even more insulated from direct pressures from civil society, and from the political issue of gender inequity in particular. A former member of the technical commission reported that it was very difficult to get gender onto the agenda of this committee. For example, the idea of unpaid work remained marginal to the discussion, despite her efforts to incorporate this concept (Larraín 2005 interview). Testament to the greater powers of the technical commission was that its head, Hernán Sandoval, was also the representative of the ministry of health on the interministerial commission on health reform. Whereas the role of the technical commission was to develop a range of potential reform proposals, the inter-ministerial commission was the place where these proposals were vetted and formulated into bills to be presented to the Congress. The inter-ministerial commission was particularly important because it included a representative from the ministry of finance (*Ministerio de Hacienda*), which holds higher authority than any other ministry in that it evaluates and approves the financial viability of any major policy decision.

A key member of the inter-ministerial commission reported that the gender mainstreaming document developed by the Gender Commission and the proposals by the working groups organized by Bachelet had no influence over interministerial commission decision-making (Anonymous C01 2005 interview). To these influential decision-makers, the reform process was confined to the technical commission, the interministerial commission, and the Congress (ibid.).

Thus the re-reform process demonstrates a politics of contestation between women's movements and the state *and* a process of gendered contestation within the state itself. Although the reform debate as a whole was contained to lateral spheres of decision-making, Minister Bachelet's more participatory and gender-conscious approach was contested by other lateral spheres with a more decisive influence over the reform process.

At about the same time that Bachelet was replaced, an "uploading" opportunity appeared that was favourable for advocates of gender equity in health. In 2002, the Pan American Health Organization (PAHO) had been funded by the Ford Foundation to commence a project on gender equity and health sector reforms in Chile. Financial support from Ford and technical support from PAHO allowed key figures from the women's health movement to continue the work begun by Bachelet's gender commission, under the auspices of the PAHO "Gender, Equity and Health Reform Project."

One of the first steps of the project was to create a road map of the reform process, identifying the key decision-makers and decision-making spaces, and interviewing informants to identify the obstacles to gender mainstreaming the health reforms (Matamala 2005 interview). The interviews exposed a need for research and public education on gender and health reforms. The project commissioned research, and each time a document was published it was released with high levels of publicity and presented to the ministry of health, the parliament, and other key decision-making centers.[6] In this way, the project attempted to raise public consciousness of the discriminatory nature of the existing health system. For example, on 21 May 2002, just before President Lagos' annual address to the nation, women's groups published a newspaper ad that outlined ten key agenda items for a gender equitable reform, with many signatories, so that the president would feel compelled to respond (Matamala 2005interview). They followed this with a meeting of 400 women on 28 May 2002, led by

PAHO and several key women's organizations, to define proposals for a gender equitable health reform ("Las Mujeres" 2002; "Mujeres" 2002).[7]

An example of the potentially positive aspects of state reconfiguration, funding from an outside, international organization gave the movement for gender equity in health reform a level of legitimacy it did not have before. At one point, the project even solicited proposals for funding gender and health projects – funds for which the ministry of health applied. Also key to the success of the women's health reform movement were its ability to make inroads into lateral spheres such as the ministry of health, even in times in which the leadership was opposed to dialogue; its ability to build a base of support around the issue of gender equity and health in civil society; and its ability to develop research that matched the requirements of state technocrats in terms of data and technical language. In other words, women had to enter the political playing field on the terms of the state technocrats. This was a long process, however, much of which took place after the re-reform proposals were passed and had moved to the implementation stage. In the next section I discuss the reforms that were debated and passed and their implications for gender equity, before returning to a discussion of the role of the women's movement during implementation.

Re-reform and social reproduction

The Lagos government began discussion of re-reform of the health sector in its first year in office, and in 2002 sent a full reform proposal to the Congress. Two of the five proposed health-reform laws would have had important consequences for gender equity. By this time enough public emphasis had been placed on the discriminatory nature of the existing system (in part through pressure from civil society via the women's movement) that ending gender and other forms of discrimination became one of the primary motivations behind these two reforms (Anonymous C01 2005 interview).

One of these proposed reforms was to create a universal package of health services that each health insurer/provider would be obligated to provide to each of its clients. This was termed the Plan for Universal Access with Explicit Guarantees, or "Plan AUGE" (*Plan de Acceso Universal con Garantías Explícitas*). The plan was envisioned as standard in its components, universal in its coverage of all Chileans regardless of insurance type, integral in that it would apply to any stage of the disease in question, and total in that it would encompass curative and preventative care. To rectify long waits for care, especially in the public FONASA system, Plan AUGE outlined timelines within which care would be guaranteed. The plan would also guarantee a standard level of quality (Biblioteca del Congreso Nacional 2002; Anonymous C01 2005 interview). AUGE had important gender implications. By requiring that all health plans, private and public, offer a uniform set of minimal services, all of which included basic reproductive health services, the AUGE essentially (without directly saying so) outlawed the infamous "no uterus plans" of the ISAPREs and required that any basic health plan cover childbirth.

The other proposed reform key to gender equity was to create a compensatory, universal health fund, the Solidarity Compensation Fund (*Fondo de Compensación Solidario*), intended to make financing of the health system more solidaristic. Under this proposal, rather than pay their ISAPRE or FONASA directly according to individual risk, individuals would contribute from their salaries to a national fund. Each consumer would pay the same percentage of salary, while the fund would pay the insurers according to risk. In this way, the fund would serve as a cross-subsidy between the rich and poor, the healthy and the sick, between the high- and the low-risk, and between the private and public sectors – thus alleviating the disproportionate costs of health care that have fallen on the Chilean public sector. Moreover, the fund would address one of the main discriminatory effects of the health system: the higher prices for insurance charged to women and the elderly (Biblioteca del Congreso Nacional 2003). Thus, the fund was designed explicitly to address gender and age discrimination.

Of these two key reforms, only Plan AUGE passed through the Congress into law. As a result of the strength of the political right in Congress, and of lobbying against the measure by the ISAPREs themselves, the fund was modified to create only a compensatory fund among the ISAPREs, rather than a fund that would bridge risk between the public and private sectors. Thus the law that did pass defeated the main objectives of the reform. Yet women's groups did gain with the passage of AUGE, which challenged many inequities. Moreover, the women's groups that organized as a result of the legal debates continued their work and sought to influence the implementation of the reforms.

Implementation and perseverance

In the implementation stage of reforms, access points to areas of "lateral loading," such as ministries, become even more important. The implementation stage, by its very nature, is not a process of debate. Yet it is the stage which has the most direct influence on people's lives, and in which policies can become remoulded on the ground. When a more sympathetic vice-minister of health took office, the women's movement was able to make three key inroads. One was its successful insistence that the effects of violence be covered by the health system. This area had been left out of reform discussion altogether, but through simultaneous pressure, women's movements and the Chilean state's executive women's agency (*Servicio Nacional de la Mujer*, SERNAM) were able to place this on the health agenda post-facto (Lamadrid 2005 interview, Matamala 2005 interview).[8] Attention to violence began on a pilot basis in some health facilities in 2004, and was required throughout the system in 2005 (Matamala 2005 interview). The women's health reform movement also succeeded in negotiating with the ministry of health for the PAHO project to train ministry health professionals in gender sensitivity over a three-year period, beginning in 2005, part of the ironic "uploading" discussed previously (Matamala 2005 interview). A final focus was to account for women's unpaid contribution to health care. The PAHO project developed a methodology for accounting for this work, and began lobbying for this unpaid work to be calculated into the national health accounts system put together by FONASA (Matamala 2005 interview).

One of the leaders of the efforts to integrate attention to gender equity into the health system put it thus: "SERNAM has been our best ally" (Matamala 2005 interview). The very existence of national women's machineries is a result of uploading – acquiescence in the UN Convention on the Elimination of All Forms of Discrimination against Women, which encouraged the creation of state women's agencies. Chile was the first country in Latin America to establish an executive level women's agency (in 1991), a move which carried through with the CEDAW accords, but which also represented the Concertación government's attempt to meet feminist demands in the democratization process (Matear 1995).

But state women's agencies are also a form of lateral loading; they are points of access for civil society only if upper-level authorities are open to these interests. The relationship between SERNAM and the Chilean feminist movement has been highly uneven, fluctuating in its degree of support of feminist objectives dependent on the minister (Franceschet 2003; Ríos Tobar 2003). In the health reform political process, the women's minister made the political decision not to become involved (Lamadrid 2005 interview). By contrast, the subsequent minister, in the implementation process, chose to work closely with women's organizations to monitor the implementation of the reforms.

Beyond the commitment of the minister, what matters for the effectiveness of women's executive agencies is the degree of real authority these have over other ministries (Stetson and Mazur 1995). In the case of Chile, SERNAM in 2002 gained special authority over other ministries through a programme begun by the ministry of finance, called the Programme to Improve Management (*Programa de Mejoramiento de Gestión*, PMG).[9] A programme unique in the Latin American region, under the PMG, SERNAM is charged with assuring that each ministry meets specific criteria for integrating gender into its programming. If a ministry does not do so, it is penalized by budget cuts enforced by the ministry of finance. While the ministry of health began a number of projects to integrate gender more carefully in its programming, its efforts in many respects fell short of SERNAM standards. As a result, in 2004, the ministry of health did not pass its evaluation for integrating gender, and was faced with budget cuts. Since 2005, it has been forced to be more responsive to questions of gender equity, and this facilitated many of the recent inroads described above made by the women's movement.[10] The PMG give the women's movement, via SERNAM, important indirect access point to the politically influential ministry of finance which controls the national budget.

Conclusion

Chile under Pinochet was among the most neoliberal nations in terms of its social policies, relying almost entirely on the market to determine costs. Health reforms under Pinochet created a two-tiered public/private health system. The flight of the best paid and healthiest individuals to the private system left the public system – in which women were concentrated – underfunded, while those women who were able to access the private system faced blatant discrimination. The private sector shifted the costs of biological reproduction to women as individual "consumers". The fight over health reform under the presidency of Ricardo Lagos was in large part a struggle over whether the responsibility for social reproduction should rest with individuals or whether this was also a collective responsibility. In the re-reform process, organized feminists and their allies in the state sought to socialize the costs of social reproduction, in particular biological reproduction, while private sector interests, in the interest of profit, and more neoliberalist parts of the state sought to maintain the neoliberal status quo of individualizing this cost.

In the period of health policy re-reform, of the two policies key to improving gender equity in the health system, only one passed. The AUGE plan, which guarantees reproductive health care for all – in private and public sectors – and seeks to equalize the quality of care among institutions, can be viewed as a major advance for gender equity. But the solidarity compensation fund, which would have pooled health care "risk" between rich and poor, men and women, young and old, and the private and public sectors, did not pass. Important reasons why it did not are the entrenched powers of the private-sector ISAPREs as a result of 20 years of growing economic and political strength; the strength of the right in Congress in 2002; and lateral loading to the technical and inter-ministerial commissions where organized feminists and their allies had limited influence.

In the implementation stage, however, the women's health reform movement developed both more powerful points of access within the state, and new modes of communicating with the neoliberal state. First, the movement used the power of "uploading," via the support and influence of the Pan-American Health Organization, to obtain greater legitimacy and to develop more concrete data and evidence of gender inequity in the existing health system. This data in turn allowed the movement to speak more directly to the state technocracy, and explain, often in quantitative terms, the discrimination that existed in current policy. In addition, via the lateral sphere of the state women's agency (SERNAM), the women's movement gained a new access point within the state. The PMGs used by SERNAM to demand that the ministry of health implement gender mainstreaming or face budget cuts proved especially effective. This tool gave SERNAM power over other ministries, and gave the agenda for gender equity an upper hand in the ongoing gender contestation within the state.

The experience of Chilean health reform demonstrates that the reconfigured state poses both limits and opportunities for women's movements to challenge the current neoliberal social policy paradigm from within. The reconfigured state itself is a space of contestation – in which different parts of the state often have competing agendas and objectives as well as shifting degrees of power. Because much of this contestation takes place in competing lateral spheres, it is particularly demanding for women's movements to identify not only access points, but also the centres of power at any particular point in time.

The neoliberal, reconfigured state reflects two major currents of the transnational globalized age: the economically oriented technocracy that has dominated the state since the economic adjustment period; and the women's machineries that have emerged as a result of pressure from the transnational women's movement. Women's machineries can provide a foothold for women's movements only if these are given significant powers over other parts of the state, and only if these lateral spheres, as with all lateral decision-making spheres, open themselves to collaboration and participation with movements in civil society. Neoliberal technocracies such as Chile's ministry of finance are much more difficult points of access for women's movements. Yet, to some degree, by speaking on their "terms" of evidence-based positions and through innovative mechanisms such as the PMG, women's movements can also make some advances in this arena.

Notes

1 Research for this chapter was made possible by the generous financial support of a Fulbright New Century Scholars fellowship and by the University of Wisconsin–Milwaukee which granted me leave from my regular teaching duties to direct their study abroad programme in Santiago during the spring of 2005. I extend thanks to the many informants in Chile for their generosity of time and insights during the course of this research. For specific comments on this chapter, I thank the participants of the "Gender, Governance and Globalization" working group, and in particular Meena Acharya for her comments at our meeting at the Rockefeller Study Center in Bellagio, Italy. At that meeting and subsequently, I also received valuable comments from Isa Bakker and Rachel Silvey, to whom I extend my warmest appreciation.

2 See the Introduction to this volume for a definition of social reproduction.

3 Williamson (1990) coined the term "Washington consensus" to refer to the informal agreement among dominant international policy-makers in the 1980s on the economic reforms necessary for improving faltering national economies.

4 With the democratic transition, the right was designated nine seats in the senate and the open list electoral system was replaced with a binomial system in which the winning slate has to win two thirds of the vote; otherwise the second seat goes to the second largest vote-getter. This system has favoured rightist party

candidates. The military was also given budgetary and political autonomy. Recently the designated seats were eliminated, and reform of the binomial system is now a point of debate. For the first 10 years following democratization, these measures and a general fear of a repetition of the economic and social chaos experienced under the presidency of Salvador Allende (overthrown by Pinochet in 1973) led democratic Chile to stick closely to the neoliberal economic model.

5 There were four working groups: (1) academics, professional associations, and public health clients; (2) ISAPREs, service providers, and unions and clients of the private system; (3) civil society; and (4) municipalities (Celedón and Orellana 2003: 16).

6 The project's research papers can be found online at www.paho.org/Spanish/DPM/GPP/GH/ChileReform.htm

7 This was called the "Parlamento de Mujeres," or Parliament of Women, to which key government policy-makers were invited. The meeting has been organized for four consecutive years by the women's organizations Foro Red de Salud and Derechos Sexuales y Reproductivos.

8 SERNAM is not precisely a ministry. It is housed in the Ministry of Planning and Cooperation (MIDEPLAN) but the head of SERNAM has the status of a minister of state (Franceschet 2003).

9 The PMG programme began in 1999, but the gender measure, carried out by SERNAM, was added in 2002. For a full explanation of the mechanics of the PMG, see Pérez (2006).

10 It is important to note that organized women in Chile have rarely made advances in the arena of reproductive rights, where conservative forces, including the Catholic Church, have been vocally opposed to feminist positions. In these areas, even when the ministry of health has been willing to make changes, outside conservative forces have made limited advances. This dynamic could be seen in early 2005, when the ministry of health was ready to make emergency contraception available in state health clinics, but conservative politicians prevented this.

9 Working women, the biological clock, and assisted reproductive technologies

Wendy Chavkin[1]

Louise Brown, the world's first test tube baby, is now 30 years old. In the two and a half decades since she was born, births such as hers have increased at a dizzying pace. In 2002, some 33,000 American women delivered babies as a result of assisted reproductive technologies (ARTs) – more than twice the number who had done so in 1996. Additionally, more than double that number used ARTs unsuccessfully. The use of ARTs is even more common in Europe. At least a million, perhaps 2 million, babies have been born worldwide as a result of these technologies (Zegers-Hochschild 2004; OECD 2005). Over the same time, there have been dramatic changes in the way people in the highly developed world are leading their most intimate lives. Women now participate in paid employment; divorce and single parenthood have escalated; and women have fewer children and at significantly later ages, often postponing childbearing until salary and career are established (Fox 1994; Orloff 1996; McDonald 2000). This delay truncates their period of opportunity to become pregnant and successfully carry to term. A rapidly increasing number are resolving the discordance between employment trajectories and the biological reproductive clock by defaulting to the technological fix of ARTs. In the context of these demographic and social trends, this chapter will examine how technology is transforming the basic conditions and capacities of one aspect of social reproduction – biological reproduction – for an increasing number of women.

Why do ARTs serve as the path of least resistance, and is this good for women – for their health, and for gender equity? To answer these questions, we must revisit several critical insights of second-wave feminism regarding the centrality of social reproduction to gender equity and the related dilemma of separate or equal treatment of maternity, as well as the concepts of gender underpinning variations of the welfare state. In the last three decades, there have been dramatic changes in demographic patterns, the shift from a bipolar to a unipolar political world, the rise of "globalization," and the rapid-fire dissemination of a host of new technologies. I argue here that the delay in childbearing and falling birthrates is one consequence of these three entwined issues. I further argue that the technological solution of ARTs is problematic for women – and for children – and does not resolve the fundamental issue of gender inequity based on social reproductive responsibilities. I build this case by first discussing changes in birthrates and explanations that link this phenomenon to the (in)adequate provision of some social reproductive functions by welfare states. Next, I look at fertility patterns in specific welfare states as they respond to the economic pressures of globalization. I then turn to ARTs and state policies regarding ARTs. Finally, I weave these together to argue that both employment and social provisioning must address female reproductive biologic patterns, as well as social reproduction, in order to achieve gender equity and support childbearing.

Fertility decline: trends and implications

First, we need to understand fertility decline, one of a cluster of profound demographic changes that transpired over the course of the 20th century, with the pace and global sweep of these changes accelerating dramatically in the last few decades. These changes comprise reduced mortality and child-bearing and prolongation of the lifespan, and have taken place all over both the developed and developing world, although least in sub-Saharan Africa. In the developed world these shifts have been so dramatic that most European and "Asian tiger" countries now have fertility rates well below the replacement level of 2.1 births per woman (Lochhead 2000; Bulatao and Casterline 2001).

While demographers had anticipated that fertility decline would follow the mortality decline attendant upon improved living conditions and medical advances, they had expected birthrates to level off at replacement rates. However, the overall European total fertility rate (number of live births per year over the total female population aged 15–44, or TFR) of 1.4 is now significantly below the replacement level of 2.1. Sixty-four countries now have fertility rates below replacement levels (UN 2003b). In fact, a new term, "very low fertility," has come into use to describe the group of countries, such as Italy and Hong Kong, whose fertility levels hover near 1.0. While fertility is still above replacement in much of the developing world, the pace of the decline follows a similar trend. For example, although average TFR in resource-poor countries in 2003 was 2.9 births per woman, 20 of these countries had TFRs below replacement level ascribed to delayed age of marriage and first birth (UN 2003b) (see Figure 9.1).

Is this a problem? Together with extended longevity, declining birthrates have led to the "aging of the population", with a shrinking working-age population available to support both children and older, retired people (Lochhead 2000; Bulatao and Casterline 2001). The shift in the population age structure will determine the size and productivity of the labor force and have consequences for the tax base, social programs, and economic growth. Hence fertility is inseparably linked to the broad macro and meso questions referred to in the Introduction to this volume. The age shift will also have

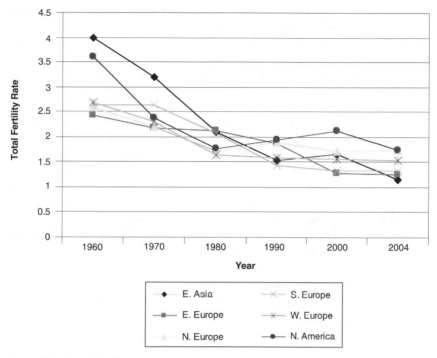

Figure 9.1 Total fertility, 1960–2004

consequences for disease patterns and health care needs, with chronic diseases and long-term care needs predominating (UN 2000; Brucker 2002). These changes, in turn, have profound implications for pension and health systems and could aggravate competition for resources between the old and the young. In fact, certain demographers argue that the focus of many current policy debates about population aging is too far downstream. For example, the US debate centers on social security, pensions, and Medicare without simultaneously addressing fertility (Garcia 2000).

Why have these changes occurred? While theorists differ regarding the contributions of specific factors, in general they agree that the decline in fertility is associated with the following demographic and social changes: mortality decline; increased longevity; urbanization; rises in female education and employment; changes in family formation, including delayed marriage and first birth, increases in divorce and out-of-wedlock childbearing; increased "individualism"; and technological advances in contraception (Sorrentino 1990; Oppenheim and Jensen 1995).[2]

Certainly, female employment has increased dramatically over the past decades, including the employment of married women and mothers of young children. Initially, higher rates of female education and employment correlated with lower birthrates (Sorrentino 1990; Oppenheim and Jensen

1995). More recently, demographers have described a new pattern in highly developed countries, termed "a world turned upside down," where very low birthrates characterize more socially conservative societies, such as those of Southern Europe. These low birthrates have been ascribed to tension among the perseverance of traditional gender roles, the lack of governmental support for female employment, and the expectations and requirements of women in these countries who do indeed want and need to work for wages (Chesnais 1996; McDonald 2000; Castles 2003). The demographers McDonald, Castles, and Chesnais see low fertility as a function of incoherence between the monetary and opportunity costs of having children and the social supports available. Put simply, it has become normative in the highly developed world for women to be educated and employed. When these opportunities are significantly reduced by motherhood, or the task of juggling work and home responsibilities is very burdensome, then women sharply reduce the number of children they have (Sorrentino 1990; Oppenheim and Jensen 1995; Chesnais 1996; McDonald 2000; Castles 2003).

Thus, certain demographers and welfare scholars now concur with feminist theoreticians that gender inequities in employment and responsibilities for biological and social reproduction are entwined and mutually reinforcing (Orloff 1996). Female responsibility for social as well as biological reproductive work is associated with occupational segregation and a gender wage gap virtually everywhere, even in the most generous welfare states.

Several decades ago, US feminists debated whether pregnancy should receive "special" or "equal" treatment. The equal treatment proponents argued that job discrimination would result if women were perceived as more expensive or less reliable workers. The special treatment advocates argued that a formal equality that did not respond to women's material circumstances was empty and failed to improve their situation. Recent experience on the ground has substantiated the warnings of both sides. Special treatment, such as maternity leave and flexible work conditions, has indeed made women less desirable to private sector employers, and has thus perpetuated occupational segregation and wage gaps by gender (Geduldig v. Aiello *et al.* 417 US 484 [1974]; CFSLA v. Garland 84–5843 [9th Cir. 1985]). Such benefits are geared to accommodate the double burden of women workers, and implicitly accept the gendered division of responsibility for childrearing and domestic life. Thus women remain disadvantaged in the workplace and therefore – circularly – have voted with their feet, so to speak, by having very few children. However, an equality model based on a male breadwinner norm, meaning one that does not acknowledge social reproductive responsibilities, has also left working women staggering under the double burden – to which they have again responded by delaying marriage and not having children.

There is emerging agreement among many European (and increasingly East Asian) policy analysts that policies most likely to support birthrates at levels close to replacement are those that enable women and men to parti-cipate both in paid employment and in childrearing responsibilities. These "work-family reconciliation" efforts include such measures as financial compensation for the costs associated with childrearing (cash grants, tax credits, subsidized childcare, access to housing, loans) and work conditions that enable employees to perform their domestic responsibilities (maternity and paternity leave, flexible work hours, subsidized childcare, tax structure that values "second" lesser income) (Cheal *et al.* 1998; Lochhead 2000; Laroque and Salanie 2003; OECD 2005). Through empirical observation of patterns of birthrates, family and work arrangements, and public support, such mainstream players as the European Union (EU), the Organization for Economic Cooperation and Development (OECD), and the United Nations (UN) have accepted feminist insights about the need to address social reproduction and gender relations simultaneously and support work-family reconciliation policies (OECD 2001; OECD 2005). These work-family reconciliation policies are, of course, predicated on a generous welfare state, one that provides some social reproductive functions, such as subsidized childcare or eldercare.

Policy responses and the current fiscal squeeze

Yet, concurrently, the rise of "globalization" – the increased role of transnational corporations and economic institutions (International Monetary Fund [IMF], World Bank, World Trade Organization [WTO], etc.), the increased interconnectedness of production and communication with reduced barriers to trade, and the increased movement of people for trade and work – has exerted pressure in the opposite direction, toward contraction of the welfare state. These "globalizing" developments have brought supranational actors into national social policy formulation, pressing individual nation states to cut taxes, regulations, and public expenditure and to increase job insecurity, and have spurred a global market of private welfare service purveyors that further undermine public welfare provision.

Analysts have debated the extent to which these pressures have actually led to significant welfare retrenchment. An emerging viewpoint is that the welfare state has proven remarkably sturdy, although resilience to these pressures has varied according to type of welfare state. While there is much scholarship and debate as to how best to characterize welfare states (Esping-Anderson 1990; Orloff 1996; O'Connor *et al.* 1999; Korpi 2003), for purposes of this discussion, the salient issue is how these varying models accommodate social reproductive needs. Welfare states vary significantly regarding such fundamental goals as redistribution or alleviation of dire need; whether the benefits are universally available or targeted to sub-populations; what the underlying ideological assumptions are regarding the desired relationships between the state, the market, the worker, and the family; and consequently whether they construct the worker, the family, or the individual as the recipient (Korpi 2003).

Welfare state models and fertility patterns

My focus of concern here is the relationship between fertility rates and welfare state provision of work-family support. Sweden provides a case of the model based on the individual, where entitlement derives from membership in the nation (including residents as well as citizens). Swedish postwar economic policy had supported high employment and wage compression, but the center-right government elected in the early 1990s responded to global economic pressures about inflation by cutting government spending and allowing increased unemployment. While Swedish benefits remained generous judged by international standards, they were significantly reduced compared to previous Swedish levels. By 1996 unemployment had risen to 7.8 percent, parental leave had been cut from 90 percent to 75 percent of salary, and child benefits had been reduced by 15 percent. Swedish birthrates, which had been among the highest in the highly developed world, dropped (Hoem and Hoem 1996). Similarly, the drastic reduction of family supports in the Eastern European countries following the end of the socialist era was associated with a precipitous decline in fertility. It is, of course, impossible to disentangle the cutbacks in social support for children and working mothers from the radical changes in the economy, governmental services in toto, and expectations for the future that transpired with the collapse of the Soviet empire.

While both examples of fertility changes are complex phenomena and one cannot simplistically, linearly ascribe cause and effect, the temporal associations between retrenchment and birthrate decline are consistent with previous observations, and certainly suggestive. In fact, it has now become mainstream opinion in the highly developed world that in order to maintain birthrates, societies must transfer some costs of childrearing from parents to the larger community, and provide supports to mothers with both employment and domestic responsibilities (OECD 2001). In other words, societies must assume some social reproductive responsibilities if they want to self-perpetuate.

Yet even this profound acknowledgment of the centrality of social reproduction to societal function can stop short of real gender equity. For example, some work-family reconciliation policies are intended to enable women to shoulder *both* domestic and workplace loads. Other such policies are more radical and tackle the gender assignment of domestic work, and thus try to restructure the relationships between biological and social reproduction and employment. France, for example, has increased paternity leave, with a small part paid for by employers and the bulk by the social security fund (Laroque and Salanie 2004). The Scandinavian countries have been pioneers in developing structural incentives for fathers to participate in childcare. For example, Sweden and Iceland mandate that fathers take a sizable portion of parental leave ("use it or lose it").

However, even the most resilient and generous of these states predicate many benefits on employment. Therefore, there are built-in structural incentives to delay childbearing until salary level and career status are well established. There is thus a discordance between employment trajectories and the female reproductive biological clock that disadvantages women both economically and biologically. The implicit assumption that the male worker is the norm goes deep. It extends beyond the question of social responsibilities and assumes male reproductive biological patterns as well.

The female biological clock and ARTs

The data on the female biological clock are incomplete but sobering. It is methodologically difficult to assess age-related changes in fertility, as a host of contributory factors complicate isolation of the age-specific component. These include behaviors, such as frequency of intercourse and use of cigarettes or other noxious agents, cumulative exposure to work or environmental hazards, and age of partner, who will have also had a similarly complicated life course trajectory. Estimates are derived from observing age-specific fertility in "natural" populations like the Hutterites (who do not use contraception) from worldwide survey data, and from studies of pregnancy rates following insemination timed in relation to ovulation. Results generally indicate that female fecundity begins to decline by the late twenties and drops very sharply after the late thirties (Frank *et al.* 1994; Dunson *et al.* 2002). Probabilities of pregnancy for women aged 19–25 are about double those of women aged 35–39. Spontaneous abortion rates also significantly increase with age, in substantial part because of age-related increases in genetic abnormalities (Frank *et al.* 1994; Dunson *et al.* 2002). The secular trend to delay childbirth thus leaves women a narrow window of biological opportunity for childbearing. Many are then demanding recourse to ARTs.

ARTs comprise a variety of measures, ranging from the simpler interventions like artificial insemination or ovarian stimulation, to ones where sperm and egg meet in the laboratory (in vitro fertilization being the most common and well known of this group). The latter group of procedures has low success rates (known in the trade as "take home baby rates") and both worrisome and inadequately studied complications. These include increased rates of pre-term delivery, low birth weight, perinatal death, certain specific rare birth defects, and twin and higher-order multiple pregnancies (Evans *et al.* 1995; Gleicher *et al.* 2000) – triplets, quadruplets, etc. Multiples are at increased risk of all the outcomes just outlined, and follow-up studies indicate neurological and cognitive deficits in long-term survivors of very low birth weight multiple births. There are heightened risks to women who carry multiple pregnancies. There are also biologically plausible theoretical reasons for concern about long-term consequences of the hormonal manipulations involved for women's health later in life, although this issue has not been well studied (Evans *et al.* 1995; Gleicher *et al.* 2000).

For Europe as a whole, about 22 percent of ART treatment cycles result in live births, of which approximately a quarter are multiple births, but success rates and multiple birthrates vary widely between countries (Anderson *et al.* 2004). In 2000, 22 European countries reported data on ARTs: approximately 856 cycles per million inhabitants (compared to 765 cycles per million in 1997), with a multiple delivery rate of 26.4 percent (compared to 29.6 percent in 1997), with wide variations by country (Anderson *et al.* 2004). The Centers for Disease Control reported a 66 percent increase in ART cycles in the USA from 1996 to 2001, with 36 percent of live births being multiple births (compared to 3 percent in the general population). Unfortunately, success for ARTs also declines with increasing maternal age (Wright *et al.* 2005).

Similar tensions are also playing out in the developing world, although very differently. As mentioned earlier, recent data demonstrate rapidly declining TFRs in much of the developing world, with 20 countries already below replacement levels (UN 2003b). In India and China, declining birthrates have exacerbated a longstanding preference for sons. People are using reproductive technologies such as ultrasound to identify fetal gender in order to selectively abort female fetuses on such a widespread basis that there is a significant imbalance in the sex ratio at birth (Mazumdar and Krishnaji 2001). In other developing regions, such as Latin America, accommodation to conservative Catholicism has restricted access to contraception, abortion, and ARTs. However, ARTs are available to those who can purchase access, are unregulated, and, because of anti-abortion pressures, can involve heightened risk for women and infants (e.g. prohibitions on freezing embryos can lead to exposing women to repeated stimulatory cycles, and prohibitions on discarding embryos can lead to transplanting less viable or too many embryos).

Policies regulating access to ARTs vary widely. One group of policies relates to public funding. For example, Singapore permits citizens to use their "medisave" accounts (semi-privatized health insurance accounts intended for old age) to pay for ARTs; Canada decided against public funding for ARTs because of low efficacy and high risk; Hungary provides public funding for ARTs despite limited funds for health and other benefit programs (Martin and Park 1999; OECD 2005). In the United States, 15 states mandate that health insurance cover ART (CDC 2004).

Other policies constrain access according to normative social values. Sweden, for example, requires applicants to demonstrate stability as a couple (Saldeen and Sundstrom 2005). Single women are not eligible for ARTs in Uruguay or Italy.

The last cluster of policies is directed toward medical practice. Sweden and Belgium permit implantation of only one embryo to avoid multiple gestations (with public funds – the private sector is not similarly con-strained) (Saldeen and Sundstrom 2005). Many countries set maternal age limits, as chances of success decline steeply past the age of 40.

These policies thus express a jumble of normative social constructs about family (which can contradict other policies – e.g. Sweden limits publicly funded ART use to "stable" heterosexual couples, even though its working family benefit structure is not similarly restrictive at all), cost, and concerns about medical safety.

Constraints on access and expense have led to the phenomenon of "reproductive tourism," where some seek treatment abroad in countries without regulation or with a less costly private sector. This pursuit leaves both purchasers and donors vulnerable to heightened medical risk and exploitation (Spar 2006).

Expanding the policy imagination

Declining fertility poses such a significant problem for the economic and social order of these highly developed nations that some have entertained structural – and political – adaptation. Thus, the EU and the OECD have sponsored conferences and commissions on work–family reconciliation, fertility decline, and gender. Both the EU and the OECD have formally stated that work–family reconciliation is a goal in itself (OECD 2001; OECD 2005). An OECD commission explains that work–family reconcilia-tion should improve the quality of life, increase the labor supply and national income, provide families with more secure income (including cases where the parents separate), lead to better child development outcomes, enable families to have the desired number of children (and thus increase fertility), and promote gender equity.

The penultimate point on the list is noteworthy. Repeated European sur-veys over the past several decades indicate that people's ideal number of children exceeds the number that they actually have and, while this average ideal number has declined over the past 40 years, it has stayed above replacement level for several decades (Bein 2000). Therefore some policy analysts argue that governments need not go the route of active pronatalism (for example, incentives for births or disincentives for contraception or abortion) to resolve the problem of fertility decline. Rather, the provision of infrastructural supports for social reproduction, to enable women and men to participate in employment and family life, will enable those who want more children to have them.

Feminists have often been suspicious of governmental concern about fer-tility levels and feared that even positive incentives might rebound to women's disadvantage and constrain their opportunities. However, one could construct the question as a human rights and reproductive rights issue, i.e. that a society should provide quality of life sufficient for its members to feel that it is possible to have children. The OECD formulation may assuage such concern, as it indicates acceptance of the Cairo-Beijing model of respect for individual decision-making and repudiation of coercion, as well as endorsement of the necessity of services and income to enable people to rear children.

The premise that social policy must address social reproduction or perpetuate gender inequity now needs extension – social policy needs to acknowledge two biological reproductive norms as well. Second-wave feminists called attention to gender as a social construction, separating the categories of biological sex and the associated social assignment of behaviors, obligations, and opportunities. I argue that now we need to explore the meaning of equity in both these domains and understand the ways in which they are interrelated. For example, policies could aim to reconcile the employment trajectory and the biological clock by providing family-supportive measures like access to housing, paid leave, and childcare through mechanisms other than the labor market, say during job training or advanced education. Such unlinking of benefits from salary attainment might enable childbearing at earlier maternal ages, which might, in turn, reduce the demand for ARTs. Currently, Singapore offers tax rebates for women who have children by specified ages; Japan provides home-based electronic continuing education and training for women on maternity leave; and the Czech Republic gives priority access and low-interest housing loans to newlyweds, with portions forgiven with each birth (Brewster and Rindfuss 2000; Sobotka 2002; OECD 2005; Library of Congress 2006). While none of these are provided within a framework that integrates the promotion of gender equity, work–family reconciliation, and fertility, they are nonetheless mechanisms meriting review for possible incorporation in a broader policy endeavor.

Conclusion

Feminist insights of the past 30 years about the centrality of gender inequity and social reproductive responsibility are being vividly confirmed by widespread declines in fertility. This is a dramatic development and one that provides us with the opportunity – and necessity – to deepen our understanding of the relationships among employment, social reproduction, gender, biology, the state, and global interactions. Even though there is uneven appreciation of the magnitude and importance of fertility declines, concern about fertility levels has led certain mainstream political players to support work–family reconciliation efforts as well as the promotion of paternal involvement in childrearing.

We need to parlay this growing concern into policies that enable women and men to choose both employment and children without financial hardship or biological risk. These demographic developments and political concerns offer the opportunity to advance strategies to redefine gender roles and norms related to social reproduction and work.

Notes

1 I am grateful to the New Century Scholars Program and the stimulating group of scholars, particularly the contributors and editors of this volume. I appreciate all those who shared their expertise in the countries I visited. Many thanks to Liza Fuentes and Molly Findlay for their help with research and logistics. My thanks to my gracious hosts in Sweden and Canada: Karin Schenck-Gustafsson and Zsuzsanna Wiesenfeld-Hallin of the Karolinska Institute and Evelyne LaPierre Adamcyk, University of Montreal.

2 Evidence suggests that increased exposure to environmental toxins has reduced sperm motility and viability, and may be a possible contributor to the global fertility decline. For further reading see Carlsen *et al.* (1992); Fisher (2004); Naha and Chowdhury (2006); and Swan (2006).

Afterword

Pregs Govender[1]

This book was conceived during a collaboration between a group of scholars and activists on "The Global Empowerment of Women," a Fulbright New Century Scholars Program (NCS). Our work is located in an increasingly unequal world characterized by militarization, war, and economic and religious fundamentalisms. As this book illustrates, contrary to general belief, the poor, particularly poor women, in fact subsidize the rich. Women and girls, as a direct consequence of their role in and responsibility for social reproduction, bear the brunt of poverty, violence, and HIV/AIDS.

At the end of our NCS collaboration, we concurred that:

> In this setting of increasing worldwide inequality, the path toward gender equality becomes more difficult. . . . Structural adjustment, state privatization and the expansion of market economies contribute to widening the gap between North and South, rich and poor, and men and women. In this context religious, ethnic and national tensions are used to obscure and justify material injustice. We see these processes as intertwined with continued violence against women, the feminization of poverty, transnational labor exploitation, the limitations on women's sexual and reproductive rights and the ongoing control of women's mobility.
>
> (Scholars' Statement 2004–5)

Our collective conclusion was that "the global empowerment of women depends upon going beyond gender neutrality and neo-liberal governance" (Scholars' Statement 2004–5).

This book is the result of continued collaboration within a smaller NCS group: Meena Acharya, Isabella Bakker, Wendy Chavkin, Christina Ewig, Gioconda Herrera, Hella Hoppe, Lakshmi Lingam, Olga Pyshchulina, Rachel Silvey, and myself.[2] We had been the NCS group on "Gender, Globalization and Governance," the "3Gs," in the contemporary nomenclature of acronyms. Our research into "social reproduction and global transformation" spans our work in India, Nepal, Ecuador, Indonesia, Chile, Ukraine, the USA, Canada, and South Africa.

This book uses "social reproduction" to refer to:

> both biological reproduction of the species (including its ecological framework) and ongoing reproduction of the commodity labour power. In addition social reproduction involves institutions, processes and social relations associated with the creation and maintenance of communities – and upon which, ultimately, all production and exchange rests (Edholm *et al.* 1977; Bakker 1999). As Bakker and Gill note: "In today's world social reproduction involves institutions that provide for socialization of risk, health care, education and other services – indeed many of the key elements of what the early Marx called 'species-being,' social institutions that distinguish the life of human beings from that of animals (Marx 1964)" (Bakker and Gill 2003 b: 18).
>
> (Bakker and Silvey)

Women's role in social reproduction is the production and maintenance of life itself. In a world that values war it should be no surprise that human life and the quality of life mean so little to those whose greed for wealth and power knows no boundaries. Those elected into government, wittingly or unwittingly, often collude with such forces, reneging on the political promise. This book highlights the contradictions between the myths and the reality of women's lives under neoliberal globalization. It reveals how the political choices of neoliberal economic policies devalue and commodify women's lives. The question is whether we and those who read this book will use our insights to contribute to global transformation. How will we use power, in whose interests and to what end? Will we use the power and leadership each and every one of us has to transform ourselves and our world?

In Lakshmi Lingam's chapter on microcredit programmes and women's empowerment, she draws on research in the Telengana region of Andhra Pradesh, the site of the 1947 "women's resistance" that demanded an end to restrictions on women's employment and called for maternity leave, the right to own property equally with men, a ban on marriage for women under 18, and women's education. Between 2004 and 2005, Lingam's research with 300 women from three villages, the majority of whom belonged to the "Hindu backward and scheduled castes," found that 92 per cent were illiterate and predominantly landless agricultural wage workers. Lingam notes that during her research, the women "'expressed the changes they experienced in being part of collectives (*sangha*) as increase in *dhairyam* (self-confidence) and *thelivi* (awareness).'" She concludes from her interviews that "definitions of empowerment encompass change within the material and ideological arenas and women's collective 'power to' bring about these changes externally as well as their 'power within'" (Lingam, Chapter 4, this volume)

Is there a role for *dhairyam* (self-confidence) and *thelivi* (awareness), for "power within" and "collective power" in redefining power to maintain and deepen the material gains women make? How are the endless vicious cycles from Telengana to the Soviet Union broken? Women win important victories at different points in history, make herstory, and then are beaten back. The changes to the constitution and laws that women like Alexandra Kollantai, the first Commissar for Social Welfare in 1917, enacted in the Soviet Union were potentially far-reaching for women. Apart from the right to vote, women won legal equality, the right to free abortion and free divorce, workplace and community crèches, two months' paid maternity leave, and paid "nursing breaks" at work. Wife beating was made illegal. Housing communes and clinics, nurseries and maternity homes were built. Yet by 1936, anti-abortion and anti-divorce laws were enacted, homosexuality was banned, and Stalin introduced the "Order of Maternal Glory" for women who had seven or more children. The erosion of the rights women had won in 1917 worsened with the transition to a market economy where the state no longer assumes responsibility for all of its citizens:

> Low wages and arduous socio-economic problems breed destitution of a huge mass of people, putting them at risk of exploitation. Women are perhaps the worst off. They are among the first to lose jobs, and they suffer from discrimination in the labour market and lack of social support.
>
> (Pyshchulina, Chapter 7, this volume)

This afterword argues that a redefinition of power and leadership is necessary to ensure that agendas and programmes for transformation are not co-opted by local or global patriarchies. It draws on research into activism based on an alternative notion of power and leadership. It challenges the current hegemonic world view and its values, priorities, and choices, which while paying lip-service to "gender equality" and "poverty eradication" directly undermine both. It argues that power and leadership can be redefined by, and in the interests of, the poorest and the "powerless." It names this the transformative power and leadership of love and courage. Such power can inspire a lifelong commitment to transforming the deeply ingrained, dominant, destructive understanding and practice of power within ourselves and in our world. An example of such practice is reflected in the words of Nelson Rohlihlala Mandela: "If 27 years in prison have done anything to us, it was to use the silence of solitude to make us understand how precious words are and how real their impact is on the way people live and die" (Mandela 2000). In this "age of information," when the World Bank markets itself as the "Knowledge Bank," when we are bombarded with "information" at every turn, we can use "the silence of solitude" to develop our ability to discern what information is in our interests, individually and collectively, and strengthen our ability and wisdom to act with love and courage. Collectives are as powerful or as weak as the individuals who constitute them. We cannot allow our movements to implode as we destroy the vision, our agenda for change, ourselves, and each other. Transforming the *internalized* authoritarianism of misogyny, racism, class, and caste is the missing objective of too many failed local and global projects for change.

At one of its simplest levels, power is defined as the energy to make change happen. The dominant understanding and exercise of power is too often premised on the negation or destruction of self and community. This authoritarian notion of power vests authority elsewhere – in the parent, husband, leader, or political, economic, religious, and other social institutions – away from self and community – away from the potential leader within every one of us. It is often coated in a benign form: the parent beats the child "for her own good"; the man gives his wife a black eye, red roses, and chocolates; the global institutions prescribe that our countries should follow the neoliberal agenda of privatization, trade liberalization, etc. with the promise that this will create jobs and increase foreign direct investment. Neither materializes; instead, unemployment and poverty worsen. War, we are told, is waged to end terror, free women, and ensure democracy, peace, and civilization, but Amnesty International and the United Nations reports expose the effects of war as the exact opposite. The religious right across the globe, in its quest to control and cover women's bodies, proclaims that its authority is derived from no less a power than "God himself," who is anti-condoms and dictates abstention and the murder of pro-choice doctors.

This hate, fear, and violence are all too often couched in some warm, fuzzy glow – "love" is deployed to justify atrocity. But we know, in the deepest part of ourselves, that our most powerful acts of courage have emerged from an understanding and experience of love that enables us to recognize, respect, and express our individual and collective humanity beyond the differences that are used to divide and destroy ourselves or each other. This is the power of life itself.

William Fulbright, the founder of the programme through which the authors of this book met each other, wrote a book entitled *The Arrogance of Power*. In it he issues a warning:

> Power tends to confuse itself with virtue and a great nation is particularly susceptible to the idea that its power is a sign of God's favor, conferring upon itself a special responsibility for other nations ... to remake them, that is, in its own shining image. Power confuses itself with virtue and tends also to take itself for omnipotence. Once imbued with the idea of a mission, a great nation easily assumes that it has the means as well as the duty to do God's work.
>
> (Fulbright 1966, cited in McCartney 2004: 423)

Fulbright's warning in relation to his own country is still as relevant today, in the unipolar world in which we live. The United States of America unilaterally declares war, positions itself as world leader, and prescribes trade liberalization and rapid deficit reduction as the sacred mantra for developing countries. Yet it maintains a highly protectionist policy towards its own agricultural industry and a deficit running into trillions that even the International Monetary Fund (IMF) acknowledges "is now among the highest in the world" (Muhliesen and Towe 2004).

In the USA, the "South" as a political construct exists in the massive numbers of poor US citizens, the majority of whom are white; in the lack of affordable health care because of the disproportionate political influence of the medical and pharmaceutical industry; in the severely limited educational and employment opportunities; in the reinstitutionalization of slavery through the privatization of prisons, in the culture of a masculinity defined by gun ownership; in the documented endemic levels of femicide, incest, and other forms of violence against women and children that are still kept well hidden; in the mainstream media that keep alive a fear of the "alien."

Given its image of the global bully boy, it is easy to develop prejudice against ordinary citizens of the USA. To counter such prejudice, it is important to acknowledge those American citizens who inspire international solidarity: the words of Sojourner Truth – "Ain't I a woman?" and Martin Luther King – "An injustice anywhere affects justice everywhere" – are still relevant today. In March 2005 I was fortunate to learn from veterans of the Civil Rights Movement, as one of 10 South African leaders who participated in the "Civil Rights Pilgrimage." Johnny Mae Carr, one of the veterans, shared the motivation for her continued commitment and activism at 94 years of age against the racism Black people in the USA continue to experience. She was clear that "this is not about one race – this is about the human race. Keep your ears and eyes open." If we open our ears and our eyes, what do we see?

Isabella Bakker and Stephen Gill describe what is being created as "a de facto constitution for global capitalism". They explain that:

> Neoliberalism is linked to social and political forces that tend to increase the human insecurity of the vast majority of the world's population, while redistributing income in an increasingly unequal world from the poor to the rich, in ways that tend to intensify a worldwide crisis of social and caring institutions (UNRISD 2005). Moreover, these mechanisms [0]are intended to be relatively permanent ones, and as such, they will frame the path of development in the future, not only in the short term, but also in the longer term.
>
> (Bakker and Gill, Chapter 1, this volume)

In the face of such power, what can we do? As someone who has been inspired and empowered by many in my country, South Africa, I maintain that we are not powerless and that we can and must use the power and leadership of love and courage to challenge the new "constitution" of global capitalism at whatever level it manifests. South Africa is a good example of a country that has been expected to conform to this "new constitutionalism." The experiences that I share illustrate how these forces and interests play out at country level. My research, conceptions, and writing on power and leadership derive directly from my experience as a feminist activist within the African National Congress (ANC) party, elected into office in 1994 as a Member of Parliament in South Africa's first democratic elections. Below, through examples of political choices on issues such as macroeconomic policy, military spending, HIV/AIDS, rural women's right to land, and privatization of water, I attempt to illustrate the choices we have in using power and leadership in the interests of our countries' citizens as opposed to global neoliberal interests.

As a result of the implementation of a quota that women had fought for, one third of the ruling party (ANC) MPs in 1994 were women. The challenge in the finance committee, to which I was deployed, was to find ways to ensure that our work had a positive impact on the lives of women and girls, who were and remain the majority of the poorest (Govender 1994). The poverty rate among female-headed households in 1995 was 60 per cent, and only 17 per cent of African women were in wage employment, with only 9 per cent self-employed. A central question was how to transform the mindsets and practice of economists and bureaucrats for whom economics and budgets were "neutral." The radar screens of such economists did not encompass poor African women because the product of their work was not (and still is not) recorded in the gross domestic product (GDP).

In democratic South Africa's first budget debates in 1994 (Hansard 1994, cited in Baden *et al.* 1998) I argued for transformative economic policy and budgets aimed at ending poverty, ensuring redistribution, and building women's empowerment and gender equality. I cited the Australian "Women's Budget" as an example for South Africa to use in developing our own "Women's Budget." Budgetary choices (from macroeconomic choices to departmental choices) that enabled women, as the majority of the poorest, to change their lives would improve the lives of those who were "above" them (a "ripple up" theory rather than the usual "trickle down" one). After this intervention, I worked with NGOs in establishing and steering the political impact of South Africa's Women's Budget Initiative.

By 1998–99, we ensured that in the national budget itself, the government was committed to gender-responsive budgeting. A good example of what this meant is the Working for Water programme, in which government declared that 60 per cent of all wages would be paid to women, 67 per cent in rural areas, with special emphasis on flexible time for single parents. In the first quarter of 1998, of 42,000 jobs created, 55 per cent went to women.

In the first term of Parliament, the Joint Monitoring Committee on the Quality of Life and Status of Women, which I chaired, identified and advocated transformative legislative priorities. At the end of the first term the committee had succeeded in enacting over 80 per cent of these legislative priorities. These included the Customary Law on Marriages, which addressed the minority status of African women, the Domestic Violence Act, and changes to the labour laws to address the specific needs of working women (from parental rights to sexual harassment).

Yet, despite all the work women in my country have done, women bear the brunt of deepening poverty, violence, and HIV/AIDS. Part of the reason lies in capitalist new constitutionalism and the policy incoherence between the rhetoric of "poverty eradication" and "gender equality," on the one hand, and the objectives of the global financial architecture on the other. An additional factor is that institutions such as parliaments (and those within them) operate within untransformed paradigms of power and leadership, and hegemonic priorities and values. Thus the ability to accurately evaluate whose interests are being promoted is often compromised.

Before the first democratic elections, the "Tripartite Alliance" of the ANC, the Congress of South African Trade Unions (COSATU), and the South African Communist Party (SACP) united around the Reconstruction and Development Programme (RDP), whose four "pillars" were building the economy, meeting basic needs, developing human resources, and democratizing the state. While working in the COSATU RDP office before the elections, I conducted a "gender-edit" of the RDP draft policy document in an attempt to reinsert the recommendations that women within the Alliance had developed, which had been excluded by male editors. Several, but not all, of these changes were incorporated into the final version of the RDP.

After the election, the South African government adopted the RDP as its developmental strategy and placed it under a minister in the presidency. Two years later, in 1996, the RDP office was shut down and the minister redeployed. The RDP was replaced by the Growth, Employment, and Redistribution Strategy (GEAR), a neoliberal macroeconomic policy designed almost exclusively by white men, several of whom are consultants to the World Bank. There was no discussion within the ANC or the Alliance of this new policy before its adoption. GEAR argued for "a faster fiscal deficit reduction programme ... a reduction in tariffs ... tax incentives to stimulate investment ... an expansion of trade and investment flows in Southern Africa ... flexibility within the collective bargaining system" (Government of South Africa 1996: 2). GEAR promised: "The strategy below attains a growth rate of 6% per annum and job creation of 400,000 per annum by the year 2000" (1996: 2). Neither of these targets has been met. The jobs created are mainly in low-paid vulnerable work, and the numbers of jobs do not match the increase in the labour force. The result is that unemployment levels as well as the numbers of the "working poor," particularly among women, have increased. With the focus on attracting foreign direct investment, taxation on the rich, on those who make and take their profits out of South Africa, has not increased, yet regressive taxation, in the form of value added taxes, continues to tax the poor. "Money is not the problem, the problem is capacity to spend the money" is the argument often used in defending GEAR. The commonsense logic of spending money to develop and retain the necessary capacity seems to escape those who articulate this line.

However, even before GEAR, South Africa had already begun trade liberalization in its implementation of the General Agreement on Trade and Tariffs (GATT). Tens and thousands of women workers in the clothing and textile sector lost jobs. Women workers to whom I had taught "workers' rights" in the Garment and Allied Workers Union as National Educator were shunted into the informal economy, where there are few or no rights or protections. What has happened to women workers in South Africa is a case study in the feminization of poverty and the casualization and informaliza-tion of women's work. What does the informal sector mean for these women? In practice it is any work to ensure their own and their family's survival – whether that work is selling fruit and vegetables at a bus stop or selling their bodies in the growing sex tourism industry.

In 1996, the government, in its post-Beijing Cabinet Commitment, com-mitted itself to "decreasing military spending and reallocating the savings to women's empowerment." Military spending decreased and socio-economic spending increased. By 1998, however, this trend was reversed, not only because of GEAR's priorities, but also because South Africa's government began negotiations for an arms deal that was initially estimated at R28 bil-lion and has since more than doubled. A premise of the arms deal was that the cost of purchasing arms would be offset by investments in South Africa that would create large numbers of jobs. The fact is that the few jobs cre-ated have not offset the costs, which have been exacerbated by loans taken from governments of countries that sold South Africa the armaments. Before this, cabinet ministers who had appeared before the Committee on Women's Hearings would constantly plead that there was no money to create a strong social security system, through for example the Basic Income Grant, or that there were not enough resources for the implementation of the Domestic Violence Act or other legislation.

The argument that there were not enough resources formed part of the rationale cited by the minister of health in response to demand for public provision of HIV/AIDS treatment. The arms deal came into effect in 2001 through the National Defence Budget vote, and I used the power of the vote to register my opposition to the deal. The gendered impact of HIV/AIDS led the Committee on Women to hold hearings even while the president was questioning the link between HIV and AIDS, negating the government's own policy and programme. Official policy, premised on the assumption that HIV causes AIDS, acknowledges the need for prevention, care, and treatment. South Africa's legislation had given gov-ernment the right to produce generic equivalents to ensure affordable treat-ment. Yet the position of the president, vociferously advocated by the minister of health, led to silencing and silence in structures such as the

ANC caucus in Parliament, the ANC's national executive committee, and the cabinet.

In the committee's hearings, the Brazilian experience offered a clear-cut example of a state acting in the interests of its citizens against the greed of pharmaceutical companies. Brazil offered to share the technology it had developed to produce generic medicine with countries that wanted to provide treatment free of charge. Through providing free treatment to all who needed it, Brazil had radically reduced its HIV/AIDS crisis to manageable levels. Brazil's example was recommended in the report of the Committee on Women. Both South Africa's Medicines Act and Brazil's free treatment programme had come under attack from the pharmaceutical industry, which had taken South Africa to the Constitutional Court and had laid a charge against Brazil at the World Trade Organization (WTO). In both instances the industry had to concede defeat, in the short term. In the long term it continues to play complex games, pitting patent rights and drug companies' right to obscene profits against patient rights to health and life. The rights that were won in both the Constitutional Court and the WTO have not been exercised by countries like South Africa, for fear of trade and investment repercussions. Instead we have been diverted into a polarizing debate (HIV does not exist and therefore does not cause AIDS. Thus if the virus does not exist, we do not need anti-retroviral treatment). Instead of this damaging digression, what is needed to end this crisis is a united, cohesive programme driven by clear political will.

The committee's report exposed the connections between the spread of HIV/AIDS, poverty, violence, and gender inequality. Sexual inequality renders women, especially poor women, relatively powerless to negotiate the terms of sex. As examples of the depth of the inequality, studies quoted in the report document the following: most young women's first sexual experience is one of coercion; asking a man to wear a condom can lead to being beaten or even death; the belief that sex with a virgin cures AIDS is widespread. The committee's report recommended both prevention and treatment, and detailed three key demands, including mother-to-child treatment, post-exposure prophylaxis after rape, and free treatment for all those who needed it (Govender 2002). In May 2002, the cabinet finally acceded to all three of the committee's recommendations on treatment, which had echoed civil society's demands. Yet the leadership continues to use its power to divert the struggle against HIV/AIDS from challenging patent rights to a phoney debate on whether HIV causes AIDS, hampering implementation of the cabinet's 2002 commitment. The consequences for women and girls have been particularly devastating.

In February 2004, over a year after I resigned as an MP, rural women's rights to land were sold down the river. Instead of the Customary Law on Inheritance and Succession Act, which the Committee on Women had prioritized, government enacted the Communal Land Rights Act (CLRA) in horse-trading with traditional leaders before the elections. One of the most devastating compromises during the constitutional negotiations was the property clause, which guarantees the inequitable rights of property holders in a country in which 85 per cent of South Africans were relegated to 13 per cent of the land through colonial and apartheid dispossession. This clause has severely constrained South Africa's ability to ensure equitable land redistribution. The consequences are reflected in the fact that 12 years into democracy, the highly unequal distribution of land is still the status quo (evidence presented by the Department of Land Affairs at hearings into the CLRA). Despite this inequity, of which rural African women bear the brunt, land reform has never been allocated more than 0.5 per cent of the national budget.

In May 2006, South Africa's parliament hosted an international conference focusing on women and economic policy in Africa, bringing together, among others, women parliamentarians, government ministers and members of civil society from across Africa. As facilitator, I explained its objectives in the introduction to the conference: "To analyze the reality facing African women, to understand why this situation exists and to identify how each of us can use our power and leadership to contribute to changing this situation." The challenge for me in conceptualizing the conference had been how to ensure that it provided participants with the necessary information to interrogate economic policy, as well as creating a space in which participants would listen to their own commonsense and shared experience, rather than slavishly believe the well worn mantras of economic fundamentalists.

The General Agreement on Trade in Services (GATS) promotes the privatization of services like water, health, and education and is undermining socio-economic rights across the globe. In the plenary and commission sessions, in MPs' and ministers' interactions with women from civil society, consensus emerged that privatization had deepened poverty and gender inequality across our continent. In our plenary dialogue, feminist economist Yassine Fall explained that her country, Senegal, had been one of the first countries in Africa to privatize water. Today, water in Senegal is of poorer quality and is very expensive. The result is that poor women today spend many more hours trying to find free water than before the water was privatized.

In the conference declaration, delegates called on African governments to

> Ensure that basic services such as water, sanitation, health, education and electricity are not privatized, and where such services have already been privatized governments must review such policies .....Ensure that budget allocations are slanted more in favour of social development spending and that such budgets value life, peace and development above war ....Review all financial and trade agreements, which impact directly on the economic rights of women, employment and women's capacity for economic self-determination ... . Establish special focus

committees, which are enabled to call the private sector to hearings to account as to how its economic decisions meet the Constitutional-legislative requirement in relation to human rights, gender equality and socio-economic rights, employment, the environment and the livelihoods of women.

(Parliament of the Republic of South Africa 2006)

Each of us has power and each of us exercises leadership, in different contexts. This book, the collective work of individual authors, can help make the connections between the everyday and the global. Women's work in social reproduction cannot be conveniently manipulated or erased – it must shape global transformation. I hope that the experiences I have shared from my country and continent will affirm the power and leadership of love and courage. Women and men can create the world of our dreams, in which no girl or boy will go hungry or homeless or die of diseases of poverty. Women and men can organize our world and our lives to meet basic needs, to ensure work of dignity, and to enable each girl and each boy to develop to their full creative human potential.

Notes

1 This chapter is based on my book, *Love and Courage, A Story of Insubordination* (2007) Johannesburg, South Africa: Jacana.
2 Two chapters also benefited from ongoing collaborative projects with Stephen Gill (Chapter 1) and Maria Floro (Chapter 2)

Bibliography

Acharya, K., Thapa, N. B. and Sharma, S. (1998) *Economic Liberalization in Nepal: sequence and process*, Kathmandu, Nepal: Oxfam GB-Nepal.

Acharya, M. (1981) *The Maithili Women of Sirsia: the status of women in Nepal*, vol. 2, part 1, Kathmandu, Nepal: Center for Development Administration.

——(2000) *Labor Market Developments and Poverty in Nepal: with special opportunities for women*, Kathmandu, Nepal: Tanka Prasad Acharya Memorial Foundation.

——(2003) "The Economic Foundations of the Current Socio-political Crisis in Nepal," in D. B. Gurung (ed.) *Nepal Tomorrow: voices and visions*, Kathmandu, Nepal: Koselee Prakashan.

Acharya, M. and Bennett, L. (1981) *An Aggregate Analysis and Summary of 8 Village Studies: the status of women in Nepal*, vol. 2, part 9, Kathmandu, Nepal: CEDA.

Acharya, M. and Ghimire, P. (2005) "Gender Indicators of Equality, Inclusion and Poverty Reduction for Measuring Program/Project Effectiveness," *Economic and Political Weekly*, 40(44–45): 4719–28.

Acharya, M., Khatiwada, Y. R. and Aryal, S. (2003) *Structural Adjustment Policies and Poverty Eradication*, Kathmandu, Nepal: Institute for Integrated Studies.

Ackerly, B. (1997) "What's in a Design? The effects of NGO programme delivery choices on women's empowerment in Bangladesh," in A. M. Goetz (ed.) *Getting Institutions Right for Women in Development*, London: Zed Press.

Acosta, A. (2004) "Ecuador: oportunidades y amenazas económicas de la migración," in F. Hidalgo (ed.) *Migraciones: un juego con cartas marcadas*, Quito, Ecuador: Ediciones Abya-Yala, ILDIS-FES, PMCD.

Acosta, A., López, S. and Villamar, D. (2005) "Las Remesas y su Aporte Para la Economía Ecuatoriana," in G. Herrera, M. C. Carrillo and A. Torres (eds) *La Migración Ecuatoriana: transnacionalismo, redes e identidades*, Quito, Ecuador: FLACSO – Plan Migración, Comunicación y Desarrollo.

Adaba, G. (2004) "A View from Labor," in C. Barton and L. Prendergast (eds) *Seeking Accountability on Women's Human Rights: women debate the UN Millennium Development Goals*, New York: WICEJ.

Ahmed, F. E. (2004) "The Rise of the Bangladesh Garment Industry: globalization, women workers, and voice," *NWSA Journal*, 16(2): 34–45.

Aman, A. C., Jr. (1993) "An Introduction," *Indiana Journal of Global Legal Studies*, 1: 1–2.

Anderson, A., Gianaroli, L. and Nygren, K. (2004) "Assisted Reproductive Technology in Europe, 2000: results generated registers by ESHRE," *Human Reproduction*, 19(3): 490–503.

Anderson, B. and Daviddon, J. O. (2004) *Trafficking – A Demand Led Problem?* Sweden: Save the Children.

Andrew, C., Armstrong, P., Armstrong, H., Clement, W. and Vosko, L. (eds) (2003) *Studies in Political Economy: developments in feminism*, Toronto: Women's Press.

Anonymous C01, Member of the Interministerial Commission on Health Reform (2 June 2005). Interview by Ewig, C., Santiago, Chile.

Antonopoulos, R. and Floro, M. (2004) "Asset Ownership Along Gender Lines: evidence from Thailand," working paper (December), Washington DC and New York: American University and Levy Economic Institute.

Antony, P. (2001) *Towards Empowerment: experiences of organizing women workers*, New Delhi: International Labor Organization.

Arat-Koc, S. (2006) "Whose Social Reproduction? Transnational motherhood and challenges to feminist political economy" in K. Bezanson and M. Luxton (eds) *Social Reproduction: feminist challenges to neo-liberalism*, Montreal and Kingston: McGill-Queens University Press.

Arestis, P. and Caner, A. (2005) "Financial Liberalization and Poverty: channels of influence," in P. Arestis and M. Sawyer (eds) *Financial Liberalization: beyond orthodox concerns*, International Papers in Political Economy, new series, Basingstoke: Palgrave Macmillan.

Arestis, P. and Demetriades, P. O. (1997) "Financial Development and Economic Growth: assessing the evidence," *Economic Journal*, 107(442): 783–99.

Arestis, P. and Sawyer, M. (eds) (2005) *Financial Liberalization: beyond orthodox concerns*, International Papers in Political Economy, new series, Basingstoke, UK: Palgrave Macmillan.

Armstrong, H. and Armstrong, P. (1983) "Beyond Sexless Class and Classless Sex: towards feminist Marxism," *Studies in Political Economy*, 10: 7–43.

Baden, S., Hasim, S. and Meintjes, S. (eds) (1998) *Report No 45, Country Gender Profile: South Africa*, report prepared for the Swedish International Development Office (SIDA), Pretoria. Online. Available at: www.bridge.ids.ac.uk/reports/re45c.pdf (accessed 13 August 2007).

Bakker, I. (ed.) (1994) *The Strategic Silence: gender and economic policy*, London and New York: Zed Books with the North-South Institute.

——(1999) "Neoliberal Governance and the New Gender Order," *Working Papers*, 1(1): 49–59.

——(2003) "Neo-Liberal Governance and the Reprivatization of Social Reproduction: social provisioning and shifting gender orders," in I. Bakker and S. Gill (eds) *Power, Production and Social Reproduction*, Basingstoke, UK and New York: Palgrave Macmillan.

Bakker, I. and Gill, S. (2003a) "Global Political Economy and Social Reproduction," in I. Bakker and S. Gill (eds) *Power, Production and Social Reproduction*, Basingstoke, UK and New York: Palgrave Macmillan

——(2003b) "Ontology, Method and Hypothesis," in I. Bakker and S. Gill (eds) *Power, Production and Social Reproduction*, Basingstoke and New York: Palgrave Macmillan.

Bakker, I. and Gill, S. (eds) (2003c) *Power, Production and Social Reproduction*, Basingstoke and New York: Palgrave Macmillan.

Balakrishnan, R. and Huang, M. (eds) (2002) *The Hidden Assembly Line: gender dynamics of subcontracted work in a global economy*, Bloomfield CT: Kumarian Press.

Baldez, L. (2002) *Why Women Protest: women's movements in Chile*, Cambridge: Cambridge University Press.

Bales, K. (1999) *Disposable People*, Berkeley CA: University of California Press.

Banaszak, L., Beckwith, K. and Rucht, D. (eds) (2003) *Women's Movements Facing the Reconfigured State*, Cambridge: Cambridge University Press.

Banerjee, N. (2002) "Between the Devil and the Deep Sea: shrinking options for women in contemporary India," in K. Kapadia (ed.) *The Violence of Development*, New Delhi, India: Kali for Women.

Banerjee, N. (ed.) (1991) *Indian Women in a Changing Industrial Scenario*, New Delhi, India: Sage Publications.

Bardhan, P. and Udry, C. (1999) *Development Microeconomics*, Oxford: Oxford University Press.

Barnett, K. and Grown, C. (2004) *Gender Impacts of Government Revenue Collection: the case of taxation*, Commonwealth Economic Papers series, London: Commonwealth Secretariat.

Barrientos, A. (2000) "Getting Better After Neoliberalism: shifts and challenges of health policy in Chile," in P. Lloyd-Sherlock (ed.) *Healthcare Reform and Poverty in Latin America*, London: Institute of Latin American Studies.

Batliwala, S. (1993) *Empowerment of Women in South Asia: concepts and practices*, New Delhi, India: Asian South Pacific Bureau of Adult Education and FAO.

Beckerman, P. and Solimano, A. (eds) (2002) *Crisis and Dollarization in Ecuador: stability, growth and social equity*, Washington DC: World Bank.

Bein, W. (2000) "Changing Values Among the Future Parents of Europe," paper presented at the annual seminar of European Observatory on the Social Situation, Demography and Family, on Low Fertility, Families, Public Policies, Seville, Spain, 15–16 September 2000.

Bendixen and Associates (2003) *Remesas e Inversión en el Ecuador*, Washington DC: Fondo Multilateral de Inversiones (FOMIN).

Benería, L. (1992) "The Mexican Debt Crisis: restructuring the economy and the household," in L. Benería and S. Feldman (eds) *Unequal Burden: economic crises, persistent poverty and women's work*, Boulder CO: Westview Press.

——(1999) "Globalization, Gender and the Davos Man," *Feminist Economics*, 5(3): 61–83.

Benería, L. and Feldman, S. (eds) (1992) *Unequal Burden: economic crises, persistent poverty and women's work*, Boulder CO: Westview Press.

Benería, L. and Floro, M. (2006) "Distribution, Gender and Labor Market Informalization: a conceptual framework and a focus on homebased workers," in L. Benería and N. Kudva (eds) *Rethinking Informalization: precarious jobs, poverty and social protection*, Ithaca NY: Cornell University Press e-Publishing.

Benería, L. and Lind, A. (1995) "Engendering International Trade: concepts, policy and action," *GSD Working Paper Series no. 5*, July, New York: GSD and United Nations Development Fund for Women.

Benería, L. and Sen, G. (1981) "Accumulation, Reproduction and 'Women's Role in Economic Development': Boserup revisited," *Signs*, 7(2): 279–98.

Benhabib, S. (1994) "From Identity Politics to Social Feminism: a plea for the nineties," *Philosophy of Education Yearbook*. Online. Available at: www.ed.uiuc.edu/eps/PES-Yearbook/94_docs/BENHABIB.HTM (accessed 25 July 2006).

Bennett, L. and Gajurel, K. (2004) *Negotiating Social Change: gender, caste and ethnic dimensions of empowerment and social inclusion in rural Nepal*, Kathmandu, Nepal: World Bank.

Benton, L. (1989) "Homework and Industrial Development: gender roles and restructuring in the Spanish shoe industry," *World Development*, 17(2): 255–66.

Bergeron, S. (2003) "The Post-Washington Consensus and Economic Representations of Women in Development at the World Bank," *International Feminist Journal of Politics*, 5(3): 397–419.

Berik, G. (2000) "Mature Export-Led Growth and Gender Wage Inequality in Taiwan," *Feminist Economics*, 6(3): 1–26.

Berik, G., Rodgers, Y. V. M. and Zveglich, J. E., Jr. (2004) "International Trade and Wage Discrimination: evidence from East Asia," *World Bank Policy Research Working Paper no. 3111*, Washington DC: World Bank. Online. Available at: http://ideas.repec.org/p/wbk/wbrwps/3111.html (accessed 11 September 2006).

Bezanson, K. (2006) *Gender, the State and Social Reproduction: household insecurity in neoliberal times*, Toronto: University of Toronto Press.

Bezanson, K. and Luxton, M. (eds) (2006) *Social Reproduction: feminist political economy challenges neo-liberalism*, Montreal and Kingston: McGill-Queens University Press.

Biblioteca del Congreso Nacional de Chile (2002) *Conceptualización del Plan de Acceso Universal con Garantías Explícitas (AUGE), Eje de la Actual Reforma de Salud*, serie de Estudios de Anticipación /CEA/BCN Year 1, no. 1, April, Valparaíso, Chile: Biblioteca del Congreso Nacional de Chile.

——(2003) *Reforma de Salud Fondo de Compensación Solidaria*, serie UAPROL/ BCN/ Year 3, no. 057, March, Valparaíso, Chile: Biblioteca del Congreso Nacional de Chile.

Boonmathya, R., Praparpun, Y. and Leechanavanichin, R. (1999) "The Situation of Women Subcontracted Workers in the Garment Industry in Bangkok, Thailand," *Working Paper*, October, Bangkok: The Asia Foundation.

Borzutsky, S. (2002) *Vital Connections: politics, social security and inequality in Chile*, Notre Dame IN: University of Notre Dame Press.

Braudel, F. (1995) *The Mediterranean and the Mediterranean World in the Age of Philip II, Vol. II*, Berkeley CA: University of California Press.

Braunstein, E. (2000) "Engendering Foreign Direct Investment: family structure, labor markets and international capital mobility," *World Development*, 28(7): 1157–73.

——(2004) "Gender-intensive FDI and Policies for Development," *PERI Working Paper*, Amherst MA: University of Massachusetts.

Braunstein, E. and Epstein, G. (2002) "Bargaining Power and Foreign Direct Investment in China: can 1.3 billion consumers tame the multinationals?" in W. Milberg (ed.) *Labor and the Globalization of Production*, London: Palgrave Macmillan. Online. Available at www.umass.edu/peri/pdfs/WP45.pdf (accessed 22 June 2006).

Brenner, J. and Laslett, B. (1991) "Gender, Social Reproduction, and Women's Self-Organization: considering the US welfare state," *Gender and Society*, special issue on Marxist Feminist Theory, 5(3): 311–33.

Brenner, S. (1998) *The Domestication of Desire: women, wealth, and modernity in Java*, Princeton NJ: Princeton University Press.

——(2005) "Islam and Gender Politics in Late New Order Indonesia," in A. Willford and K. George (eds) *Spirited Politics: religion and public life in contemporary Southeast Asia*, Ithaca NY: Cornell Southeast Asia Program Publications.

Bretton Woods Project (2003) *Harmonisation and Coherence: white knights or Trojan horses?* Washington DC: Global Policy Forum.

Brewster, K. and Rindfuss, R. (2000) "Fertility and Women's Employment in Industrialized Nations", *Annual Review of Sociology*, 26: 271–96.

Brodie, J. (2005) "Globalization, Governance and Gender: rethinking the agenda for the twenty-first century," in L. Amoore (ed.) *The Global Resistance Reader*, London and New York: Routledge.

Brown, L. (1995) *Gender and the Implementation of Structural Adjustment in Africa: report prepared for the Africa and Middle East Division*, Canadian International Development agency, Washington DC: International Food Policy Research Institute.

Brucker, H. (2002) "Can International Migration Solve the Problems of European Labour Markets?" *Economic Survey of Europe*, Geneva, Switzerland: UN Economic Commission for Europe, Economic Analysis Division.

Bulatao, R. and Casterline, J. (eds) (2001) *Global Fertility Transition*, New York: Population Council.

Caffentzis, G. (2005) "On the Notion of a Crisis of Social Reproduction: a theoretical review," *The Commoner* (www.thecommoner.org) no. 5 (autumn).

Çağatay, N. (2001) "Trade, Gender and Poverty," background paper for *United Nations Development Programme*. Online. Available at www.undp.org/poverty/ publications/wkpaper/wp5/wpf-nilufer.pdf (accessed 2 June 2006).

Çağatay, N. and Erturk, K. (2004) "Gender and Globalization: a macroeconomic perspective," technical background paper for the final report of the World Commission on the Social Dimension of Globalization, *A Fair Globalization: creating opportunities for all*, Geneva, Switzerland: International Labor Organization.

Çağatay, N., Elson, D. and Grown, C. (eds) (1995) *World Development*, special issue: Gender, Adjustment and Macroeconomics, 28(7).

Caliari, A. (2004) *The 'Coherence' Agenda of International Finance and Trade Institutions is Tightening Industrial Country Control over Developing Countries*, Washington DC: World Hunger Education Service. Online. Available at: www. worldhunger.org/articles/global/Trade/caliariwto.htm (accessed 23 June 2006).

Caliari, A. and Williams, M. (2004) "Capacity of International Financial Institutions to Support Trade Liberalisation in Low-income and Vulnerable Countries," civil society briefing paper prepared for the 2004 Commonwealth finance ministers meeting. London: Commonwealth Foundation. Online. Available at: www.igtn. org/pdfs//328_cfmm2004briefingpaper.pdf (accessed 23 June 2006).

Carlsen, E., Giwercman, A., Keiding, N. and Skakkebaek, N. (1992) "Evidence for Decreasing Quality of Semen During Past 50 years," *British Medical Journal*, 305: 609–13.

Carr, M., Chen, M. and Jhabvala, R. (1996) *Speaking Out: women's economic empowerment in South Asia*, New Delhi, India: Vistaar Publications.

Carr, M., Chen, M. and Tate, J. (2000) "Globalization and Home Based Workers," *Feminist Economics*, 6(3): 123–42.

Cartin, B. (1998) "Chile: the effectiveness of reform," in M. A. Cruz-Saco and C. Mesa-Lago (eds) *Do Options Exist? The reform of pension and health care systems in Latin America*, Pittsburgh PA: University of Pittsburgh Press.

Casas, L. (1999) *La Salud Sexual y Reproductiva en el Sistema Privado de Salud Previsional*, Santiago, Chile: CORSAPS.

Castles, F. (2003) "The World Turned Upside Down: below replacement fertility, changing preferences and family-friendly public policy in 21 OECD countries," *Journal of European Social Policy*, 13: 209–27.

Celedón, C. and Orellana, R. (2003) *Gobernancia y Participación Ciudadana en la Reforma de Salud en Chile*, serie Estudios Socio/Económicos no. 17, Santiago, Chile: CIEPLAN.

CDC (Centers for Disease Control and Prevention) (2004) *Commonly Asked Questions About the U.S. ART Clinic Reporting System*, Atlanta GA: CDC.

CBS (Central Bureau of Statistics)/NPC (1995) *Population Monograph*, Kathmandu, Nepal: HMG.

——(1999) *Nepal Labor Force Survey*, Kathmandu, Nepal: HMG.

——(2001) *Population Census 2001, The National Report*, Kathmandu, Nepal: HMG.

——(2004) *Nepal Living Standards Survey, 2003/2004*, vols. 1 and 2, Kathmandu, Nepal: HMG.

Chanana, K. (2003) "Female Sexuality and Education of Hindu Girls in India," in S. Rege (ed.) *Sociology and Gender*, New Delhi, India: Sage Publications.

Chaney, E. M. and Castro, M. G. (1989) *Muchachas No More: household workers in Latin America and the Caribbean*, Philadelphia PA: Temple University Press.

Chang, H-J. and Grabel, I. (2004) *Reclaiming Development: an alternative economic policy manual*, London: Zed Press.

Charmes, J. (1998) "Informal Sector, Poverty and Gender: a review of empirical evidence," background paper for the *World Bank World Development Report 2000*, Washington DC: World Bank.

Cheal, D., Wooley, F. and Luxton, M. (1998) *How Families Cope and Why Policymakers Need to Know*, Ottawa: Canadian Policy Research Networks.

Chen, M., Sebstad, J. and Connell, L. O. (1999) "Counting the Invisible Workforce: the case of homebased workers," *World Development*, 27(3): 603–10.

Cheru, F. (2001) "Overcoming Apartheid's Legacy: the ascendancy of neoliberalism in South Africa's anti-poverty strategy," *Third World Quarterly*, 22(4): 505–27.

Chesnais, J. (1996) "Fertility, Family, and Social Policy," *Population and Development Review*, 22: 729–39.

Colectivo, I. (2001) *Mujer, Immigración y Trabajo*, Madrid, Spain: IMSERSO, Ministerio de Trabajo y Asuntos Sociales.

Congress, Library of (2006) "Czechoslovakia – Health and Social Welfare," *Country Studies*, Washington DC: Library of Congress.

Connell, R. (1987) *Gender and Power: society, the person and sexual politics*, Stanford CA: Stanford University Press.

——(1990) "The State, Gender and Sexual Politics: theory and appraisal," *Theory and Society*, 19(3): 507–44.

——(2001) "Masculinities and Globalization," in M. S. Kimmel and M. A. Messner (eds) *Men's Lives*, Meedham Heights MA: Allyn and Bacon.

——(2005) "Change Among Gatekeepers: men, masculinities and gender equality in the global era," *Signs*, 30(1): 1801–25

Cornelius, W. (2004) "Spain: difficult transition from emigrant to immigrant country," in W. Cornelius, T. Tsuda, P. Martin and J. Hollifield (eds) *Controlling Immigration: a global perspective*, 2nd ed., Stanford CA: Stanford University Press.

Cranny-Francis, A., Waring, W., Stavropoulos, P. and Kirby, J. (2003) *Gender Studies: terms and debates*, New York: Palgrave Macmillan.

Creevey, L. (1996) *Changing Women's Lives and Work*, London: IT Publications.

Daskalova, K. (2001) "Manipulated Emancipation: representations of women in post-communist Bulgaria," in G. Janhart, J. Gohrisch, D. Hahn, H. M. Nickel,

I. Peinl and K. Schafgen (eds) *Gender in Transition in Eastern and Central Europe Proceedings*, Berlin: Trafo Verlag.

Date-Bah, E. (1985) "Technologies for Rural Women of Ghana: role of socio-cultural factors," in I. Ahmed (ed.) *Technology and Rural Women: conceptual and empirical issues*, London: George Allen and Unwin.

Datta, R. and Kornberg, J. (eds) (2005) *Women in Developing Countries: assessing strategies for empowerment*, New Delhi, India: Viva Books.

della Porta, D. (2003) "The Women's Movement, the Left and the State: continuities and changes in the Italian case," in L. Banazak, K. Beckwith and D. Rucht (eds) *Women's Movements Facing the Reconfigured State*, Cambridge: Cambridge University Press.

DEPNAKERTRANS (Departemen Tenaga Kerja dan Transmigrasi) (2006) *Website of the Indonesian Department of Labour and Transmigration*. Online. Available at: www.nakertrans.go.id/pusdatinnaker/tki/ index_tki.php (accessed 26 June 2006).

DFID (Department for International Development) and World Bank (2005) *Citizens With (Without) Rights: Nepal gender and social exclusion assessment* (final draft, June), Kathmandu, Nepal: DFID/World Bank.

DMN (Dirección Nacional de Migración) (2004) *Flujos migratorios en el Ecuador*, Quito, Ecuador: DMN.

Druz', O. V. and Hryshynska, O. O. (1999) *Trafficking in Young Women, Observation of Women's Human Rights and Relevant Tasks of Law Enforcement Bodies in Ukraine*, University of the Interior of Ukraine and International Women's Human Rights Protection Center (ed.), Kharkiv-Kyiv, Ukraine: La Strada Ukraine.

Dunson, D., Colombo, B. and Baird, D. (2002) "Changes with Age in the Level and Duration of Fertility in the Menstrual Cycle," *Human Reproduction*, 17: 1399–1403.

Edholm, F., Harris, O. and Young, K. (1977) "Conceptualizing Women," *Critique of Anthropology*, 3(9–10): 101–30.

Ehrenreich, B. and Hochschild, A. R. (eds) (2004) *Global Woman: nannies, maids and sex workers in the new economy*, New York: Henry Holt.

Elson, D. (ed.) (1991) *Male Bias in the Development Process*, Manchester and New York: Manchester University Press and St. Martin's Press.

——(2001) "Gender Responsive Budget Initiatives: some key dimensions and practical examples," paper presented at the Conference on Gender Responsive Budgeting, Brussels, 16–17 October 2001.

——(2005) *Monitoring Government Budgets for Compliance with CEDAW: a report to the United Nations Development Fund for Women (UNIFEM)*, mimeo, January.

Elson, D. and Çağatay, N. (2000) "The Social Content of Macroeconomic Policies," *World Development*, 28(7): 1347–64.

Erturk, K. and Darity, W. (2000) "Secular Changes in the Gender Composition of Employment and Growth Dynamics in the North and the South," *World Development*, 28(7): 1231–38.

Esping-Anderson, G. (1990) *The Three Worlds of Welfare Capitalism*, Princeton NJ: Princeton University Press.

Espínola, Rosa, Foro Red de Salud y Derechos Sexuales y Reproductivos (12 May 2005) Interview by Ewig, C., Santiago, Chile.

Evans, M. I., Littmann, L., Louis, L. S., Leblanc, L., Addis, J., Johnson, M. P. and Ewig, C. (1999) "The Strengths and Limits of the NGO Women's Movement Model: shaping Nicaragua's democratic institutions," *Latin American Research Review*, 34(3): 75–102.

——(2006a) "Global Processes, Local Consequences: gender equity and health sector reform in Peru," *Social Politics*, 13(3): 427–55.

——(2006b) "Hijacking Global Feminism: feminists, the Catholic Church and the family planning debacle in Peru," *Feminist Studies*, 32(3): 632–59.

Federici, S. (2004) *Caliban and the Witch: women, the body and primitive accumulation*, New York: Autonomedia.

Fernando, J. L. and Heston, A. L. (eds) (1997) "The Role of NGOs: charity and empowerment," *The Annals of the American Academy of Political and Social Science*, 554.

Fisher, J. S. (2004) "Environmental Anti-Androgens and Male Reproductive Health: focus on phthalates and testicular dysgenesis syndrome," *Reproduction*, 127: 305–15.

Fisher, T. and Sriram, M. S. (2002) *Beyond Micro-Credit: putting development back into micro-finance*, New Delhi, India: Vistaar Publications.

FLACSO (Facultad Latinoamericana de Ciencias Sociales Sede Ecuador) and Banco Central del Ecuador (2004) "Módulo de migración," *Encuesta de Coyuntura del Mercado Laboral Ecuatoriano*, January.

Floro, M. (1995) "Economic Restructuring, Gender and the Allocation of Time," *World Development*, 23(11): 1913–30.

——(2001) "Gender Dimensions of Financing for Development," background paper prepared for the United Nations Development Fund for Women, New York.

Floro, M., Çagatay, N., Erturk, K. and Willoughby, J. (2004) "Gender Issues and Distributional Concerns of Financing for Development," background paper prepared for the United Nations International Research and Training Institute for the Advancement of Women (INSTRAW), June 2004.

Floro, M. and Messier, J. (2004) "Credit, Gender and Debt Servicing: the case of urban poor households in Ecuador," paper presented at the Southern Eastern Economics Association Meetings, New Orleans LA, 19–20 November 2005.

Floro, M. and Miles, M. (2003) "Time Use and Overlapping Activities: evidence from Australia," *Cambridge Journal of Economics*, 27(6): 881–904.

Folbre, N. (1994) *Who Pays For the Kids? Gender and the structures of constraint*, New York: Routledge.

——(2001) *The Invisible Heart*, New York: New York Press.

Fontana, M. (2002) "Modelling the Effects of Trade on Women: the case of Zambia," IDS Working Paper 155, March, Brighton: Institute of Development Studies at Sussex. Online. Available at: www.ids.ac.uk/ids/bookshop/wp/wp155.pdf (accessed 23 June 2006).

Fox, C. (1994) "Changing Japanese Employment Patterns and Women's Participation: anticipating the implications of employment trends," *Manoa Journal*, 3: 1–5.

Franceschet, S. (2003) "'State Feminism' and Women's Movements: the impact of Chile's Servicio Nacional de la Mujer on women's activism," *Latin American Research Review*, 38(1): 9–40.

Frank, O., Bianchi, P. and Campana, A. (1994) "The End of Fertility: age, fecundity and fecundability in women," *Journal of Biosocial Science*, 26: 349–68.

Fraser, A., Kamal-Smith, M. and Watkins, K. (2004) "The Cost of Childbirth," *Oxfam Briefing Paper*, 52 (March): 1–29.

Frohmann, A. and Valdés, T. (1995) "Democracy in the Country and in the Home: the women's movement in Chile," in A. Basu (ed.) *The Challenge of Local Feminisms: women's movements in global perspective*, Boulder CO: Westview Press.

Fulbright, J. W. (1966) *The Arrogance of Power*, New York: Random House.

FWLD (2003) *Shadow Report to CEDAW Monitoring Committee*, Kathmandu, Nepal: Forum for Women, Law and Development.

Garcia, B. (ed.) (2000) *Women, Poverty, and Demographic Change*, New York: Oxford University Press.

GDS/FES (1997) *Women in Garment Industries*, Kathmandu, Nepal: GDS/FES.

GEFONT (2001) *Women's Participation in Nepali Labor Movement*, Kathmandu, Nepal: GEFONT.

Gender Monitoring Group of the World Summit (2005) *Women Cite Successes in UN World Summit Agreements on Gender Equality, but Underscore Lack of Political Will to Tackle Poverty, Foster Peace, and Ensure Human Rights*, unpublished document, September, New York. Online. Available at: www.cwgl.rutgers.edu/globalcenter/policy/millsummit/Sept14.pdf (accessed 22 June 2006).

Ghimire, F. (2005) *The Contemporary Global Social Movements: emergent proposals, connectivity and development implications*, Geneva, Switzerland: UNRISD.

Gideon, J. (2003) "Understanding Economies as Gendered Structures: examples from Central America," in M. Gutierrez (ed.) *Macro-Economics: making gender matter*, London and New York: Zed Press.

Gill, S. (1998) "New Constitutionalism, Democratization and Global Political Economy," *Pacifica Review*, 10(1): 23–38.

——(2002) "Constitutionalizing Inequality and the Clash of Globalizations," *International Studies Review*, 4(3): 47–65.

——(2003) *Power and Resistance in the New World Order*, Basingstoke: Palgrave Macmillan.

Gill, S., and Bakker, I. (2006) "New Constitutionalism and the Social Reproduction of Caring Institutions." *Theoretical Medicine and Bioethics*, 27: 35–57.

Gleicher, N., Oleske, D. M., Tur-Kaspa, I., Vidali, A. and Karande, V. (2000) "Reducing the Risk of High-Order Multiple Pregnancy after Ovarian Stimulation with Gonadotropins," *New England Journal of Medicine*, 343: 2–7.

Glick Schiller, N. (1999) "Transmigrants and Nation-States: something old and something new in the U.S. immigrant experience," in C. Hirschmann, P. Kasinitz and J. DeWind (eds) *The Handbook of International Migration*, New York: Russell Sage Foundation.

Glick Schiller, N., Basch, L. and Blanc-Szanton, C. (1992) "Towards a Transnational Perspective on Migration: race, class, ethnicity, and nationalism reconsidered," *Annals of the New York Academy of Sciences*, 645.

Goetz, A. M. and Gupta, R. S. (1996) "Who Takes the Credit: gender, power and control over loan use in rural credit programmes in Bangladesh," *World Development*, 24(1): 45–63.

Gómez, A., Red de Salud de las Mujeres Latinoamericas y del Caribe (8 May 2005) Interview by Ewig, C., Santiago, Chile.

González de la Rocha, M. (1995) "The Urban Family and Poverty in Latin America," *Latin American Perspectives*, 22: 12–31.

Govender, P. (ed.) (1994) *Beijing Conference Report: 1994 country report on the status of South African women*, Pretoria, South Africa: Government of South Africa.

——(2002) "How Best Can South Africa Address the Horrific Impact of HIV/AIDS on Women and Girls?" Report by the government of South Africa's Committee on Women, tabled and published by the South African Parliament, available from author.

Government of South Africa (1996) "Growth, Employment and Redistribution: a macroeconomic strategy." Online. Available at www.polity.org.za/attachment.php? aa_id = 4396 (accessed 13 August 2007).

Gratton, B. (forthcoming) "Women and Work: Ecuadorians in the United States and Spain," *Journal of Ethnic and Migration Studies.*

Grewal, I. and Kaplan, K. (1994) *Scattered Hegmonies: postmodernity and transnational feminist practices,* Minneapolis MN: University of Minnesota.

Grunberg, I. (1998) "Double Jeopardy: globalization, liberalization and the fiscal squeeze," *World Development,* 26(4): 591–605.

Gurung, J. D. (ed.) (1999) *Searching for Women's Voices in the Hindu Kush Himalayas,* Kathmandu, Nepal: ICIMOD.

Gutierrez, M. (ed.) (2003) *Macro-Economics: making gender matter,* London and New York: Zed Press.

Haddad, L., Hoddinott, J. and Alderman, H. (eds) (1995) *Intrahousehold Resource Allocation in Developing Countries: models, methods, and policy,* Baltimore MD and London: Johns Hopkins University Press for the International Food Policy Research Institute.

Hagan, J. (1988) *Structural Criminology,* New Brunswick NJ: Rutgers University Press.

Harper, M., Esipisu, E., Mohanty, A. K. and Rao, D. S. K. (1998) *The New Middle Women,* London: Intermediate Technology Publications.

Hart, G. (1992) "Household Production Reconsidered: gender, labor conflict and technological change in Malaysia's Muda region," *World Development,* 20(6): 809–23.

Hartmann, H. (1981) "The Unhappy Marriage of Marxism and Feminism: toward a more progressive union," in L. Sargent (ed.) *Women and Revolution,* Boston MA: South End Press.

Helleiner, E. (1997) "Braudelian Reflections on Economic Globalization: the historian as pioneer," in S. Gill and J. Mittelman (eds) *Innovation and Transformation in International Studies,* Cambridge: Cambridge University Press.

Herrera, G. (2005a) "Remesas, Dinámicas Familiares y Estatus Social: una mirada de la emigración ecuatoriana desde la sociedad de origen," in N.Z. García-Falces (ed.) *La migración, un Camino Entre el Desarrollo y la Cooperación,* Madrid, Spain: Centro de Investigación para la Paz (CIP-FUHEM).

——(2005b) "Dall'altra parte delle riva: percezioni e pratiche fra i figli di migranti rimasti in Ecuador," in A. Torre and L. Queirolo Palmas (eds) *Il Fantasma Delle Bande: Giovanni dall'America latina a Genova,* Genoa, Italy: Fratelli Frilli Editori.

Hirway, I. (2002) "Indian Experience of Time Use," proceedings of the National Seminar on Applications of Time Use Statistics, organized by the Department of Statistics, Government of India, in collaboration with UNIFEM, New Delhi and Centre For Development Alternatives (CFDA), Ahmedabad, 8–9 October 2002.

Hoem, B. and Hoem, J. (1996) "Sweden's Family Policy and Roller-Coaster Fertility," *Jinko Mondai Kenkyu,* 52: 1–22.

Hondagneu-Sotelo, P. (1994) *Gendered Transitions: Mexican experiences of immigration,* Berkeley CA: University of California Press.

——(2001) *Doméstica: immigrant workers cleaning and caring in the shadows of affluence,* Los Angeles CA: University of California Press.

——(ed.) (2003) *Gender and U.S. Immigration: contemporary trends,* Berkeley CA: University of California Press.

Hossain, H. (1988) "Industrialization and Women Workers in Bangladesh: from home-based work to the factories," in N. Heyzer (ed.) *Daughters in Industry*, Kuala Lumpur, Malaysia: Asia Pacific Development Center.

Hugo, G. (1995) "Labour Export from Indonesia," *ASEAN Economic Bulletin*, 12 (2): 275–98.

——(2005) "Indonesian International Domestic Workers: contemporary developments and issues," in S. Huang, B. Yeoh and N. A. Rahman (eds) *Asian Women as Transnational Domestic Workers*, Singapore: Marshall Cavendish Academic.

Hughes, D. M. (2000) "The Natasha Trade: transnational shadow market of trafficking women," *Journal of International Affairs*, 53(2): 653–72.

INEC (Instituto Nacional de Estadística y Censos)/SIISE (Sistema Integrado de Indicadores Sociales del Ecuador)/EMEDINHO (Programa Nuestro Niños, Instituto Nacional del Niño y la Familia, Centro de Estudios de Población y Desarrollo) (2000) *Encuesta de Medición de Indicadores de la Niñez y los Hogares*, Quito, Ecuador: SIISE.

International Helsinki Federation for Human Rights (2000) *Women: an investigation into the status of women's rights in Central and South-Eastern Europe and the newly independent states*: IHF. Online. Available at: www.ihf-hr.org/cms/cms.php?sec_id = 72&pag_id = 107 (accessed 20 August 2007).

ILO (International Labor Organization) (1996) *ILO Convention on Homework*, Geneva, Switzerland: ILO.

——(1999) *World Employment Report 1998–99: women and training in the global economy*, Geneva, Switzerland: ILO.

——(2002) *Women and Men in the Informal Economy*, Geneva, Switzerland: ILO.

IMF (International Monetary Fund) (1997) *World Economic Outlook*, Washington DC: IMF.

Jackson, C. (1996) "Rescuing Gender from the Poverty Trap," *World Development*, 24(3): 489–504.

Jackson, C. and Pearson, R. (eds) (1998) *Feminist Visions of Development: gender analysis and policy*, London and New York: Routledge.

James, S. and Dalla Costa, M. (1973) *The Power of Women and the Subversion of Community*, Bristol: Falling Wall Press.

Jones, C. (2004) "Whose Stress? Emotion work in middle-class Javanese homes," *Ethnos*, 69(4): 509–28.

Jones, C. W. (1986) "Intra-household Bargaining in Response to the Introduction of New Crops: a case study of North Cameroon," in J. L. Moock (ed.) *Understanding Africa's Rural Households and Farming Systems*, Boulder CO and London: Westview Press.

Kabeer, N. (1999) *The Conditions and Consequences of Choice: reflections on the measurement of women's empowerment*, UNRISD Discussion Paper no. 108, Geneva, Switzerland: UNRISD.

——(2000) *The Power to Choose*, London: Verso.

——(2005) "Is Microfinance a 'Magic Bullet' for Women's Empowerment? Analysis of findings from South Asia," *Economic and Political Weekly*, 40(44–45): 4709–18.

Kabeer, N. and Subrahmanian, R. (1999) *Institutions, Relations and Outcomes*, New Delhi, India: Kali for Women.

Kapadia, K. (ed.) (2002) *The Violence of Development*, New Delhi, India: Kali for Women.

Kapadia-Kundu, N. and Dyalchand, A. (2005) *The Pachod Paisa Scale: A new scale for measuring attitudes, client satisfaction, beliefs and intentions*, unpublished paper, Pachod, India: Integrated Health Management.

Katz, C. (2001a) "On the Grounds of Globalization: a topography for feminist political engagement," *Signs: Journal of Women in Culture and Society* 26(4): 1213–34.

——(2001b) "Vagabond Capitalism and the Necessity of Social Reproduction," *Antipode*, 33(4): 709–28.

Keck, M. E. and Sikkink, K. (1998) *Activists Beyond Borders: advocacy networks in international politics*, Ithaca NY: Cornell University Press.

Kelkar, G., Nathan, D. and Jahan, R. (2004) "Redefining Women's 'Samman': microcredit and gender relations in rural Bangladesh," *Economic and Political Weekly*, 39(32): 3627–40.

Kofman, E. and Raghuram, P. (2004) "An Introduction from the Guest Editors," special issue: Gender and International Migration, *Feminist Review*, 77(1): 4–6.

KOMNAS Perempuan (Komisi Nasional Anti Kekerasan terhadap Perempuan) [National Commission against Violence against Women] and Solidaritas Perempuan/CARAM Indonesia (Women's Solidarity) (2003) "Indonesian Report to the United Nations' Special Rapporteur for Migrants' Human Rights", *Buruh Migran Pekerja Rumah Tangga (TKW-PRT): Kerentanan dan Inisiatif-inisiatif baru untuk perlindungan hak asasi*. TKW-PRT [Migrant Domestic Workers: New Sensitivity and Initiatives to Protect Basic Rights], Jakarta, Indonesia: KOMNAS Perempuan and Solidaritas Perempuan/CARAM.

Konig, I. (ed.) (1997) *Trafficking in Women*, Vienna, Austria: Federal Chancellery.

Korpi, W. (2003) "Welfare State Progress in Western Europe: politics, institutions, globalization, and europeanization," *Annual Review of Sociology*, 29: 589–609.

Krisnawaty, T. R., Tagaroa, R., Indriati, E., Wibawa, Y. B., Muchsin, A., Khusnaeni, A., Kuswandari, K., Chandrakirana, K., Trimayuni, P. and Achnas, G. (2003) *Buruh Migran Pekerja Rumah Tangga Indonesia (TKWPRT): kerentanan dan inisiatif-inisiatif baru untuk perlindungan hak asasi TKW-PRT* (Indonesian Overseas Migrant Domestic Workers: sensitivity and new initiatives for the protection of the human rights of overseas migrant domestic workers), report for the UN Special Rapporteur on Migrant Human Rights, Jakarta, Indonesia: Komnas Perempuan (National Commission for Women's Human Rights).

Kucera, D. (2001) "The Effects of Core Worker Rights on Labour Costs and Foreign Direct Investment: evaluating the conventional wisdom," Decent Work Research Programme Working Paper no. 130, Geneva, Switzerland: International Institute for Labor Studies, ILO.

Kucera, D. and Milberg, W. (2000) "Gender Segregation and Gender Bias in Manufacturing Trade Expansion: revisiting the 'wood asymmetry,'" *World Development*, 28(7): 1191–210.

Kumar, S. K. (1994) "Adoption of Hybrid Maize in Zambia: effects on gender roles, food consumption and nutrition," Research Paper no. 100, Washington DC: International Food Policy Research Institute.

Kurtz, M. J. (1999) "Chile's Neo-liberal Revolution: incremental decisions and structural transformation, 1973–1989," *Journal of Latin American Studies*, 31: 399–427.

Labra, M. E. (2002) "La Reinvención Neoliberal de la Inequidad en Chile: el caso de la salud," *Cadernos de Saude Pública*, 18(4): 1041–52.

Lamadrid, S., SERNAM, health sector division (19 May 2005). Interview by Ewig, C., Santiago, Chile.

Laroque, G. and Salanie, B. (2003) *Fertility and Financial Incentives in France*, Paris: CREST-INSEE and CNRS USA.

——(2004) "Fertility and Financial Incentives in France," *CESifo Economic Studies*, 50: 423–50.

Larraín, S., former member of the technical commission on health reform (13 June 2005) Interview by Ewig, C., Santiago, Chile.

Larrea, C. and Sánchez, J. (2002) *Pobreza, Empleo y Equidad Social en Ecuador: perspectivas para el desarrollo humano sostenible*, Quito, Ecuador: ONUD.

"Las Mujeres y la Reforma de Salud" (2002) *Argumentos Para el Cambio*, 51 (May), Santiago, Chile: Centro de Estudios de la Mujer.

Laslett, B. and Brenner, J. (1989) "Gender and Social Reproduction: historical perspectives," *Annual Review of Sociology*, 15: 381–404.

Leitner, H. (2000) "The Political Economy of International Labor Migration," in E. Sheppard and T. Barnes (eds) *A Companion to Economic Geography*, Malden MA and Oxford: Blackwell.

Levchenko, K. (1999) "Combat of Trafficking in Women for the Purpose of Forced Prostitution," *Ukraine Country Report*, 1999, Vienna, Austria: Ludwig Boltzmann Institute of Human Rights.

Levitt, P. (2001) *The Transnational Villagers*, Berkeley CA: University of California Press

Levitt, P. and Glick Schiller, N. (2004) "Conceptualizing Simultaneity: a transnational social field perspective," in A. Portes and J. DeWind (eds) *International Migration Review: conceptual and methodological developments in the study of international migration*, Staten Island NY: Center for Migration Studies of New York, Inc.

Lind, A. (2005) *Gendered Paradoxes: women's movements, state restructuring and global development in Ecuador*, University Park PA: Penn State Press.

Lingam, L. (2006) "Gender, Households and Poverty: tracking mediations of macro adjustment programmes," *Economic and Political Weekly*, 41(20): 1989–98.

Lipton, M. and Longhurst, R. (1989) *New Seeds and Poor People*, Baltimore MD: Johns Hopkins University Press.

Lochhead, C. (2000) "The Trend Toward Delayed First Childbirth: health and social implications," *Isuma*, 1: 41–44.

López, D. (1999) *Salud Previsional y Cobertura Femenina*, Documento no. 61, Santiago, Chile: SERNAM.

McCartney, P. (2004) "American Nationalism and U.S. Foreign Policy from September 11 to the Iraq War," *Political Science Quarterly*, 119(3): 399–423.

McDonald, P. (2000) "The 'Toolbox' of Public Policies to Impact on Fertility: a global view," paper presented at the annual seminar of European Observatory on the Social Situation, Demography and Family, on low fertility, families, and public policies. Seville, Spain, 15–16 September 2000.

McDowell, L. (1991) "Life Without Father or Ford: the new gender order of post-Fordism," *Transactions of the Institute of British Geographers*, 16(4): 400–19.

Malhotra, A., Schuler, S. R. and Boender, C. (2002) "Measuring Women's Empowerment as a Variable in International Development," background paper prepared for the World Bank Workshop on Poverty and Gender: New Perspectives. Gender and Development Group, Washington, DC: World Bank.

Mandela, N. (2000) "Closing Address," 13th International AIDS Conference, Durban, South Africa, 14 July 2000. Online. Available at: http://lists.kabissa.org/lists/archives/public/pha-exchange/msg00006.html (accessed 13 August 2007).

Manning, L. and Graham, P. (2000) "Banking and Credit," in J. Petersen and M. Lewis (eds) *The Elgar Companion to Feminist Economics*, Cheltenham: Edward Elgar.

Martin, J. and Park, M. (1999) "Trends in Twin and Triplet Births: 1980–97," *National Vital Statistics Report*, 47: 1–16.

Martínez, U. (2004) *Trabajadores Invisibles: precariedad, rotación y pobreza de la immigración en españa*, Madrid, Spain: Editorial Catarata.

Marx, K. (1964) *Economic and Philosophic Manuscripts of 1844*, D. J. Struik (ed.), trans. M. Milligan, New York: International Publishers.

——(1976) *Capital Volume I*, Toronto: Penguin Books Canada Ltd.

Matamala, M. I., Coordinator of the Gender, Equity and Health Reform Project of the Pan American Health Organization in Chile (18 May 2005). Interview by Ewig, C., Santiago, Chile.

Matear, A. (1995) "The Servicio Nacional de la Mujer (SERNAM): women and the process of democratic transition in Chile 1990–94," in D. E. Hojman (ed.) *Neoliberalism with a Human Face? The politics and economics of the Chilean model*, Liverpool: Institute of Latin American Studies.

Mayoux, L. (2000) *Microfinance and the Empowerment of Women: A review of the key issues*, Geneva, Switzerland: International Labor Organization, Social Finance Unit. Online. Available at: www.ilo.org/public/francais/employment/ finance/papers/mayoux.htm (accessed 1 December 2006).

——(2001) "Jobs, Gender and Small Enterprises: getting the policy environment right," *Working paper no. 15*, series on Women's Entrepreneurship Development and Gender in Enterprises, Geneva, Switzerland.

——(2006) "Women's Empowerment through Sustainable Micro-Finance: rethinking 'best practice,'" discussion draft, February 2006. Online. Available at: www.genfinance.info/Documents/Mayoux_Backgroundpaper.pdf (accessed 1 December 2006).

Mazumdar, V. and Krishnaji, N. (eds) (2001) *Enduring Conundrum: India's sex ratio*, Delhi, India: Rainbow Publishers Ltd.

Meltzer, E. (2004) "Assuring Development Gains from Trade," *International Trade Forum*, 2: 14.

Merino, R., ex-president of the Association of Isapres of Chile (7 July 2005). Interview by Ewig, C., Santiago, Chile.

Meyers, D. T. (1997) *Feminist Social Thought: a reader*, New York and London: Routledge.

Mies, M. (1986). *Patriarchy and Accumulation on a World Scale*, London: Zed Books.

MINSAL (Ministerio de Salud) (2001) *Transversalización de la Perspectiva de Género en las Políticas de Reforma de Salud en Chile*, Santiago: Gobierno de Chile.

"Ministra Bachelet: afinan bases para reforma global de salud" (2001) *El Mercurio*, 22 April: A1, A19.

Minnesota Advocates Group (2000) *Trafficking in Women: Moldova and Ukraine*. Minneapolis: Minnesota Advocates Group.

Mishra, S. (2006) "Farmers' Suicides in Maharashtra," *Economic and Political Weekly*, 41(16): 1538–45.

Mitchell, D. (2000) *Cultural Geography: a critical introduction*, Malden MA and Oxford: Blackwell.

Mitchell, K. (2004) *Crossing the Neoliberal Line: Pacific Rim migration and the metropolis*, Tempe AZ: Tempe University Press.

Mitchell, K., Marston, S. and Katz, C. (2003) "Introduction: Life's Work: an introduction, review and critique," *Antipode*, 35(3): 415–42.

Moghadam, V. (2005) *Globalizing Women: transnational feminist networks*, Baltimore MD and London: Johns Hopkins University Press.

Moghissi, K. S. (1995) "Evolving Patterns of Iatrogenic Multifetal Pregnancy Generation: implication for the aggressiveness of infertility treatments," *American Journal of Obstetrics and Gynecology*, 172: 1750–55.

Mohanty, B. B. (2005) "'We Are Like the Living Dead': farmer suicides in Maharashtra, Western India," *Journal of Peasant Studies*, 32(2): 244–76.

Molyneux, M. (1979) "Beyond the Domestic Labor Debate," *New Left Review*, 116: 3–27.

Molyneux, M. and Razavi, S. (2002) *Gender Justice, Development and Rights*, New York: Oxford University Press.

Moock, J. L. (ed.) (1986) *Understanding Africa's Rural Households and Farming Systems*, Boulder CO and London: Westview Press.

Mooij, J. (2002) "Welfare Policies and Politics: a study of three government interventions in Andhra Pradesh, India," Working Paper no. 181, London: Overseas Development Institute.

Muhliesen, M. and Towe, C. (eds) (2004) "U.S. Fiscal Policies and Priorities for Long-Run Sustainability," IMF Occasional Paper 227. Online. Available at: www.imf.org/external/pubs/nft/op/227/ (accessed 13 August 2007).

"Mujeres en Pie de Guerra" (2002) *Punto Final*, 545. Online. Available at: www.puntofinal.cl/545/reformadesalud.htm (accessed 7 April 2006).

MWCSW/MGEP/UNDP and SAHAVAGI (2004) *Gender Assessment and Gender Budget Audit of the Ministry of Local Development (Nepal)*, Kathmandu, Nepal: MWCSW/MGEP/UNDP and SAHAVAGI.

Nageer, F. (2004) "What You Need to Know About Trade-Finance Policy Coherence," Working Paper, Fact Sheet no. 4, Washington DC: IGTN. Online. Available at: www.igtn.org/pdfs/21_CoherenceFacts.pdf (accessed 22 June 1996).

Naha, N. and Chowdhury, A. R. (2006) "Inorganic Lead Exposure in Battery and Paint Factory: effect on human sperm structure and functional activity," *Journal of the University of Occupational and Environmental Health*, 28: 157–71.

Narasimha Rao, P. and Suri, K. C. (2006) "Dimensions of Agrarian Distress in Andhra Pradesh," *Economic and Political Weekly*, 41(16): 1546–52.

Navarro, V. (2006) *El Subdesarrollo Social de España: causas y consecuencias*, Barcelona, Spain: Editorial Anagrama.

Nesiah, V. (1993) "Toward a Feminist Internationality: a critique of US feminist legal scholarship," *Harvard Women's Law Review*, 16: 189–210.

Nguanbanchong, A. (2004) "Gender Effects on Savings: evidence from urban poor households in Thailand," unpublished doctoral dissertation, American University.

Nguyen, A. and Zampetti, A. B. (eds) (2004) *Trade and Gender: opportunities and challenges for developing countries*, New York: United Nations.

North, L. and Cameron, J. D. (2003) *Rural Progress Rural Decay: neoliberal adjustment policies and local initiatives*, Bloomfield CA: Kumarian Press.

NPC/UNDP (2004) *Nepal Human Development Report 2004: empowerment and poverty reduction*, Kathmandu, Nepal: United Nations Development Program.

NRB (Nepal Rastra Bank) (1988) *Multipurpose Household Budget Survey: a study on income distribution, employment and consumption patterns in Nepal*, Kathmandu, Nepal: Nepal Rastra Bank.

O'Connor, J., Orloff, A., and Shaver, S. (1999) *States, Markets, Families*, Cambridge: Cambridge University Press.

OECD (Organization for Economic Cooperation and Development) (2001) "Balancing Work and Family Life: helping parents into paid employment," *OECD Employment Outlook*, Paris: OECD.

——(2005) "Babies and Bosses: balancing work and family life," policy brief, Paris: OECD.

Ong, A. (1999) *Flexible Citizenship: the cultural logics of transnationality*, Durham NC: Duke University Press.

Oppenheim, K. and Jensen, A. (eds) (1995) *Gender and Family Change in Industrialized Countries*, New York: Oxford University Press.

OPS-Chile (Organización Panamericana de Salud en Chile) (2003) *Health Profile of Men and Women in Chile*, Santiago: OPS/World Health Organization Gender Equity and Health Reform in Chile Project.

Orloff, A. (1996) "Gender in the Welfare State," *Annual Review of Sociology*, 22:51–78.

Oxfam (2002) "Cultivating Poverty: the impact of US cotton subsidies on Africa," Oxfam Briefing Paper no. 30, Oxford. Online. Available at: www.oxfam.org.uk/what_we_do/issues/trade/downloads/bp30_cotton.pdf (accessed 23 June 2006).

Parliament of the Republic of South Africa (2006) "Conference Declaration," Women and the Economic Recovery of Africa, Cape Town, 4–7 May 2006. Online. Available at: www.parliament.gov.za/live/splash.php (accessed 13 August 2007).

Parreñas, R. (2004) "The Care Crisis in the Philippines: children and transnational families in the new global economy," in B. Ehrenreich and A. R. Hochschild (eds) *Global Woman: nannies, maids and sex workers in the new economy*, New York: Henry Holt.

——(2005) *Children of Global Migration: transnational families and gendered woes*, Stanford CA: Stanford University Press.

Peck, J. and Tickell, A. (2002) "Neoliberalizing Space," *Antipode*, 34(3): 380–404.

Pedone, C. (2003) "Tu Siempre Jalas a los Tuyos: cadenas y redes migratorias de las familias ecuatorianas en españa," unpublished doctoral dissertation, Universidad Autónoma de Barcelona.

Pérez, C. (2006) *La Transversalidad de Género al Servicio del Fortalecimiento Institucional de los Mecanismos de Adelanto de la Mujer: la experiencia del SERNAM con el PMG de género en Chile*, Santiago, Chile: CEPAL.

Pérez-Sainz, J. P. (2000) "Labor Market Transformation in Latin America During the 1990s: some analytical remarks," working paper, Facultad Latinoamericana de Ciencias Sociales (FLACSO), Costa Rica.

Petchesky, R. P. (2003) *Global Prescriptions: gendering health and human rights*, New York and London: Zed Books.

Picchio, A. (1992) *Social Reproduction: the political economy of labour markets*, Cambridge: Cambridge University Press.

Pichetpongsa, A. (2004) "Work Intensity and Individual Well-Being: evidence from Thailand," unpublished thesis, American University.

Polanyi, K. (1957) *The Great Transformation*, Boston MA: Beacon Press.

Pollack, M. E. (2002) *Equidad de Género en el Sistema de Salud Chileno*, no. 123, serie Financiamiento del Desarrollo, Santiago, Chile: CEPAL, Unidad de Financiamiento para el Desarrollo.

Powis, B. (2003) "Grass Roots Politics and 'Second Wave of Decentralization' in Andhra Pradesh," *Economic and Political Weekly*, 38(26): 2617–22.

Pratt, G. (2004) *Working Feminism*, Philadelphia PA: Temple University Press.

Pribytkova, I. (2002) "Trudovyje Migranty v Socialjnoj Ijerarhiji Ukrainskogo Obshchestva" (Labor Migrants in the Social Hierarchy of Ukrainian Society), *Sociologija: teorija, metody, marketing*, 4: 159.

Prügl, E. (1999) *The Global Construction of Gender: home-based work in the political economy of the 20th century*, New York: Columbia University Press.

Pyshchulina O. (2004) "An Evaluation of Ukrainian Legislation to Counter and Criminalize Human Trafficking," in S. Stoecker and L. Shelley (eds) *Human Traffic and Transnational Crime*, Lanham MD: Rowman and Littlefield.

——(2007) *Information Campaign Against Trafficking in Women from the Ukraine*, Online. Available at: www.american.edu/traccc/resources/publications.html (accessed 3 July 2007).

Radcliffe, S. A. (1999) "Race and Domestic Service: migration and identity in Ecuador," in J. H. Momsen (ed.) *Gender Migration and Domestic Service*, London: Routledge.

Rai, S. (1999) "Democratic Institutions, Political Representation and Women's Empowerment: the quota debate in India," *Democratization*, 6(3): 84–99.

——(2002) *Gender and Political Economy of Development: from nationalism to globalisation*, Cambridge: Polity Press.

Ramirez, F. and Ramirez, J. (2005) *La Estampida Migratoria*, Quito, Ecuador: Abya-Yala, CIUDAD,UNESCO.

Ramírez Caballero, A. (2001) *Género y Sistema Isapre*, Santiago, Chile: Minsal, SERNAM.

Reddy, G. K. (2002) "New Populism and Liberalisation: regime shift under Chandrababu Naidu in AP," *Economic and Political Weekly*, 37(9): 871–83.

Ríos Tobar, M. (2003) "Chilean Feminism(s) in the 1990s," *International Feminist Journal of Politics*, 5(2): 256–80.

Robinson, K. (1991) "Housemaids: the effects of gender and culture in the internal and international migration of Indonesian women," in G. Bottomley, M. De Lepervanche and J. Martin (eds) *Intersexions: gender/class/culture/ethnicity*, Sydney, NSW: Allen and Unwin.

——(2000) "Gender, Islam, and Nationality: Indonesian domestic servants in the Middle East," in K. Adams and S. Dickey (eds) *Home and Hegemony: domestic service and identity politics in South and Southeast Asia*, Ann Arbor MI: University of Michigan Press.

Rocha, G. (1995) "The Urban Family and Poverty in Latin America," *Latin American Perspectives*, 22(2): 12–31.

——(2001) "From the Resources of Poverty to the Poverty of Resources? The erosion of a survival model," *Latin American Perspectives*, 28(4): 72–100.

Rodrik, D. (2001) "The Global Governance of Trade: as if development really mattered," background paper prepared for United Nations Development Programme, *Making Trade Work for People*, New York: UNDP.

Rogers, B. (1983) *The Domestication of Women*, New York: Tavistock Publications.

Roldan, M. (1988) "Renegotiating the Marital Contract: intrahousehold patterns of money allocation and women's subordination among domestic outworkers in

Mexico City," in D. Dwyer and J. Bruce (eds) *A Home Divided: women and income in the third world*, Palo Alto CA: Stanford University Press.

Rose, G. (1993) *Feminism and Geography: the limits of geographical knowledge*, Minneapolis: University of Minnesota Press.

Rudnyckyj, D. (2004) "Technologies of Servitude: governmentality and Indonesian transnational labor migration assimilation," *Anthropological Quarterly*, 77: 407–34.

Safa, H. (1996) "Gender Inequality and Women's Wage Labor: a theoretical and empirical analysis," in V. Moghadam (ed.) *Patriarchy and Development*, Oxford: Clarendon Press.

SAHAVAGI (2006) *Gender Equality and Empowerment of Women: an update*, Kathmandu, Nepal: UNFPA.

Salaff, J. W. (1981) *Working Daughters of Hong Kong*, Cambridge: Cambridge University Press.

Saldeen, P. and Sundstrom, P. (2005) "Would Legislation Imposing a Single Embryo Transfer be a Feasible Way to Reduce the Rate of Multiple Pregnancies After IVF?," *Human Reproduction*, 20: 4–8.

Sanghatana, S. S. (1989) *We Were Making History: life stories of women in the Telengana people's struggle*, New Delhi, India: Kali for Women.

Sassen, S. (1998) *Globalization and its Discontents: essays on the mobility of people*, New York: The New Press.

——(2004) "Global Cities and Survival Circuits," in B. Ehrenreich and A. R. Hochschild (eds) *Global Woman: nannies, maids and sex workers in the new economy*, New York: Henry Holt.

Sayad, A. (2004) *The Suffering of the Immigrant*, Cambridge: Polity Press.

Schild, V. (1998) "New Subjects of Rights? Women's movements and the construction of citizenship in the 'new democracies'," in S. Alvarez, E. Dagnino and A. Escobar (eds) *Politics of Culture, Cultures of Politics*, Boulder CO: Westview Press.

Schneiderman, D. (2000) "Investment Rules and the New Constitutionalism," *Law and Social Inquiry*, 25(3): 757–87.

Scholars' Statement (2004–5), "Global Empowerment of Women: beyond gender neutrality and neoliberal governance," *Fulbright New Century Scholars Program*. Online. Available at: www.cies.org/NCS/2004_2005/download/2004_05_statement.pdf (accessed 13 August 2007).

Scholte, J. A. (2005) *The Sources of Neoliberal Globalization*, Geneva, Switzerland: UNRISD.

Scott, C. V. (1995) *Gender and Development: rethinking modernization and dependency theory*, Boulder CO and London: Lynne Rienner.

Sebstad, J. and Cohen, M. (2001) *Microfinance, Risk Management and Poverty, Consultative Group to Assist the Poorest*, Washington DC: United States Agency for International Development.

Seccombe, W. (1974) "The Housewife and Her Labour Under Capitalism," *New Left Review*, 83: 3–24.

Seguino, S. (2000) "Gender Inequality and Economic Growth: a cross-country analysis," *World Development*, 29(7): 1211–30.

Seguino, S. and Floro, M. (2003) "Does Gender Have any Effect on Aggregate Savings? An empirical analysis," *International Review of Applied Economics*, 17(2): 147–66.

Sen, G. (1997) "Globalization, Justice and Equity: a gender perspective," *Development*, 40(2): 21–26.

Sheinin, D. (c.1996) *The Organization of American States*, Piscataway NJ: Transaction Publishers.

Shelley, L. (1999) "Sex Trade: trafficking of women and children in Europe and the United States," hearing before the Commission on Security and Cooperation in Europe (the Helsinki Commission), 28 June 1999.

Silvey, R. (2007) "Unequal Borders: Indonesian transnational migrants at immigration control," *Geopolitics*, special issue: Contradictory Borders, 12(2): 265–79.

Silvey, R. and Lawson, V. (1999) "Placing the Migrant," *Annals of the Association of American Geographers*, 89(1): 121–32.

Singh, A. (1994) "Openness and the Market-Friendly Approach to Development: learning the right lessons from development experience," *World Development*, 22 (12): 1811–23.

Smith, J., Barau, A. D., Goldman, A. and Mareck, J. H. (1994) "The Role of Technology in Agricultural Intensification: the evolution of maize production in the Northern Guinea savanna of Nigeria," *Economic Development and Cultural Change*, 42(3): 537–54.

Sobotka, T. (2002) *Ten Years of Rapid Fertility Changes in the European Post-Communist Countries: evidence and interpretation*, Gröningen, the Netherlands: Population Research Centre.

Sorrentino, C. (1990) "The Changing Family in International Perspective," *Monthly Labor Review*, 113: 41–58.

Spaan, E. (1999) *Labour Circulation and Socioeconomic Transformation: the case of East Java, Indonesia*, Gröningen, the Netherlands: Rijksuniversiteit Gröningen.

Spar, D. L. (2006) *The Baby Business: how money, science, and politics drive the commerce of conception*, Boston MA: Harvard Business School Press.

Sparke, M. (2006) "A Neoliberal Nexus: economy, security and the biopolitics of citizenship on the border," *Political Geography*, 25: 151–80.

Standing, G. (1999) *Global Labour Flexibility: seeking distributive justice*, New York: St. Martin's Press.

Stetson, D. McBride and Mazur, A. G. (eds) (1995) *Comparative State Feminism*, Thousand Oaks CA: Sage.

Stone, K. (1995) "Labour and the Global Economy: four approaches to transnational labour regulation", *Michigan Journal of International Law*, 16: 987–1028.

Stree Shakti Sanghatana (1989) *"We Are Making History" life stories of women in the Telengana People's Struggle*, New Delhi, India: Kali for Women.

Suri, K. C. (2006) "The Political Economy of Agrarian Distress," *Economic and Political Weekly*, 41(16): 1523–29.

Suryakusuma, J. (1996) "The State and Sexuality in New Order Indonesia," in L. Sears (ed.) *Fantasizing the Feminine in Indonesia*, Durham NC and London: Duke University Press.

Swan, S. H. (2006) "Semen Quality in Fertile US Men in Relation to Geographical Area and Pesticide Exposure," *International Journal of Andrology*, 29: 62–68.

Tagaroa, R. and Sofia, E. (2002) *Buruh Migran Indonesia: mencari keadilan* (Indonesian Migrant Workers: Searching for Justice), Bekasi, Indonesia: Lembaga Advokasi Buruh Migranand Solidaritas Perempuan (Migrant Workers Advocacy Institute–Women's Solidarity).

Taylor, I. and Jamieson, R. (1999) "Sex Trafficking and the Mainstream of Market Culture," *Crime, Law and Social Change*, 32: 257–78.

Tinker, I. (ed.) (1990) *Persistent Inequalities: women and world development*, New York: Oxford University Press.

Titelman, D. (1999)). "Reforms to Health Systems Financing," *CEPAL Review*, 69, available at: www.eclac.org/publicaciones/xml/1/20101/titelman.pdf (last accessed 5 December 2007).

——(2000) *Reformas al Sistema de Salud en Chile: desafíos pendientes*, no. 104 serie Financiamiento del Desarrollo, Santiago, Chile: CEPAL, Unidad de Financiamiento para el Desarrollo.

Todaro, R. and Yanez, S. (eds) (2004) *El Trabajo Se Transforma: relaciones de produccion y relaciones de genero*, Santiago, Chile: Centro de Estudios de la Mujer.

TPAMF (Tanka Prasad Acharya Memorial Foundation) (2005) "Analysis of Caste, Ethnicity and Gender Data from 2001Population Census in Preparation for Poverty Mapping and Wider PRSP Monitoring," a report submitted to DFID, Kathmandu, Nepal: unpublished mimeo.

Tsing, A. (2005) *Friction: an ethnography of global connection*, Princeton NJ: Princeton University Press.

Ul Haque, I. (2004) "Commodities as a Development Issue," discussion paper presented at the United Nations Informal Hearings of Civil Society on Financing for Development, New York, 22 March 2004.

UN (United Nations) (2000) *Replacement Migration: is it a solution to declining and aging populations?* New York: UN Population Division, Department of Economic and Social Affairs.

——(2003a) *Making Global Trade Work for People*, New York: UN.

——(2003b) *Partnership and Reproductive Behavior in Low-fertility Countries*, New York: UN Population Division, Department of Economic and Social Affairs.

——(2004) *Report of the Secretary General: follow-up to and implementation of the outcome of the International Conference on Financing for Development*, UN General Assembly, 16 August.

——(2005) *Resolution adopted by the General Assembly [without reference to a Main Committee (A/60/L.1)] 60/1: 2005 World Summit Outcome*, New York (A/RES/ 60/1).

UNCTAD (United Nations Conference on Trade and Development) (2003) *Report of the Meeting of Eminent Persons on Commodity Issues (TD/B/50/11)*, 30 September 2003, Geneva, Switzerland: UNCTAD.

UNIFEM (United Nations Development Fund for Women) (2000) *Progress of the World's Women 2000, UNIFEM Biennial Report*, New York: UNIFEM.

UNDP (United Nations Development Programme) (1995) *Human Development Report*, New York: UNDP.

——(2004) *Human Development Report*, New York: UNDP.

——(2005) *Human Development Report*, New York: UNDP.

UNRISD (United Nations Research Institute for Social Development) (2005) *Gender Equality: striving for justice in an unequal world*, Geneva, Switzerland: UNRISD.

US Department of State (2006) *Victims of Trafficking and Violence Prtoection Act 2000: Trafficking in persons report*. Online. Available at: www.state.gov/g/tip/rls/ tiprpt/2006 (accessed 3 July 2007).

Valiente, C. (2003) "The Feminist Movement and the Reconfigured State in Spain (1970s–2000)," in L. Banazak, K. Beckwith and D. Rucht (eds) *Women's*

Movements Facing the Reconfigured State, Cambridge: Cambridge University Press.

van Staveren, I. (2002) "Global Finance and Gender," in J. A. Scholte and A. Schnabel (eds) *Civil Society and Global Finance*, London and Tokyo: Routledge/United Nations University Press.

Vanders, L., Owen, S. and Yeros, P. (eds) (2000) *Poverty in World Politics: whose global era?* New York and London: St. Martin's Press/Macmillan Press, in association with *Millennium: Journal of International Studies*.

Vásconez, A. (2005) *Género, Pobreza y Trabajo Informal en el Ecuador*, Quito, Ecuador: International Labor Organization.

Ventura-Dias, V. (1985) "Modernization, Production Organization and Rural Women in Kenya," in I. Ahmed (ed.) *Technology and Rural Women: conceptual and empirical issues*, London: George Allen and Unwin.

von Struensee, V. (2000) "Wired, Globalized: sex trafficking of Russian and Ukrainian women," online. Available at: www.geocities.com/vanessavonstruensee_2000/traff.html (last accessed 5 December 2007).

Vos, R. (2003) *¿Quién se Beneficia del Gasto Social en el Ecuador?* Quito. Ecuador: SIISE-STFS.

Wahyudi, S. S. (2002) "Kajahatan TerorganisasiTterhadap TKI Pada Tahap Pemulangan Dari Luar Negeri dan Penanganannya Oleh Polri" (Organized Crime faced by Indonesian Workers at their Homecoming and Securitization by the Indonesian Police), unpublished master's thesis, University of Indonesia.

Walby, S. (2000) "Feminism in a Global Age," *Economy and Society*, 31(4): 533–57.

Walker, S. (2004) "Human Rights, Gender and Trade: a legal framework," in United Nations Conference on Trade and Development (UNCTAD) (ed.) *Trade and Gender: opportunities and challenges for developing countries*, Geneva, Switzerland: UNCTAD.

Waylen, G. (1994) "Women and Democratization: conceptualizing gender relations in transition politics," *World Politics*, 46(3): 327–54.

Webb, P. (1989) *Intrahousehold Decisionmaking and Resource Control: the effects of rice commercialization in West Africa*, Working Papers on Commercialization of Agriculture and Nutrition, no. 3, Washington DC: International Food Policy Research Institute.

Weber, H. (2002) "The Imposition of a Global Development Architecture: the example of micro-credit," *Review of International Studies*, 28: 537–55.

Wichterich, C. (2002) *The Globalized Woman*, London and New York: Zed Books.

WIDE (2002) "Globalisation and Gender: the privatisation of social services," workshop at the Belgian Social Forum, 21 September. Online. Available at: www.eurosur.org/wide/Globalisation/Report_BSF.htm (accessed 22 June 2006).

Williams, M. (2001) "The General Agreement on Trade in Services (GATS): the debate between the North and the South," paper for *International Gender and Trade Network*. Online. Available at: www.igtn.org/pdfs/34_GATSNorthSouth.pdf (accessed 22 June 2006).

——(2003a) "Economic Policy, Social Reproduction and Gender in Latin America and the Caribbean," *International Gender and Trade Network Briefing Note*, December. Online. Available at www.genderandtrade.net (accessed 21 March 2006).

——(2003b) *Gender Mainstreaming in the Multilateral Trading System, Commonwealth Secretariat and the GATS*, London: Commonwealth Secretariat.

——(2004) "Gender, the Doha Development Agenda and the Post Cancún Trade Negotiations," *Gender and Development*, 12(2): 73–81.

Williams, P. (1997) "Trafficking in Women and Children: a market perspective," *Transnational Organized Crime*, special issue on Illegal Immigration and Commercial Sex – The New Slave Trade, 3–4: 145–70.

Williamson, J. (1990) "What Washington Means by Policy Reform," in J. Williamson (ed.) *Latin American Adjustment: how much has happened?*, Washington DC: Institute for International Economics.

"Women's Eyes on the World Bank: a global network to transform the bank and to meet women's needs" (1997) *Women's International Network News*, 23(1): 14.

World Bank (1990) *World Development Report 1990: poverty*, New York: Oxford University Press.

——(1998) *East Asia: the road to recovery*, Washington DC: World Bank.

——(2001) *Engendering Development Through Gender Equality in Rights, Resources and Voice*, Washington DC: Oxford University Press and the World Bank.

——(2002) *Initiatives in Legal and Judicial Reform*, Washington DC: International Bank for Reconstruction and Development.

——(2003) *World Development Report 2003: sustainable development in a dynamic world – transforming institutions, growth and quality of life*, New York: Oxford University Press.

——(2005) "Poverty Trends in Nepal Between 1995–96 and 2003–04," background paper for Nepal poverty assessment, Kathmandu, Nepal: World Bank (unpublished mimeo).

World Commission on the Social Dimension of Globalization (2004) *A Fair Globalization: creating opportunities for all*, Geneva, Switzerland: International Labor Organization.

WTO (World Trade Organization) (2001) "Doha Development Round," 4th Ministerial Meeting of the World Trade Organization, Doha, Qatar, 9–13 November 2001.

Wright, V. C., Schieve, L. A., Reynolds, M. A. and Jeng, G. (2005) "Assisted Reproductive Technologies Surveillance, United States, 2002," *Morbidity and Mortality Weekly Report*, 54: 1–24.

Yeoh, B., Huang, S. and Rahman, N.A. (2005) "Asian Women as Transnational Domestic Workers," in S. Huang, B. Yeoh and N. A. Rahman (eds) *Asian Women as Transnational Domestic Workers*, Singapore: Marshall Cavendish Academic.

Young, B. (2003) "Financial Crises and Social Reproduction: Asia, Argentina and Brazil," in I. Bakker and S. Gill (eds) *Power, Production and Social Reproduction* Basingstoke, UK and New York: Palgrave Macmillan.

Young, B. and Hoppe, H. (2003) *The Doha Development Round, Gender and Social Reproduction*, New York and Berlin: FES.

Zampetti, B. (2004) "The Impact of WTO Rules on the Pursuit of Gender Equality," in UNCTAD (ed.) *Trade and Gender: opportunities and challenges for developing countries*, Geneva, Switzerland: UNCTAD.

Zegers-Hochschild, F. (2004) "The Latin American Registry of Assisted Reproduction," in E. Vayena, P. J. Rowe and P. D. Griffin (eds) *Current Practices and Controversies in Assisted Reproduction*, Geneva, Switzerland: World Health Organization.

Index